Explaining Computers in Plain English

for Seniors®

Secrets to Understanding Online Security, the Cloud, Apps, Streaming, Google®, and More

Publisher's Note

This book is intended for general information only. It does not constitute medical, legal, or financial advice or practice. The editors of FC&A have taken careful measures to ensure the accuracy and usefulness of the information in this book. While every attempt has been made to assure accuracy, errors may occur. Some websites, addresses, and telephone numbers may have changed since printing. We cannot guarantee the safety or effectiveness of any advice or treatments mentioned. Readers are urged to consult with their professional financial advisors, lawyers, and health care professionals before making any changes.

Any health information in this book is for information only and is not intended to be a medical guide for self-treatment. It does not constitute medical advice and should not be construed as such or used in place of your doctor's medical advice. Readers are urged to consult with their health care professionals before undertaking therapies suggested by the information in this book, keeping in mind that errors in the text may occur as in all publications and that new findings may supersede older information.

The publisher and editors disclaim all liability (including any injuries, damages, or losses) resulting from the use of the information in this book.

And do not forget to do good and to share with others,
for with such sacrifices God is pleased.

Hebrews 13:16

FC&A Publishing®
103 Clover Green
Peachtree City, GA 30269

Produced by the staff of FC&A

ISBN 978-1-935574-71-2

Table of Contents

The wonderful world of apps: Tap into better health, bigger savings, and more fun

Stay in touch online: Connect through email, Facebook, Skype, and more

The magic of streaming: Cheap and easy entertainment at your fingertips

Online security: Expert help to battle internet threats

Google software: The free suite that does it all

The amazing cloud: Work, play, and share from anywhere

The wonderful world of apps
Tap into better health, bigger savings, and more fun

Apps may seem scarier than the Wicked Witch of the West from *The Wizard of Oz*. But many apps (short for applications) are as valuable and helpful as Dorothy's ruby slippers. Here are just a few ways you can use these powerful software programs.

- exchange messages with friends while you wait at the doctor's office — and see the vacation pictures your cousin just posted online

- find new ways to save money and get free stuff

- read the news or check your email while you're in a check-out line

- find the long-lost manual for a kitchen gadget in less than five minutes

You may be surprised to learn that apps have been around since 1994. The first apps were go-anywhere "software applications" created for small handheld computers. Later, apps referred primarily to smartphone programs that were somewhat less powerful than desktop software.

Today, when you use an app, you may be operating any of these three types of software.

- mobile applications

- desktop applications

- web applications

Read on to find out all you need to know about working with — and enjoying — the wonderful world of apps.

Unlock the secrets of these powerful programs

3 ways to use apps that will change your life

You may be familiar with the apps on your smartphone and tablet represented by those tiny icons lined up in neat little rows. But those are just a small part of the applications universe. By taking advantage of desktop and web apps as well, you'll have the world at your fingertips.

Mobile apps deliver easy, go-everywhere computing. Mobile apps are "native apps." That means they can only run on the operating system they were designed for.

Apple iPhones and iPads include apps made for the iOS operating system. Android smartphones and tablets use apps for the Android operating system. An Android app can't run on iPhones or iPads, and an iOS app won't run on Android devices. Fortunately, many apps come in both iOS and Android versions.

When an app comes in three choices, check the features of each before deciding which version you want. Sometimes you're better off with a desktop app, and sometimes the mobile app or web app may do everything you need.

Mobile apps work differently than desktop software. Why? Imagine struggling to type in a long website address or a username and password on your smartphone's tiny keyboard. That is as miserably slow as trying to view a desktop-sized document or web page on your small smartphone screen. App designers simplify and repackage desktop websites, software, and other products so they are:

- simple to use and read on smaller screens.

- easy to navigate using a finger and small keyboard.

- won't run too slowly.

Sometimes that means mobile apps have fewer features. But don't worry — you'll also find full-featured mobile apps loaded with all kinds of special powers. For example, the Waze smartphone app can speak the directions to your destination while you drive and even adjust those directions on-the-fly to avoid traffic jams.

"Go native" with desktop apps. These applications run on desktop and laptop personal computers (PCs). They include apps created for Windows or for Mac OS. Desktop apps range from full-featured software packages like Microsoft Office and Apple iWorks to "specialist" apps that do a few things very well.

Like mobile apps, desktop applications are native apps, so they can only run on the operating system they were made for — either Windows or Mac. Some apps are only available for one operating system, while others maintain one version for Windows and another for Mac OS.

Some apps may contain viruses or carry other security threats to your desktop, laptop, tablet, or smartphone. See the chapter *Smart defense against spyware, viruses, and other malware* to learn how you can safeguard your device and still enjoy using apps.

Use web apps on any device, anywhere. Web apps are software programs located on a website, so you need a browser and an internet connection to use them. All the information you exchange with a web app has to pass over an internet connection.

If your connection can't handle as much data as it needs to, you'll have problems running the app. It's one reason many web apps have fewer features than a typical desktop or laptop computer app — it helps keep the app up to speed.

In most cases, the online program will still do all you need. Plus it has a big advantage. While some mobile or desktop apps may not be available for your device, you can run a web app on anything — even a computer at your local library.

How to connect to the wonderful world of apps

You know that apps can make your life easier, and you're ready to get started. All you need now is your device — a computer, smartphone, or tablet — and an internet connection. To make the magic happen, you'll require:

- an Internet Service Provider (ISP). For a monthly fee, your ISP can provide an internet connection that works with desktop computers, laptops, tablets, and more. You may also need a router and modem to set up a home network.

- a mobile carrier. Most smartphones and some tablets use this wireless cellular connection that does not require a modem. The mobile carrier charges one monthly fee for the cellphone service plan and another fee based on the amount of data your device downloads or uploads from the internet.

Problem-solving apps that rival the best desktop software

Need to attach glass to metal or wood for a repair or craft project? What kind of glue should you use? A web app can help you find out.

Or do you simply want to be creative and draw a picture of your best friend's cat for a birthday surprise? A web app can help you with that, too.

Web apps are the most convenient kind of app to get and use. If you buy desktop software from the web, you need to download and install the software and check for updates from time to time. You never need to install or update a web app — you just surf to its website.

Want to try it? Open a web browser — such as Edge, Safari, or Chrome — on your device. In your browser's address bar, type the address of the website of the app you want, go to the site, and follow the instructions for using the app.

Unlike regular web apps, the new progressive web apps (PWAs) will run without a constant internet connection. PWAs load quickly and keep working even if you're offline. They'll also send notifications and use location services if given permission. Yet you still won't need to download or install them.

Find the right kind of glue for your DIY project. All you have to do is visit *thistothat.com*. This handy web app was created because someone decided people could use expert advice on how to glue things together. Simply click in the **Attach** and **To** boxes to select the two kinds of material you need to bond. When you click the **Let's Glue!** button, the app recommends the best product to use.

Don't need to glue anything? Here is a more fun web app to try.

Be the artist you always dreamed of. To draw amazing, computer-assisted sketches, visit *autodraw.com*. After you take a brief tutorial, use your mouse to make a rough sketch of the picture you want. Autodraw transforms your sketch into a polished, professional-looking line drawing. Add text, color, and other details, and download your auto-drawn picture.

Web apps can do even more surprising things than this. Just be aware that some apps may require you to register with an email address or other personal information.

App stores — instant access to everything you need

Your phone or tablet comes with some apps pre-installed, but that's just the beginning. Thousands of other apps are available, and many are free. You just need to visit your device's online app store.

The Apple App Store offers 2 million apps for the iPad, iPhone, and other devices that use the iOS operating system, while the Google Play Store serves up slightly more than 2 million apps for Android tablets, phones, and more. So you shouldn't have a problem finding something you like.

To open the app store for your device, find its icon on your Home screen.

If you don't see your app store's icon, swipe left or right to check your other Home screens. If you run out of Home screens to check in Android, tap the app drawer icon.

All your apps appear in the app drawer, so just swipe vertically or horizontally until you spot the Google Play Store icon. Open the app store the same way you launch any other app on your mobile device. Tap the app's icon once with your finger.

7

Both mobile app stores have several features in common.

- They offer more than just apps, so make certain you are viewing apps before you browse the store. To be sure, tap the **Home** tab in Android's Google Play Store or the **Apps** tab in the Apple App Store.

- You can view apps by category, such as **Food & Drink**, or **Health & Fitness**.

- Both stores offer useful lists like **Top Free Apps** or **Apps We Love**.

- Tapping an app's icon shows a details page or product page packed with valuable information about the app.

- Each store includes a search box so you can search for an app name or for a description of the app you want.

Before you get your first new app, see *'Mal' cop: 8 easy ways to guard against malware* in the *Online Security* section to learn how to avoid malware and security threats.

Super simple steps to downloading an app

Don't be nervous about downloading apps to your tablet or phone. The process is super easy, and it's similar in both the Apple App Store and the Google Play Store. Here's an example if you have an Android phone.

1. Tap the icon for the Google Play Store app to open it.

2. Type either the name of an app or a description of what you want in the search box. (You may need to tap a magnifying glass icon to see the search box in the Apple App Store.)

3. If suggestions appear below the search box, tap the one you want. If none of the suggestions seem right, tap the magnifying glass icon to start the search.

> If you search online for apps to download, you'll find various websites that offer them. To help avoid malware and viruses, only download mobile apps from the Google Play Store or Apple App Store.

4. Scroll through the search results, and tap the icon of the app you want.

5. If you are sure this is the right app, check the price. If the app is free, you'll see a button labeled **Install** (or **Get** in iOS devices). Paid apps display a button labeled with a price such as $0.99.

6. To get the free app, tap the **Install** button. (If you tap **Get** in the Apple App Store, you may be asked to enter your Apple ID and password.) If you need to buy the app, click the button with the price on it. Paid mobile apps usually cost anywhere from 99 cents to just under $10, but some apps may require a subscription.

7. If a free app has costs attached to it later, or if you buy a paid app, you may be asked to sign in to your Google Account or Apple ID account and add payment information.

8. You may be asked to grant permissions for the app. Look permissions over carefully to determine if you are comfortable how that may affect your privacy. Tap **Allow** to grant permission or **Deny** to refuse.

9. After the app downloads and installs, the **Open** button and **Uninstall** button appear. Tap the **Open** button to open the app.

The app automatically installs its icon on one of your phone's Home screens or in Android's app drawer. To open the app next time, just tap its icon. That's all there is to it.

Manage your payment info like a pro

If you buy a mobile app, you must connect a payment method to your Apple ID account or Google account. If you have never entered payment information for those accounts, you may be prompted to do so when you buy an app. You can connect a credit card, PayPal account, or the appropriate gift card to your Google or Apple ID account.

For detailed information about checking a gift card balance or changing payment information in the Google Play Store app or your iPhone Settings app, visit *support.google.com* (Android) or *support.apple.com* (for iPhones).

Pick the best apps every time

Like cars, apps can range from Cadillac to clunker. Clunker apps may hog your battery, crash or freeze, ask for too much personal information, or even slow down your device. Before you choose an app, use these easy tricks to help you cruise with the Cadillacs and leave the lemons behind.

Listen to the experts. Read reviews and top app lists at technology sites like *pcmag.com*, *lifehacker.com*, *softpedia.com*, and *cnet.com*. Hint — at *cnet.com*, click the **Reviews** tab. The app reviews are listed under **Software**.

Find bestsellers, fan-favorites, and crowd-pleasers. Visit the app store for your device, and look for lists with titles like **Top Free**

Apps, Top-Rated Apps, Staff Picks, Editor's Favorites, or **Most Popular.** You may even find lists for individual categories such as **Health & Fitness** or **Productivity.**

Get trusted offline recommendations. Ask friends and family about which apps they have used for a while and really like.

Verify the price. Think an app sounds promising? Go to the app store and check its price on the app's product page.

Check for twins and triplets. Sometimes several apps may have the same name. Check the app's name, icon and other information on the product page to make sure you have the right one.

Screen out clunkers with user reviews. On a mobile app's product page, see how many downloads or installs it has and how many reviews. The more downloads, the better. If it has thousands of downloads, read the reviews, and check the app's ratings.

If a mobile app earns less than four stars, move on. Otherwise, the reviews can reveal what people like and dislike about the app. You may also notice if the app maker is quick to respond to problems mentioned in reviews.

User reviews aren't foolproof. Some app makers have been nabbed for packing their app pages with fake five-star reviews. You should still read plenty of reviews before downloading an app, but don't depend on reviews alone.

Look for key features you can't do without. Read the description and reviews carefully to see if you get all your must-have features.

- Do you want an app you can use on both your smartphone and computer? You may need a mobile app that also has a web or desktop version.

- Do you want an app that only stores its data on your phone, so it is more private?

- If this app stores information, can you back up that information or download it if you need to give up the app?

Is help readily available? Check for tutorials, Frequently Asked Questions lists, or troubleshooting tips on the app's product page, at the app store, or the app maker's website.

Double-check the product page for details. Make sure you haven't missed any information about permissions, system requirements, additional terms and conditions, or anything else.

Put security first. Always download apps from authorized app stores like Google Play or Apple, or other websites you trust. If you're not sure it's a safe site, don't take any chances.

Watch out for the hidden costs of free apps

Make sure you can genuinely enjoy free apps. Learn how to tell which apps are truly free, and which ones could end up costing you.

Which apps should you check? Your computer, tablet, or mobile phone comes with some apps already installed. Although many of these apps are free, other apps may be pre-installed by your mobile carrier or the maker of your device or operating system. These may or may not be free.

You may find a similar problem in the Apple App Store for iOS, Google Play Store for Android devices, desktop app stores, and free software sites. A surprising number of these apps are listed as free, but you may be shocked at how many definitions of free you'll find.

Which kind of free is it? Some apps are more free than others. Here is what free can mean.

- Free, but ad supported. Ad-supported apps work like radio stations. Instead of charging you, app makers charge advertisers for placing an ad in the app where (hopefully millions) of users see it. If you don't mind ads, you can download and use the app for free. If they drive you crazy, some apps let you pay a one-time fee to permanently remove them.

- Free trial version. The app is free to download and try for a limited time so you can decide whether you like it. When the trial period ends, you must either pay for the app or uninstall it.

- The simple Freemium. A basic version of the app is free to use, but you'll need to pay to get the premium version that has more and better features.

- The feature picker's Freemium. Another version of the Freemium is often seen in games. The app is free to use, but you must pay for each extra feature you want. For example, gamers may need to pay to move up to a more challenging level of the game or give their character extra abilities.

> Another hidden cost? Ads use your device's computing power, memory, and battery life when they display. They may also affect how much data your phone uses. As you add apps, pay close attention to how your data usage and battery life are affected, and notice whether your device slows down.

- Free of charge. Some apps are genuinely free, while others demand personal information. For example, you may be required to register with your email address.

4 ways to check for hidden costs. If you watch closely, hidden costs may not be hard to catch. Pay close attention to these tip-offs.

- Check the details or product page in the app store for information about potential costs of purchases. Read all the information on those pages including reviews and links.

- Look for information next to the **Get** or **Install** button.

- Read the license agreement or terms and conditions. Check for a link to that information on the product or details page, or find it on the app maker's website. Otherwise, read the license agreement during installation, or as soon as the app makes it available.

- A warning box about possible fees or purchase requirements may appear when you begin using the app or when a trial period ends.

This 'good habit' is draining your battery

Have you ever closed a bunch of apps to keep from using up too much battery power? If you double tap your Home button and swipe away your apps, Apple suggests you stop. If you tap your Android **Recent Apps** button and swipe apps away, Google also suggests you stop.

Unlike the old days, both Android and iOS have now gotten so good at minimizing the power your apps consume that it takes more energy to reopen an app after you have swiped it away, than it does to just let the app keep running.

So unless an app freezes, Google and Apple recommend you just let it keep running in the background. It's better for your battery and your phone.

Are you helping apps spy on you? Fix that today

At first, the Unroll.me app sounds like a great idea. Sign in with your email address and password, and the app helps you easily unsubscribe from email you no longer want. Yet many Unroll.me users recently discovered they had unknowingly given the app permission to mine data from their email, strip out the personal information, and sell it to marketers.

Privacy experts suggest this happens far more often than it should, but you can take these steps to prevent it.

Read the privacy policy and catch what others miss. Unroll.me did not deceive its users. The app's privacy policy explained how it would collect data.

Before you download an app, read the privacy policy and the terms of service. In spite of the confusing language, you may still learn many interesting things. Pay close attention to what data the app may collect about you and how that data may be used.

Sometimes, the privacy policy or license agreement even offers a way to opt out of having your information collected. If not, reading it can still help you decide whether to install the app. Read the policies and license agreements for apps you have already installed, too.

Prune your permissions and prioritize privacy. Before you download an app, check its product page on the app store to find out which permissions it requires. For example, apps may ask permission to:

- access personal data such as your email address or phone number.

- track your location.

- record audio.

- make and receive calls.

- send and receive SMS and MMS messages.

- read information from your list of contacts.

- read your phone call log.

These are often legitimate requests. For example, a weather forecast app wants to track your location so it can tell you the forecast no matter where you go. A bar code reader app needs access to your camera because it uses the camera to "see" the bar code. Likewise, any app that accepts spoken commands needs to use your device's microphone to hear them.

Still, if you see a permission that seems unnecessary or suspicious, don't install the app. Another similar app may work just as well.

Permissions aren't necessarily permanent. If you have already installed the app, you can revoke permissions in both Android and iOS. Here's how to do it on an Android device.

1. Tap the Settings icon and tap **Apps**.

2. Scroll to the app you want and tap its name.

3. Tap **Permissions** to see which permissions you granted.

4. To revoke one, tap that permission so the toggle dims. Now that permission is revoked.

To see the types of permissions you can revoke in iOS, tap the Settings icon and tap **Privacy**.

Don't sign in with Facebook, Google, Twitter, etc. Signing in to an app with a Google or social networking account is convenient because it's quick, and that's one less username and password to worry about. It's also a way to give up the app information to Google or social media. To stop signing in with:

- Google — visit *myaccount.google.com* and tap Apps with account access > Manage Apps to remove apps from the sign-in-with list.

- Facebook and Twitter — find the sign-in-with list in Settings > Account or Settings and privacy > Account.

Keep your PC apps secure — don't forget to update

App makers may make improvements, fix problems with the app, patch security holes, or add new features at no charge. These updates may happen automatically, or you may need to visit the app store to trigger an update.

- In the Mac OS App Store, click on **Update** in the sidebar. You can update each app individually or all of them at once.

- In the Microsoft Store, click the Menu button (three horizontal dots) in the upper right corner, and click **Downloads and updates**. When the list of apps appears, click the **Get updates** button.

Learn the smarter way to delete a mobile app

You want to delete that game app you no longer play to make room for newer apps. But hold on. You need to take steps to prevent potential disasters first.

Before you delete an app, check whether it has any data you want to keep. For example, if you want to switch to a new note-taking app, can you download your old notes as text files, or import them to your new note-taking app?

Also, before deleting a free trial app, paid app, or an app with a paid subscription, read the terms and conditions or license agreement. You need to determine whether uninstalling the app is enough to prevent you from being billed in the future.

Say adios to an Android app. Once you're sure you can safely delete the app, here's how to do it on an Android device.

1. Tap Settings > Apps.

2. Move through the app listing to find the app you want to uninstall. Tap its name.

3. On the app's information page, tap the **Uninstall** button. If asked, tap to confirm you want to uninstall the app.

4. If the Uninstall button is missing, this app cannot be deleted. You can only tap the **Disable** button to remove the app from your apps list.

Delete an app from your iPhone if you can. Although a few apps on your iPhone can never be removed, you can uninstall most apps — and their data — with these steps.

1. On your Home screen, find the icon of the app you want to delete. Swipe left or right to see additional Home screens.

2. Tap and hold the app's icon. When all the icons wiggle, an "X" appears at the upper left corner of each icon.

3. Tap the "X" on the icon of the app you are deleting.

4. If asked, tap to confirm that you want to uninstall the app.

Bought a bad one? Yes, you can get a refund!

The app you just bought is so faulty that you feel as if you lit your money on fire. Get that money back. Ask for a refund right away.

Act fast with Android apps. If less than two hours have passed since you bought the app, you can get a no-questions-asked refund. Tap the Google Play Store icon to open the app store.

1. Type the exact name of the app in the search box, and tap the magnifying glass icon on your keyboard.

2. Found the app? Make sure it is labeled **Installed**, and then tap its icon.

3. Tap the **Refund** button.

4. Confirm that you want the refund, and it happens immediately.

Don't give up if that doesn't work. After the two-hour window, you can no longer get a refund in the Google Play Store app. Instead, open a web browser on your computer or Android device. Type *play.google.com* in the address bar. If asked, sign in to your Google account.

1. Tap **Account**.

2. Scroll down to **Order History**.

3. Find the order that needs a refund, and scroll right until you see the More symbol, which is three vertical dots.

4. Tap the More symbol and then tap **Report a Problem**.

5. Tap the option for the problem which caused your refund request.

6. Scroll down and tap **Submit**.

You won't have to wait long to find out whether your request is approved. An email usually arrives within two business days.

Turn an iPhone app receipt into a refund. When you buy a new app from the Apple App Store, keep the email receipt. Apple gives you 90 days to request a refund on a mobile app.

1. To make that request, find the email receipt for that app. After opening the receipt, find the line for the faulty app purchase, and click **Report a Problem** on that same line.

2. Your web browser will open. If asked, sign in with your Apple ID and password to open Apple's problem-reporting website.

3. Tap the **Choose Problem** drop-down list. Choose the option that describes the problem with your app, and tap **Submit**. Within a week, Apple will let you know whether your refund request has been approved.

How to get computer apps for free

Shopping for computer applications has changed in the last 10 years. Although you can still get software from freeware sites and individual app makers, you can also get free and paid software from the Mac OS App Store on your Apple computer or the Microsoft Store on a Windows PC.

This means some software may come in two versions, one from the software vendor and one from your computer's app store. Other apps may only be available from the original software maker.

Apps from the software maker are usually still available from a CD, flash drive, or by download from the web. Apps from the app store are downloaded directly from the store app on your computer.

Why go to the store? Each app store has designed its apps to be more secure.

- Mac OS. Apps from the App Store are "sandboxed" to help stop malware. That means the software can't access certain sensitive parts of the operating system.

- Windows. Apps from the Microsoft Store must get your permission before they can access key parts of your hardware and operating system. In addition, Microsoft reviews each app for security before the app appears in the store.

Ready, set, shop! Go to the Start Menu in Windows and click the Microsoft Store icon, or the dock or Launchpad in Mac OS, and click on the icon for your store app.

You may be asked to sign in with your Apple ID account or Microsoft account. If you do not have an account yet, you will be prompted to create one and link a credit card or PayPal information to the account.

When the main store page opens in Windows, click on the **Apps** tab to view the available apps. The Mac OS App Store shows apps and games automatically. In both stores, you can:

- browse the featured offerings.

- browse app lists such as the **Top Free** apps list.

- choose a category to browse.

- search for an app by name or by description.

Examine the merchandise. When you find an app you want, click the app's icon to see its product page. This page tells you a lot about the app including:

- what the app does, including its available features.

- its seller or publisher.

- release date and size.

- rating and reviews.

- price.

- which hardware it can run on.

- which permissions you must grant to use the app.

If the app is free, a button labeled **Get** or **Install** appears. Otherwise, the button is labeled with a price. Click on the button, and the app store will download and install it.

When the installation completes, you may see an **Open** button you can click to open the new app. If not, find the app in the Start Menu (Windows) or in LaunchPad (Mac OS).

Try this legitimate site for free software galore

"You will never find a more wretched hive of scum and villainy," says Obi-wan Kenobi in the movie *Star Wars*. That could just as well describe some websites that offer free desktop apps full of malware.

Fortunately, some software sites get high ratings for making sure their apps are free of scams and security threats. Here's where to find the real free stuff online, and avoid the hucksters who just want to get your email address and spam you back to the stone age.

Softpedia is one of the good sites. It offers loads of free and paid desktop apps for Mac and Windows. To use it, point your browser to *www.softpedia.com*. When the page appears, don't be tempted by the enticing search box near the top of the page. You can do better. Instead, look above the box and click either **Windows** or **Mac**.

On the Mac or Windows home page, another tempting search box displays, but that's not the way to free software. Instead, scroll down until you see the **Mac Application Finder** or **Windows Application Finder**. It will look like this.

Click in the **Keywords** box, and type in the kind of desktop app you'd like to find. For example, you can search for the free VLC media player for both Mac OS and Windows. This media player can play CDs, DVDs, streaming movies, and almost any format of video or audio files.

To make sure the app is free, click the drop-down arrow in the **License Type** box, and click **Free**. That ensures you only see free software in your search.

To get good quality software, you can also click the arrow in the **Rating** box and choose **Good or Better**, **Very Good or Better**, or **Excellent**. If

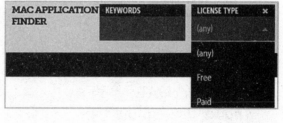

you want to limit your search to recently updated software, click in the **Updated** box, and click a choice.

To set download and file size options, click on the circular plus button. Software that has been downloaded by many people may be very good. If you'd like the most popular choices, click the plus button, click **Downloads**, and click **10,000** or **100,000**. When you have made all your choices, click **Find it!**

One of your search results might look like this example. When software is free, you'll see the **Free** label on the right side of its icon.

To learn more about an app, click on its icon to see a detail page packed with valuable information. Plenty of advertisements may display on the page as well, so be careful where you click.

Finally, to download, click the blue **Download** button just beneath the name of your software.

Here is how the download process works in Windows.

- Click the correct choice in the list. For example, if you chose VLC Media Player, you must choose an x86 site or an x64 site. (See box.)

- A web page with advertisements may appear, but don't click there. If you look closely, you may notice that buttons labeled **Download, Get Started**, and **Start Now** are actually part of advertisements. Be patient, wait for a dialog box to appear, and then follow the prompts.

> If you're not sure which Windows software to choose, go to your Windows Start Menu and click Settings > System > About, and look for **System type**. The x86 or x64 number should tell you which version of the software you want.

Delete a computer app in a snap

Some free apps are free for a reason. If you need to get rid of an app on your computer, here's how to do it.

Throw it out of Windows. Whether you got your app from the Microsoft Store or downloaded it from the web, you delete an app the same way. It's as easy as 1-2-3.

1. Hit Windows key + letter i to open **Settings**.

2. Click **Apps**.

3. In the apps listing, click the app you want to uninstall, and click the **Uninstall** button.

Move it off of Mac. For apps downloaded from the Mac OS App Store, open Launchpad.

Use your mouse to press and hold (long click) the icon of the app you want to delete. When all the apps jiggle and display an "X" in the upper corner, click the "X" on your app's icon to uninstall the app.

If the app did not come from the App Store, try dragging the app to your Trash icon.

Beware of security problems in desktop apps

Although Apple and Microsoft work hard to keep scams, malware, and other security threats out of their stores, app store customers sometimes stumble across a problem before the company can remove it.

For example, Microsoft Store users reported suspicious activity after downloading a fake "Google Photos" app that asked for their Google password. Microsoft removed the app from the store.

Meanwhile, Apple's App Store users have reported problems with some free trial and subscription apps. According to TechCrunch.com, some apps are free to try, but the free trial may only last three days before high subscription rates start.

Other apps design their screens so that your opportunity to avoid subscribing is very hard to see. Apple depends on user reports to help find potentially deceptive apps, so just be careful.

Your health toolkit
An app a day keeps the doctor away

3 sites to help you choose the right doctor

More than 60 percent of doctors say they spend 16 minutes or less with each patient. Only 11 percent of doctors spend 25 minutes or more. That's why finding the right doctor or surgeon is so important.

Start your search with recommendations from family and friends, but don't stop there. Whether you need a new doctor or surgeon — or just want vital knowledge about your regular doctor — don't miss out on the important information from the websites below.

Search doctor databases to find key facts fast. To customize your search for a local doctor to fit your needs, just visit *healthgrades.com* and *vitals.com*. Search by doctor name, medical specialty, a particular health condition, or by the test or surgery you need.

Click the profile of an individual doctor to view critical information such as:

- which insurance the office accepts.

- whether the doctor is board certified, has won awards, or had malpractice claims.

- how much experience the doctor has.

- which hospitals she is affiliated with.

- patient reviews and ratings of the doctor and office staff.

Learn the smartest way to use reviews. If you find enough reviews for a doctor, look for common or repeated themes such as "took time to explain" or "hurried too much."

If you only see four or five reviews, that means dozens of happy or unhappy patients have not weighed in. A handful of reviews may not give you a complete picture of the doctor, so don't take chances.

If you can't find enough reviews for a doctor, try the websites of local hospitals. Hospitals often collect reviews and ratings from patient satisfaction surveys. Thanks to these surveys, hospitals offer more reviews per doctor than review websites do.

> Nervous about the next doctor visit? Be prepared with an appointment guide. Just visit *healthgrades.com* and click **Health A to Z**. Click on the reasons for your visit, and get a customized list of questions your doctor is likely to ask, plus a list of smart questions you should ask.

Uncover little-known secrets doctors never tell you. Visit *projects.propublica.org/vital-signs* to find out how your doctor's fees and services compare to the average doctor's fees and services. You can also learn how your doctor's prescribing record compares with others.

Look up your surgeon's track record. If you need surgery, you can also check the Surgeon Scorecard at *projects.propublica.org/vital-signs/*. Based on Medicare records from recent years, this database shows surgeons' complication and mortality rates for eight of the most common surgeries including knee replacement, gallbladder removal, and hip replacement. Discover how much experience the surgeon has and how her fees compare to the average for this type of surgery.

If the Surgeon Scorecard does not include your surgery, visit *www.surgeonratings.org*. This site covers 14 kinds of surgery including heart surgery and spine surgery. To be listed on the site, a surgeon must have a good record of preventing complications and deaths after surgery and must be highly recommended by fellow doctors in their local area.

11 essential medical sites you need to know

Want a quick guide to the best health websites on the internet? Keep this list handy. It could save your health — or even your life.

- ProPublica's Vital Signs database
  (*projects.propublica.org/vital-signs*)

- SurgeonRatings.org (*surgeonratings.org*)

- Consumer Medication Safety (*consumermedsafety.org*)

- Drugs.com (*drugs.com*)

- GoodRx (*goodrx.com*)

- Rx Saver (*rxsaver.retailmenot.com*)

- BlinkHealth (*blinkhealth.com*)

- U.S. National Library of Medicine (*nlm.nih.gov*)

- Cleveland Clinic Health Library
  (*my.clevelandclinic.org/health*)

- Centers for Disease Control and Prevention (*cdc.gov*)

- Consumer version of Merck Manual
  (*merckmanuals.com/home*)

Physical problems? Let your computer help

If you or someone you love is hard of hearing, or has low vision, arthritis, or other physical limitations, using a computer does not have to be difficult. In fact, your computer can help. Visit *microsoft.com*, scroll to the bottom of the page, and click the **Accessibility** link. You'll find great tips on how to make the computer easier to use.

For example, you can change the screen colors to make it easier to see or use **Magnifier** to enlarge text. You can also use **Narrator** to read what's on your screen or announce notifications. Windows even offers settings to help you avoid using the keyboard or the mouse. Check for similar settings and tools on your Mac OS computer.

Powerful health apps that go everywhere you do

You already know how to use websites to make a difference in your health, but you can't always be at your computer. Whether you need to look up a disease, call for help, or keep up with prescriptions, these apps can help almost anywhere you go.

Pack a portable toolkit for health. Need to understand the medication you were just prescribed or that infection the doctor says you have? You can read about it before you leave the doctor's office. The free WebMD app is like a health reference book and toolkit in a single package. Here are just a few things it can do for you.

- guide you through first aid

- set medication reminders

- find nearby doctors, hospitals, or pharmacies no matter where you are

- display your area's cold and flu map

You can also use the app to catch up on the latest health news.

Be prepared with personal safety apps for emergencies.
Everyone hates the idea of wearing a necklace with an alert button,
so use apps to contact help if you need it. With free apps like bSafe
or Red Panic button, you can easily set up at least one person to
notify instantly if you have an emergency. If the worst happens,
just open the app, and tap a big red button to send a message for
emergency help.

- To get started with bSafe, log in with your phone number,
  and provide your email address, and a photo. When your
  location displays on the screen, tap the angel icon to ask your
  guardian to download the app and serve as your emergency
  contact. If a crisis comes, tap the SOS button to send an
  alarm to your guardian angel. The app sends a message and
  your location to that person immediately.

- The Red Panic Button app works a little differently. When
  you give permission to track your location, the app lists your
  location by address and by GPS. You can add the email
  address or phone number of one contact to notify by email or
  text message. If trouble comes, open the app, tap the red button, and a message with your location is instantly sent to
  your contact.

Be sure to test emergency apps once or twice to make sure each
one works well in your area.

Manage medications effortlessly. The free Medisafe app makes
managing your medications ridiculously easy.

You can set a medication reminder for each pill you take no matter
how complex your dosing schedule gets. That includes medications
you take every other day or antibiotics you only need to take for
two weeks. For each medicine, you can make a note of the dose,

any special instructions, and what the pill looks like. You can also set refill reminders so you don't run out.

Meanwhile, Medisafe may help you track whether you've taken your medication. You can also track your health measurements like blood pressure, blood sugar, or pain level, plus lab test results like cholesterol.

7 things you didn't know Drugs.com could do

Even if you have visited the website before, you might be surprised at all the useful things you can find at *drugs.com*. To save time when you're on the go, get the free app for your smartphone. Here are some things you can do.

- Find out if your medicine interacts with over-the-counter medicines or foods.

- Check on whether you can switch to a cheaper medication to treat a chronic health problem.

- Use the Pill Identifier to identify a loose pill by its shape, color, and imprint.

- Figure out whether that mysterious new symptom could be a drug side effect.

- See drug reviews posted by others who take the same medicine.

- Check out the latest FDA alerts about medication, or subscribe to email alerts that come to you.

- Look up information about your pet's drugs. In addition to Fido and Fluffy, you'll find meds for everything from bees to dairy cows.

Prescription drug secrets: How to save money, solve problems, and stay safe

Take some prescription medications with a glass of milk, and your body might miss out on half the drug. Strangely enough, that glass of milk might help when you take other medications. Where can you get answers? For expert tips on making your medications cheaper, safer, and better, check out these three fantastic drug websites.

Keep yourself safe from medication mistakes. One out of every 1,000 prescriptions is given to the wrong person. This may occur as often as seven times a month at some pharmacies. Make sure this never happens to you.

Visit *consumermedsafety.org* for easy ways to protect yourself. You can also take advantage of safety tips for high-alert medications like insulin or blood thinners. Check back often for smart hints and breaking news about prescription and over-the-counter medications.

Find the best prescription deals in town. Try GoodRx and RxSaver to see which one gives you a lower price. Both are free services with no registration required, and each has a mobile app you can try. What's more, both programs are accepted at many pharmacies such as CVS, Walmart, Walgreens, Kroger pharmacy, independent pharmacies, and some warehouse clubs. Just be sure to read each site's privacy policy, and check whether using the service will apply toward your insurance deductible.

Start by visiting *goodRx.com*, and follow these steps.

- Search with the name of your medicine and your zip code.

- Look above your search results to change the amount and dose to match your prescription, and to switch to a search for generic drug prices.

- Compare your search result prices with your insurance copay to see which is cheaper.

If your best price appears next to a **Get Coupon** or **Get Discount** button, make sure you print out your coupon or discount, and show it at the pharmacy when you present your prescription.

If the GoodRx price isn't low enough, point your browser to *RetailMeNot.com*, and click the **Rx Saver** link. Follow the same search steps you used at GoodRx.

If the price is cheaper than both GoodRx and your insurance copay, print the coupon or drug discount card to show when you give the pharmacist your prescription.

If your insurance copay is cheaper than GoodRx or RxSaver, don't give up hope yet.

Shop, compare, and find a new low price. Visit *blinkhealth.com*, type the name of your medicine in the search box, and see your results. Click **See nearby participating pharmacies** to make sure one of those pharmacies is within driving distance.

Scroll back to the top of the page to adjust the dose and strength in the search filters. When they match your prescription, search again. If Blink offers a better price than your insurance copay, GoodRx, or RxSaver, follow the prompts. You can buy the medicine online and pick it up when you present your prescription at a participating pharmacy. Just be sure to print a proof of purchase to show the pharmacist.

> Medications purchased through Blink may not count towards insurance deductibles or Medicare cost sharing.

Why the zombie apocalypse might make you healthier

The Centers for Disease Control and Prevention (CDC) once published a blog post humorously titled *Preparedness 101: Zombie Apocalypse*. In spite of the funny headline, the post gives valuable tips to help prepare for hurricanes, disease, and other potential hazards.

You can still see that post at the CDC website today. You can also learn more about sleep problems, food safety, and diseases ranging from arthritis to the Zika virus.

Want more? Click the **More** link on the CDC page, and click **CDC-TV** for a large library of videos you can watch to learn more about various health topics. You can even find podcasts about women's health, diabetes, and healthy aging.

New content is added every day so visit *cdc.gov* regularly. Even easier, download the CDC's mobile app, and you'll have a wealth of information at your fingertips.

Learn what your doctor wishes you already knew

People who learn how to manage diabetes keep better control over their blood sugar than those who don't study up. Doctors know how much a little learning can do for your health, but your doctor can't say everything you need to know during a 15-minute visit. To discover what your doctor doesn't have time to tell you, visit these websites.

Welcome to the biggest health library on Earth. Get all your questions answered from the world's largest collection of medical information, and every bit is free. To get started, visit the U.S. National Library of Medicine at *nlm.nih.gov*.

- Click the link for **MedlinePlus** to see a medical encyclopedia, videos, plus extra information on hundreds of health topics. You can also clear up the mysteries of your lab test results, medications, and supplements.

- On the library's home page, click **Resources for You** to read about clinical trials, household product safety, and more.

Seek expert health advice from a world-famous hospital. Cleveland Clinic is one of the top three hospitals in the U.S. and number one for heart health. Visit its health library site for thousands of videos, articles, podcasts, and more to help you take control of your health. If that's not enough, you can also:

- try free quizzes, calculators, and newsletters.

- download free treatment guides.

- find out what to expect from treatments and diagnostic tests.

- get details about medical devices, surgeries, medication, and health conditions.

To see all this and more, visit *my.clevelandclinic.org/health*.

How to translate doctor-speak to English. Your doctor says you have decrudescence. Say what? Doctors are notorious for using confusing terms like this, so the Medical Library Association has created a glossary to help. Just visit *mlanet.org*, and click the **For Patients** link. Scroll down and click **What Did My Doctor Say?** for your doctor-speak definitions. (By the way, decrudescence is a good thing — it means you have fewer symptoms than before.)

See the doctor's textbook anyone can read. The Merck Manual is the world's most widely used medicine textbook, and now you can see the consumer version for free. Just visit *merckmanuals.com/home*. You'll find medical topics, symptoms, emergencies, news, and resources. Hint — the **Resources** tab includes first aid information, quizzes, medical terms, and self-assessment tools.

Transferring records? Piece of cake

If you are one of the many people who has no iPhone, try this if you need to see your records or show them to a new doctor.

First, ask whether your current doctor or hospital has a patient portal on the web. Find out how to get a sign-on for the portal and whether the portal allows you to download all your records as PDF files.

If your new doctor can't easily get to these records, you can print them or carry them on a flash drive. Just remember, medical records should be kept as private as credit card numbers. If you carry them on a flash drive, protect them with a password, and encrypt the files with Preview (Mac OS) or PDFMate Free PDF Merger from *pdfmate.com* (Windows).

How to get your medical records in 45 seconds

Requesting medical records has been difficult and time-consuming — until now. Discover a great way to have access to your medical records any time you need them. You can even share them with a new doctor without the hassle of numerous phone calls.

Having access to your medical records makes you more satisfied with your care, a recent study found. Thousands of patients reported that reading their records helped them understand their medical care better and made it easier to follow doctor's instructions.

Checking your records could also help you answer questions, share lab results with a new doctor, or even deal with your insurance company. How is this possible? Through an app, of course!

What you need to know to get your records. Starting with iOS 12, Apple has upgraded the Health app that comes with the iOS operating system. The app can merge all your health records from multiple providers into a single timeline. For example, you can check:

- results from blood tests or lab tests.

- your prescriptions and any shots you have had.

- records of surgeries or other procedures.

- details about your health conditions.

Any time new records are added to your medical file, you get a notification on your iPhone.

Of course, this is not information you want just anyone to see, but don't worry. Your health records are encrypted to keep them private, and your iPhone passcode adds extra security protection.

It's easy to get started. Find the Health app icon with the heart on your iPhone, and tap the icon to open the app.

At the bottom of your screen, tap **Health Data**. Tap **Health Records** and then tap **Get Started**. Follow the prompts until you see a list of health institutions, hospitals, and systems. Choose yours and log in.

Before you link anything, it's a good idea to read the privacy section. Just above the **Get Started** button, tap **About Health Records**

37

& Privacy. When you finish, tap **Done** in the upper right corner of the screen.

Hundreds of hospitals and health systems already make records available through this app, and more are expected. If your provider does not offer this benefit, ask if it will be available soon.

Caregivers: Find help and training at last

Unpaid family caregivers are the largest source of long-term-care services in the United States, and research has found that's likely to continue as the population ages. At least 4 out of every 5 family caregivers say they'd like more information and training. If you are one of them, find help at the Family Caregiver Alliance at *caregiver.org*.

The website's caregiver education section includes advice for:

- dealing with medication or disturbing behaviors.

- managing dementia issues like bathing, personal grooming, or incontinence.

- getting help from apps for caregiving.

- hiring outside help.

- dealing with legal issues.

You can also view recorded webinar videos on topics like long-distance caregiving, making a home safe for dementia patients, pain assessment, and financial assistance for caregiving.

To help make caregiving easier, the website also includes information about caregiver support groups and each state's resources for caregivers.

Money-saving apps
Easy-to-find freebies, discounts, and rock-bottom prices

Get tons of free coupons without buying a newspaper

Buying the newspaper for coupons can cost anywhere from $50 to $360. Save that money. Get tons of free grocery coupons from these websites and apps.

What your newspaper won't tell you. Visit *SmartSource.com* and *RetailMeNot.com/everyday* for many of the same manufacturer's coupons you would find in your Sunday paper — plus a few extra. At SmartSource, you can even search by location, category, and brand.

Check the websites early in the week. The coupons may only be offered for a limited time. Print these coupons to take to the grocery store.

Bypass the middle man. Visit the website of your favorite brand or product to see if coupons or special offers are available. If the brand has no website, find the name and website of the company that makes the brand, such as Procter & Gamble or Pillsbury. For example, you can find coupons at Procter & Gamble's *pgeveryday.com* or at Pillsbury's website, *pillsbury.com/coupons/printable*.

Score sweet supermarket savings. Your grocery store probably has a free app along with its website. Download the app or visit the website to discover whether digital or printable coupons are available. Some apps and websites may help you add coupons to your store loyalty card.

Don't just check the apps or websites for traditional supermarkets. Target, Walmart, drugstores, or your favorite dollar store may also have grocery coupons on its free app or website.

Find coupons faster. Download the free Coupons.com app or visit *Coupons.com* for a treasure trove of printable coupons. You can also select digital coupons to add to your supermarket's store loyalty card. If you buy the coupon's product, the savings ring up at the register when you use your loyalty card.

Get help from a Grocery Pal. Discover a pile of printable and digital coupons when you download the Grocery Pal app. Just create an account and tap the **Coupon** tab to mine for coupon gold.

If your smartphone cannot print directly to your printer, don't worry. Grocery Pal sends the coupons to your email, so you can print them from your laptop or home computer. Want more discounts? Provide your zip code to root out the best specials in your area.

Some websites and apps ask you to register with an email address before you can print or receive coupons. Experts recommend you do not use your personal email just in case spam becomes a problem. Instead, create a free email address with Gmail or Yahoo, and use it only for deals and coupons.

For more grocery coupons, keep an eye out for the following free apps and websites later in this chapter — Flipp, Krazy Coupon Lady, and Hip2Save.

See up to 2,000 new bargains every week

Discounts up to 80 percent are just waiting for you if you visit *dealnews.com* or download the free app. You can view more than 350 new bargains on most days, without even registering for an account.

Deals for clothes, furniture, luggage, computers, and home and garden supplies are just the beginning. If you don't spot the product category you want in the categories menu, don't give up. The list can't cover everything, so do a search for the deal you want and see if it comes up.

When you find a great deal, click or tap the **Buy Now** or **Shop Now** button to go directly to the seller's site. If you don't find a deal, look for coupons or coupon codes to help you save.

Discover the secret grocery stores hope you never learn

Combine coupons with rebates and sales, and you may get many grocery items for pennies or even for free. Rebate and cash-back apps make this faster and easier so you can save more money than ever before.

Make grocery store rebates as easy as pie. To start, visit *savingstar.com* or download the free app. Attach your store loyalty cards from supermarkets and drugstores, and you can submit rebates through the cards. Here's how.

- Before you shop, pick out rebates to add to each store's card. Weekly rebates may include a healthy offer on produce or a "100% freebie." After you ring up your rebate purchases, submit your rebates by using your loyalty card. The rebates will be added to your SavingStar account within two weeks.

- If you shop at stores that can't attach rebates to a loyalty card, scan each rebate product's UPC code and receipt to submit rebates to your SavingStar account.

- When your account totals $20 or more, you can cash out your rebates to a bank account, PayPal account, or gift card.

  For a similar free app that may offer different rebates, try the free Checkout 51 app or visit *checkout51.com*.

Stack coupons with rebates and sales. Stacking can mean using a manufacturer's coupon with a coupon issued by your supermarket, or you can stack a coupon with a rebate or sale. To easily find these cost-cutting combos, use coupon match-up sites and apps.

- Visit *thekrazycouponlady.com* or download the free Krazy Coupon Lady app.

- Download the Favado app.

- Visit *5dollardinners.com*.

Each time you sign up for a coupon, rebate, or cash-back app, read the Terms of Use and Frequently Asked Questions or Help carefully. These can help you learn how to save more money with the app and may prevent problems with unexpected deadlines or inactivity fees.

If you can't find an online rebate, visit the manufacturer's website to check for mail-in rebates.

3 ridiculously easy ways to turn receipts into cash

Cash-back apps can help you save even more money. Combine them with a sale or coupon, or use them to save money on full-price items.

Rack up the points and earn a gift card. Download the free Fetch Rewards app, and use the app's built-in scanner to scan your receipts after you shop. If you sign up with an email address, the app adds rewards points to your accounts when you buy participating brands.

To score even more rewards points, see the app's list of participating brands, and look for specials that include bonus points. The app not only accepts receipts from supermarkets, but also warehouse stores, dollar stores, drugstores, convenience stores, and more. Just be aware that information from your receipt is used in market research.

When you earn enough points, you can exchange them for a gift card from Amazon, Target, Kohl's, or many other stores, restaurants, and businesses.

Consider a combination app for bigger savings. If you don't mind taking part in market research, you may save up to $20 each month with the free Ibotta app.

Ibotta works differently from other cash-back apps. Before you shop, open the app and choose the cash-back offers you want. Buy the offered product at one of Ibotta's many participating stores. After shopping, you must take a photo of your receipt. But you'll also be asked to contribute to market research by scanning a QR code or bar code, taking a brief survey, watching a video, or performing other quick tasks.

You may be allowed to scan your receipt even if you have already scanned it for another cash-back or rebate app. When you accumulate $20 of cash-back savings, you can receive a gift card or payment to your PayPal account.

Use this Hog to protect your piggy bank. Receipt Hog is another free receipt-scanning app that offers cash back, in exchange for receipt information and answering market research surveys.

Scan in paper receipts from stores that carry groceries, and you earn coins. Scan in receipts from other stores for opportunities to earn additional coins. These coins pile up until you have enough to earn a gift card or cash back.

How to pay rock-bottom prices on everything you buy

Never pay full price again? It may just be possible with these websites and apps that find sale prices near your home for just about anything.

Don't be fooled by scammers offering free samples. For genuine freebies, visit *MyFreeProductSamples. com, SampleADay.com,* or *SampleSource.com.*

Remember when you could have saved money, but didn't? Don't let that happen again. The free Shopular app shows you the sale circulars, special deals, and coupons for any store you select. Add specific deals to your **Saved Deals** list so you won't miss a bargain. It's easier than you think.

If you don't have time to study the sales circulars, go to **Settings** for deal alerts, and choose which offers come to you. Select bargains from nearby shopping centers, deals from only your favorite stores, or the hottest specials for the weekend.

Strike instant gold with discounts for your favorite stores. Use *RetailMeNot.com* or the free RetailMeNot app to get cash-back offers, coupons, and other bargains in-store and online.

- Search for promotional codes to get online shopping discounts. If you want a store's best cash-back offers and promotional codes to automatically appear while you shop online, download the Genie browser plug-in for Chrome and Firefox, and sign up for a free *RetailMeNot.com* membership.

- Find deals and thousands of coupons for restaurants and both online and local shops. This includes stores for clothing, electronics, home goods and furniture, office supplies, crafts, home improvement, sporting goods, and oodles more.

- Buy discounted gift cards for your favorite shop, but spend the card's full value. It's an extra discount on top of any sales or coupons you use.

Save as much as 80 percent no matter where you shop. Visit *DealHunting.com* to get great quality as well as low prices. Search for deals by store or by item, or search for discount promotional codes. *DealHunting.com* lists discounts and deals from many familiar retail names ranging from Ace Hardware to Zales. You can even find bargains on travel and eyeglasses.

See all your local sales in one place and rake in more coupons. Want to see the circulars for your favorite supermarkets and retail stores without slogging through the newspaper? Download the free Flipp app or visit *us.flipp.com*.

Tell the app your location and get all the local ads at your fingertips. Visit the app's **Coupons** tab to choose from dozens of digital coupons you can attach to your store loyalty card.

Find the biggest and best bargains every day. You can't hire hundreds of people to hunt down the best deals of the day, but you can download the free slickdeals app, or visit *slickdeals.net*. On this deal-sharing website, people post the best deals they find and vote on which deals are good enough to get top billing.

To view the best deals for you, create a free membership, and pick your favorite stores and product categories. Need a particular product? Create a deal alert to save both time and dollars.

Mine this rich source of money-savers. Visit *hip2save.com* or download the free Hip2Save app to catch the latest money-saving deals at your favorite stores, both in-store and online. It also lists restaurants plus entertainment discounts on movies, music, and more. Don't forget to check for freebies and printable coupons.

Hidden gems: 2 little-known ways to save big on Amazon

Did you know Amazon has two not-so-known spots that can save you money on tons of items? See where Amazon hides jaw-dropping price reductions and huge discounts.

Prices plummet in Amazon's bargain basement. Discover the backdoor to the Amazon Warehouse where you can find like-new, returned, open-box, or used products discounted up to 70 percent.

If you shop on your laptop or home computer, find the Amazon Warehouse link hidden near the very bottom of Amazon's main page. On the Amazon app, search for "Amazon Warehouse" in the search box, and then tap the **Amazon Warehouse** link or ad.

Browsing the Amazon Warehouse is like shopping in a giant flea market or thrift mall. You can browse through items from up to 30 different departments including Arts, Crafts, and Sewing; Garden and Outdoor; Electronics; Clothing, Shoes, and Jewelry; and Home and Kitchen.

The products range from **Like New** to **Acceptable** condition, but you can return them under Amazon's usual 30-day return policy. Not every deal is worth having, but browse carefully, and you may find bargains to smile about for years to come.

What smart warehouse shoppers know. When you find a product you want, pay close attention to the item's condition. It is often listed above the **Add to cart** button. The less perfect the product is, the bigger your savings may be. Here is what each condition means.

- **Used: Like New.** The product is in good working order, but may have damaged packaging.

- **Used: Very Good.** The product may have small scratches or cosmetic blemishes, show slight signs of use, or have minor accessories missing.

- **Used: Good.** The product works well but shows some wear and signs of use. It may have minor cosmetic damage or missing instructions, parts, or accessories.

- **Used: Acceptable.** The product is worn, has signs of use, or may have scratches, dents, or other cosmetic damage. Manuals, parts, or accessories may be missing.

Amazon often gives specific descriptions of any shortfalls a product may have, but you sometimes have to click **Details** to see that information. Although the items do not come with a warranty, Amazon claims to inspect and test each product before it goes on sale in the Amazon Warehouse.

Keep in mind that Amazon Warehouse items may not be available for long and their prices may fluctuate.

Find the screaming discounts Amazon keeps under wraps.
If you can't find the right deal at Amazon Warehouse, try the Amazon Outlet. You can save up to 50 percent on overstocked and marked-down products and sometimes even up to 80 percent. Score bargains on all kinds of items including home goods, kitchen items, electronics, and much more.

Unfortunately, the outlet is even more hidden than the warehouse. You can't find this store on Amazon's main page. Instead, type "Amazon outlet" in the search box. When you find a great deal, keep an eye out for a timer or deadline because some deals may be limited-time offers.

Learn, play, and grow with fun-tastic apps

Don't miss these 8 super sites for seniors

You could spend hours hunting down the valuable information that makes life easier as you age. But you don't need to climb every mountain and turn over every rock. Just visit these websites instead.

SavvySenior.org — smart steps to a brighter future. You may have seen the Savvy Senior column in your local paper, but columnist Jim Miller has also created a website. Visit *SavvySenior.org* for news and columns about topics of interest to baby boomers and others who weren't born yesterday.

Click the **Senior Resources** tab for an immense list of links including finances, retirement, Medicare, volunteering, insurance, and travel.

SeniorLaw.com — where legal links nest. Ever wish you could get a few tips from Perry Mason? Whether you are worried about power-of-attorney issues or just want to figure out legal aspects of Medicare, wills, or disabilities, this site can help.

Their list of the web's legal resources includes websites with information about advance directives, health care proxies, nursing homes, reverse mortgages, estate planning, and much more. They also list Federal and state resources. Find answers about legal issues at *seniorlaw.com/elder-law-legal-resources-on-the-web*.

Next Avenue — advice for the road ahead. Designed for anyone over age 49, this site offers great practical advice about personal finance, work before and after retirement, health, caregiving, security, and more.

For example, you may find information about how to regain strength after age 50 or the benefits of learning a skill later in life. The site's high-quality articles are sometimes reprinted by famous financial publications such as *Forbes* or *MarketWatch*. Visit *nextavenue.org* to see why.

AARP — the site that started it all. Visit *aarp.org* for a comprehensive website for older adults, featuring articles, senior discounts, videos, and research. For example, you may find information about which medical screening tests you might not need or how to fight fraud on the cheap.

Road Scholar — broaden the mind without breaking the bank. Formerly known as Elderhostel, the site now promotes "lifelong learning" through affordable educational travel, for adults age 55 and over. Visit *roadscholar.org* to learn more.

Workforce50 — career advice for non-rookies. This premier site provides expert articles to help you market your skills, get ready for a job search, change careers, and discover free resources. You can even sign up for job alerts and learn which companies want older workers. For details, visit *workforce50.com*.

SeniorCitizenDiscountlist — a treasure trove of bargains. Don't miss this super site for checking out all the senior discounts available to you in your area. Visit *SeniorCitizenDiscountlist.org* to uncover senior discounts at the grocery store, restaurants, theaters, and more. Want more? Visit *SeniorDiscounts.com*, too.

RetiredBrains — skills for pre-retirement and beyond. For those planning to retire or already retired, this site covers a lot of ground. Information about travel, jobs, retirement resources, healthcare, insurance, and discounts are just the beginning.

Visit *retiredbrains.com* to find a full-time or part-time job, temporary work, or even volunteer opportunities. Be sure to check the bottom of the home page for a fantastic list of resources that covers ways to save, continuing education, identity theft, and more.

Got game? Test yourself with these brain-teasers

Could childhood games make you happier and healthier? Spoiler alert — some studies suggest they can. Challenge yourself and improve your thinking with these free puzzles, brain-teasers, and games.

You may find in-app purchases buried in some of these games, so click or tap carefully. By taking your time, you can avoid making unplanned purchases that could take the fun out of playing.

Try the Neuro Nation app for iPhone and Android. Chosen as an Editor's Choice by the Google Play Store, this free app starts with a few questions so it can choose the best games for you. After an "assessment" game for practice, you may start with a pathfinder game or another game tailored to your specifications. You can play three games for free every day.

See why people love the WordBrain app. At first, you might think WordBrain's tantalizing puzzles are child's play, but don't be fooled. These clever word puzzles start off easy and get harder.

You may be surprised at how time flies while playing through the levels of all the free games.

Tricky Test 2 Genius Brain is tantalizing fun. Like brain teasers? This is the app you have been waiting for. This free app is full of clever trick questions that will keep you challenged, entertained, and amused.

Print new puzzles fresh off The Griddle. When you want a change from electronic games, try the free printable puzzles at *thegriddle.net*. You do not have to register to print one out. Just meander through the menu, and pick a Sudoku, maze, or other puzzle. Click the red PDF button to see each one and print the ones you like. A new puzzle is added every week, but you can check the archives for more brain-teasers to play between updates.

Save your money on brain-training apps

Are you tempted to pay for an app that claims it will make you smarter and slow down brain issues from aging, dementia, and other health problems? The Federal Trade Commission (FTC) says to save your money. It recently charged several brain-training app companies with deceptive advertising for claiming research had proven their games can do just that.

The FTC says that research by these companies hasn't proven any boost in mental performance outside of a lab. Does this mean brain-stimulating games don't prevent mental losses as you age? It's too early to tell so it doesn't hurt to continue playing. Just stick with the free apps.

2 easy — and fun — ways to challenge your mind

Interested in speaking a new language? Love getting outdoors? Games are not the only way to stimulate your brain. Research suggests learning a language and taking walks may also help protect your aging mind, so try these apps to keep your brain sharp.

Start learning French in five minutes. Dreaming of going to Paris in the spring? Visit *duolingo.com*, choose French as your language, and select how many minutes a day you'd like to spend learning. Duolingo turns the lessons into a delightful game, so don't be surprised if you have fun while you learn. Duolingo is also available as a free smartphone app.

Does a daily walk sound boring? Not anymore. Map My Walk is a free smartphone app that can make your daily walk more interesting. The app tracks how far and how long you walk, how many calories you burn, and how many steps you take. It can even help you get back home again if you wander off the beaten track.

9 websites that actually make your life easier

The internet isn't just for news and email — it can solve problems, end hassles, and get you free stuff galore. Visit these helpful websites and see what they can do for you today.

Savings secret: Discover recipes for ingredients you already have. Stop letting pantry items go to waste. Find recipes that fit the ingredients you already have on hand. Visit *supercook.com*, type in the ingredients, and Supercook lists recipes that might work for you. You can even filter the results by diet, such as gluten-free or vegan, by cuisine type, or by the type of dish you want. For added savings, try searching for sale items from your local grocery ads.

Breeze past the automated phone menu with secret helpline shortcuts. Slogging through the customer service phone menu is such a time-waster. Press this, say that, and repeat.

Want to speak to a real person and bypass endless button pushing? Visit *GetHuman.com* to find customer service numbers for almost any company as well as tips to help you reach a representative faster. If the company handles customer service through live chat, Twitter, Facebook messenger, or Facebook, GetHuman provides contact details for those, too.

Find a missing product manual almost instantly. When you desperately need the manual for that kitchen gadget, you can't find it. Instead of wasting time hunting, just download the manual from *Manualslib.com*. The site includes manuals for more than 2 million products. Just make sure you have an app or software that can read PDF files.

Make web page ads vanish like magic. That fascinating article has so many ads and banners you can scarcely read it, let alone share it with anyone. To fix that, copy the web address, and surf to *printfriendly.com*.

Paste the address into the **PrintFriendly** box, click **Preview**, and be pleasantly surprised at the page that appears. Gone are the ads and distractions. What's left is an easy-to-read document you can print or turn into a PDF just by clicking on a button above the document.

Free printable games, signs, and forms galore. Print your own music sheets, calendar, brochure templates, weekly budget forms, cross stitch graph paper, lined paper, postcards, knitting graphs, or one of 1,700 other forms and templates. Visit *printablepaper.net* to see them all.

This site knows what you're thinking before you do. When you can't think of a word, go to *onelook.com/thesaurus*. Type in an idea or definition to get a list of possible answers.

The real reason that website refuses to load. Don't waste your precious time scrambling to figure out what's wrong with your browser or computer. The problem might not be at your end. To find out if a website is down, visit *DownForEveryoneOrJustMe.com* or *IsItDownRightNow.com*.

How to find the best charities for your donations. To make sure a charity is legitimate before you donate, check the charity's rating at *charitywatch.org* and *charitynavigator.org*.

Will the real superfood please stand up? Some delicious foods are good for your health, while others are just pretenders. How do you choose between two tasty treats? Visit *twofoods.com*. Type in your two food choices, click **Compare**, and get your answer just like that.

Trace your family tree for free

Are you related to someone famous or even someone royal? Thanks to free websites, you may find out without leaving your house. Trace your family tree back to its roots, even if your tree was planted in another country. Start with these sites.

Check cemeteries to find missing graves. Surf to *interment.net* to see records from more than 5,000 cemeteries around the globe, including some graveyards that are no longer available. Your price for this information? Zero.

If Interment.net didn't help, visit *billiongraves.com*. You can search transcribed records of graves from more than 50 countries for free. Volunteers add more records every month, so check back often.

Make a virtual visit to any county. Want local information right down to the individual county? USGenWeb can guide you to plenty of state and county sites. These sites may have free records that include cemetery transcriptions, legal documents, and more.

The USGenWeb archives also feature special projects for marriages, pensions, maps, court cases, and other records. Search an individual county or search through all the counties at once. Visit *usgenweb.org* and *usgwarchives.net* to see all the valuable resources volunteers have found.

Search billions of international records, pictures and links. Over 5 billion records are just waiting for you on the free FamilySearch site. That includes millions of images you can browse. In addition to U.S. records, see information from Europe, Argentina, and Mexico. Visit *familysearch.org*, or get the smartphone app.

For even more, visit *worldgenweb.org* for free links and resources for countries ranging from Albania to Zimbabwe.

Are your ancestors lurking at the library? If you can't find information anywhere else, try this. Heritage Quest Online is only free if your local library subscribes to it. Check whether you can use your library card for free online access.

You'll be able to look at U.S. Census information, immigration records, files from the Revolutionary War, local history books, and an index of thousands of genealogical journals.

Super useful apps you need to download now

The hands-down best thing about apps is how much easier they make your life. Check out this list of the 15 most useful — and free — cellphone apps for seniors.

AccuWeather. See local weather forecasts, severe weather warnings, and up-to-the-minute rain alerts.

A Soft Murmur. Tailor a mix of nature sounds to help you sleep, relax, or concentrate.

Facebook. Easily share personal news and photos with friends and family.

FaceTime. Make video calls to friends and family from your iPhone or iPad.

Flashlight. Turn your iPhone screen into a flashlight.

Flightradar24. Track flights on a map as they happen, and get details for individual flights.

GasBuddy. Find the cheapest gas anywhere you travel.

Google Keep. Make notes, checklists, sketches, and more.

Krazy Coupon Lady. Find sales and hundreds of coupons.

MapMyWalk. Track your walk on a map, including distance, time, and more.

Medisafe. Manage even complicated medications with fun reminders and more.

Pocket. Save an ad-free copy of a web page or article to read later, or have the app read it aloud.

Snapseed. Quickly tidy up photographs with this easy-to-use photo editor.

Tip Calculator Free. Calculate the total tip and how much each person owes.

Waze. Reach your destination faster with turn-by-turn directions that avoid traffic jams.

Organization secrets you'll wish you'd known years ago

At last, you can organize projects, control your schedule, and keep the information you need conveniently within reach everywhere you go. Try these three popular apps for astonishing results.

Keep dozens of notes in the palm of your hand. Need to write down a phone number or make a checklist? Don't lug a pen or paper around. Just open the free Google Keep app, and type or dictate a note.

Google Keep is a note-taking app where you can create and store all kinds of notes. Like other note-taking apps, it can replace a notebook or even an accordion file full of papers. What's more, you can create text notes, checklists, sketches, or even pictures as notes.

To keep your notes organized, use labels or color coding — or just search to find the note you want. You can even add a reminder to a note. If you have a Google account, your notes may also be available on the web, too.

Other good note-taking apps include Apple Notes and Microsoft OneNote.

Turbocharge your to-do list. Free to-do list apps like Remember The Milk are like granting your to-do list new super powers. For example, you can add a task, and then:

- assign a due date.

- give it a priority (low, medium, or high).

- set a reminder.

- estimate how long the task should take.

You can also give each task a reference tag such as "home" or "work." You can even set a task to repeat if you expect to do it regularly. When you sign up for Remember The Milk, the app assigns you a special Inbox email address. Send email to this address and it becomes a task in your Inbox task list. It's that easy.

Remember the Milk also has a web app so you can use the app with a regular keyboard and larger screen. Other good to-do apps include Todoist and Any.do. Both are free.

Organize your projects like a pro. Free apps can help you get organized with ease. For example, Trello is a great way to organize a project or a process like Christmas gift-giving. Here is how it might work.

Say you create a Trello "bulletin board" called **Christmas**. Because each board contains at least one list, you start with a list of gift recipients. You assign each recipient a "card" (like an index card) where you list your gift ideas for that person. Perhaps you'd call that first list **Ideas**.

You can pack a lot of ideas and other information into each card. When you open a card, you see space for comments, a description, checklists, a due date, and even a place to attach a file.

To track your progress, you could make lists like the ones shown in the graphic on the next page. As you get things done, you drag cards from one list to the next.

For example, if you order a gift, you move that person's card to the **Ordered** list, and assign a reminder to make sure the gift arrives when expected. When an order arrives, or you buy a gift, you move that card to the **Bought/Delivered** list. After wrapping or mailing someone's gift, you drag that person's card to the **Wrapped** or **Mailed** list. Nothing gets forgotten or lost.

This is just one example. People have used Trello to manage meal planning, projects at work, collections, parties, weddings, home renovation, and much more.

Never wait for news, weather, and traffic again

Remember when you had to wait for news, weather, and traffic reports on your TV or car radio? Today, you can get instant information from your smartphone, even with no TV or radio in sight. Try these apps to see what they can do.

Keep a forecast at your fingertips. More than 50 million people have downloaded the free AccuWeather app. This app delivers seven-day forecasts, hour-by-hour forecasts, radar, and current conditions. If rain is coming soon, the app tells you — down to the minute — when rain will arrive. Check the settings and name your location to make sure you get notified about storm warnings.

Other good — and free — weather apps include The Weather Channel app, and Weather by WeatherBug. You can even help the National Weather Service fine-tune their forecasts. Just download the free mPing app to anonymously report rain, snow, and more to the National Weather Service.

Steer clear of sudden traffic jams. What if your navigation app could not only plot the best way to get somewhere, but also route you around bad traffic? Waze can do that. Everyone with the app can report traffic jams, road closures, objects in the road, and other hazards, so the app includes that information when it plots your route. Naturally, it also speaks each turn aloud right when you need to hear it.

Check breaking news on the go. Choose top news apps like CNN or Fox News to read or watch the latest national or international news wherever you go. You can also get news alerts about breaking stories or top headlines as they happen.

News and weather videos use a lot of data on your phone plan. Stick to reading your news and weather apps when you're out and about. Save the videos for when you can watch using free Wi-Fi or your home Wi-Fi network.

For local news, try the apps from your local TV stations. Some offer both news and weather in a single app, and you can often choose whether to read the news or watch videos.

Stay in touch online
Connect through email, Facebook, Skype, and more

Communication has come a long way since the days of dial-up phones. Today you can connect with friends and family through all sorts of technology — cellphones, computers, even tablets. Just the click of a button puts you in touch with loved ones all over the world — for free!

- You can email your son in Atlanta and send birthday greetings to your sister in Cincinnati.

- Send an instant message to a former coworker.

- Share pictures of your trip to the Grand Canyon on Facebook and Instagram.

- Make a phone call to your family across the country — even across the ocean — from your computer or tablet.

- See how much your grandchildren in Philly have grown thanks to video software like Skype and Facetime.

The world of communication is changing constantly. If you've kept up even a little bit, good for you. It's time to take the next step and learn how much more you can do.

Email problems solved
Tips and tricks to master your inbox

Type emails without using your hands

Let's face it, typing all those emails to your grandchildren can get a little tedious. Not to mention painful when your arthritis kicks in. How would you like to have your computer do the task for you?

The secret is voice-recognition software, which is available for free on both Windows and Mac. With this high-tech feature, you can type emails and other documents by simply talking to your computer. And you set it all up with just a few simple steps. Then you can toggle the feature on and off as you need it.

On both Windows and Mac, you can choose between an online or a computer-based speech-recognition feature. The online version uses data it gathers from your speech and others' speech to improve the way it works. The computer-based version learns only from you, so it takes longer to learn how to type what you say. But it offers more privacy.

How to get your computer talking. On a Windows 10 computer, open **Settings** and choose Privacy > Speech, Inking, and Typing. Then turn on **speech services and typing suggestions**. If you want to use the computer-based feature, open **Settings**, choose Ease of Access > Speech, and turn on **Speech Recognition**.

Windows then guides you through the setup process for whichever version you choose.

On a Mac, open the Apple menu and select System Preferences > Keyboard > Dictation. To use the online feature, select the **Dictation** radio button, but leave the **Use Enhanced Dictation** checkbox clear. To use the offline feature, select **Dictation** and the **Use Enhanced Dictation** checkbox.

When you set up the dictation app, you'll see a tip sheet with basic commands for using your operating system's tool. Be sure to save the link or guide so you can easily refer to it as you learn the basic voice commands you need to know.

> Need to fax a document to your doctor's office? Surprise — you don't need a fax machine anymore to do it. With online services like eFax.com, you can easily create an account and send and receive faxes via email.

Easy-peasy way to write an email. After you set up voice recognition on your computer, you can turn it on to write an email and turn it off when you're done. Make sure the cursor appears in your email message where you want to begin adding text. Then simply begin to talk, and like magic, your words will appear on the screen.

- On a Windows computer, you can toggle voice recognition on or off using keyboard shortcuts. To toggle the online version, press the Windows key+H. To toggle Speech Recognition (the computer-based version), press the Windows key+Ctrl+S.

- On a Mac, you turn on Dictation by pressing the **Fn** key twice or choosing Edit > Start Dictation. To stop using Dictation, press the **Fn** key once or click **Done**, which appears under the microphone icon.

It may take a little time for the computer to learn your voice and for you to adjust to this new way of typing. Stick with it, and before long you'll be a dictation pro.

Save time by personalizing your messages

When you write an email, you want your message to reflect your style. But it's a hassle to type the same information and apply the same formatting options each and every time. You can save your preferences if you spend a little time upfront saving your settings.

Create a personalized email signature. An email signature is text that automatically appears at the end of every email you send. You can use a signature to share practical information, like your name, phone number, and email address. But you can also add personal touches, like a quote you love, a small image, or a special font or color for your name.

You'll probably need to set up your signature in your email program and your smartphone separately. In most browser-based email programs, like AOL or Gmail, simply open **Settings** and look for **Signature** to create and save an email signature.

On your smartphone, look for the email signature option in your email app settings. For example, on an iPhone, tap the Settings icon > Mail > Signature. You'll most likely see the phrase "Sent from my iPhone." Savvy smartphone manufacturers know the signature block is another good way to promote their product. But you can delete that text and customize the signature block with something that reflects your personal style.

Change the formatting to suit your needs. Most email services choose a default font, text size, and color that works well for most people reading on a computer or smartphone. But it may not be what's best for you. You can easily change these options and save them for all the messages you send. Look under your email **Settings** to edit the styles.

But remember, simple is usually best. You may love a blue and yellow color scheme, but black text on a white background is still the most readable. And although writing in a fancy script font may appeal to your old-fashioned nature, your grandkids may give up reading it after the first paragraph.

Email programs typically provide several basic options that look nice and are easy to read, so you should find one that appeals to you.

Magnify text so emails are easy to read

Have you ever received an email with text that was too small to read? Bet you didn't know your computer has its very own magnifying glass that can solve that problem instantly.

To use the magnifier, you typically need to turn it on first. On Windows, open the **Start** menu, select the **Settings** icon, and choose **Ease of Access**. In the window that appears, toggle the **Magnifier** option to the **On** position.

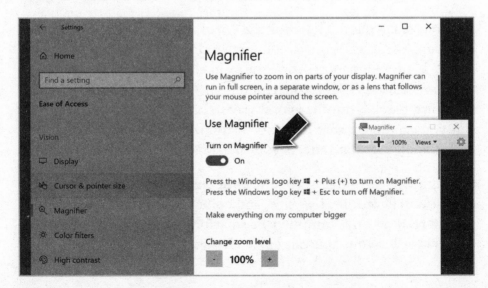

On a Mac, the magnifier is called **Zoom**. To turn it on, choose Apple menu > System Preferences > Accessibility > Zoom. Then select the checkboxes for the Zoom options you want to use, such as keyboard shortcuts or mouse scroll gesture plus a modifier key.

After you turn on the magnifier, you can turn it on and off as you need it. On Windows, press the Windows key and the plus sign (+) to turn on the Magnifier feature. Then move your cursor over the text you want to magnify. When you're done, turn off the Magnifier by pressing the Windows key+Esc.

On a Mac, you can turn Zoom on or off using whichever options you enabled during the setup process.

Need help typing? Let your email program supply the words

Predictive text is a feature that tries to guess the next word you want to type. You may have used a predictive text keyboard on your smartphone. Now, online email services are beginning to add predictive text, too.

Choose whether to use the suggested text. Unlike an autocomplete feature, predictive text lets you choose whether you want to use its suggestions.

On a smartphone keyboard, predictive text allows you to select a word from the options it presents by tapping the word you want. Then the word you tap is added to your text message. When you type an email on your computer, predictive text lets you click or press **Tab** to accept its suggestions.

Because predictive text lets you control what you want to say, rather than overriding your typing like autocomplete, it can be a handy tool. On a smartphone, it's especially helpful when you need to use a long word that's difficult to type on a tiny smartphone keyboard.

On your computer, predictive text often suggests whole phrases or completes common sentences. If the suggestion isn't useful, you simply keep typing.

If at first you don't succeed... On both smartphones and online email services, predictive text will learn your preferences as you use it. So if you like the idea of the feature, but it's not working well for you at first, keep using it. The more you type, the more it will learn.

For example, as you correspond with your favorite cousin, Bob, predictive text will eventually figure out whether you like to begin with "Hi Bob," "Hello Bob!" or "Dear Bob." Think how much more quickly you'll get those emails out!

Where to find this helpful feature. In some online email programs, you may need to turn on predictive text before you see suggestions. Look for an option that uses terms like predictive, smart, or suggested.

Gmail calls its predictive-text feature **Smart Compose**. Outlook has an option called **Suggest Replies**. If you don't see this option now, keep an eye out for it. Predictive text is fairly new to online email services and may be coming to your email soon.

3 tips to organize and find messages quickly

Keeping your email organized can be tedious and time-consuming. Your email service probably offers lots of tools and features to help, but what's the easiest way to use them? Every person and email program are a little different, but a few basic tips can help you organize a cluttered inbox and keep only the messages you need.

Cut clutter by deleting messages in bulk. Marketing emails can contain money-saving discounts, and newsletters are a helpful way to hear the latest about a topic or organization that interests you.

But if you don't keep up with reading and deleting all those messages, they can take over your inbox.

By deleting messages in bulk, you can clean out your inbox quickly. Outlook has a feature called Sweep that lets you select one message and then move all the messages from the same sender to the trash.

With other email services, you can simply search for a term that's unique to the messages you want to delete. On the search results page, look for a checkbox or radio button that lets you select all the messages in your search results at once. Then click the **Delete** or **Trash** button on the toolbar to get rid of all those messages.

Make a simple system with minimal folders. A complicated system is hard to maintain. For example, if you try to organize your messages into 25 different folders, it's harder to make snap decisions about where to put each message you want to keep. Many people find that limiting the number of organizational tools they use helps them use those tools more consistently.

You can create a simple system that works for you in lots of different ways. Some people have just one folder called **Keep**. Any message they want to save for later goes into that folder, and all other messages are deleted.

Other people use a four-folder system based on how urgent the message is. A letter from a friend you want to save forever might go into a **Keep** folder. Any message you need to follow up on goes into a folder based on how quickly you need to respond — **Urgent**, **This Month**, or **This Year**.

The **Urgent** folder helps you quickly identify the messages you want to act on right away. The monthly messages are ones to resolve by the end of each month or discounts you want to keep for later but will expire by the end of the month. The yearly folder might hold receipts you want to save for your tax preparer.

Find messages quickly with search. Instead of hunting through your inbox or folders to find a message, use your email's search feature. The trick is to choose a search term that's specific enough to narrow your messages down to the one you're looking for. Here are some tips for choosing a search term.

- Combine a contact's email address with a term. If you're looking for your sister's Christmas list, you might enter her email address and the word "Christmas" or "list" in the search box.

- Use quotes to find an exact phrase. To tell your search tool to look for two words right next to each other in a message, add quotes around the two words.

- Use a minus sign to exclude a word. For example, if you're on a committee for a local organization but you're not looking for the meeting minutes, type the organization's name and "-minutes" to exclude those messages.

Take control — fight back against email spam

Don't be a victim of computer spamming. Try these five tips to block the intrusive emails from getting to you.

Change your marketing email settings. After you make an online purchase or sign up for a newsletter, you might receive too much email from that organization. You can prevent unwanted junk mail by clicking a link labeled **Manage Settings** or something similar at the bottom of an email from that organization. Then choose an option to receive fewer messages, such as weekly or monthly messages instead of daily emails.

To tell the organization to stop sending you messages, click an **Unsubscribe** link. An easy-peasy way to slash the number of emails you receive.

Remember — click email links only if you're certain the email is legitimate. It should contain items you know you ordered or thank you for signing up for a newsletter to which you know you subscribed.

Train your spam filter. Popular email services like Outlook, AOL, and Gmail include a spam filter. To help that filter work effectively, report spam in your inbox. If a message you want ends up in your spam folder, you need to tell your filter that message isn't spam. To mark messages as spam or not spam, look for a button in the toolbar above your list of email messages. It may refer to it by another name, such as junk.

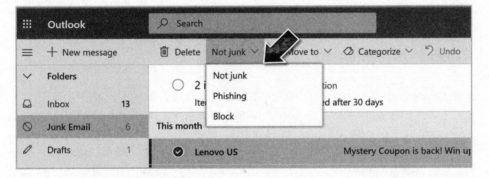

Block an email address. Most email services let you block an email address, which sends future messages to your spam email folder. To block an address, you can usually select the message in your inbox and then click a **Block** button in the toolbar at the top of your email window.

Create an approved list of contacts. Want a quick trick to prevent junk mail from cluttering up your inbox? Create a whitelist. This is a list of email contacts from which you always want to receive messages. With some email services, you can set up your inbox so you see only messages from whitelisted addresses, such as friends and family. To add an email address to a whitelist, create a filter in your email so that messages from that sender never go to spam.

Use a third-party tool to manage spam. If your email service's built-in spam tools don't work well for you, a third-party tool designed to manage spam can help. Most third-party tools work with specific email services, so look for one that works with yours. You can find free and paid options.

For example, BoxBe works with AOL, Yahoo!, Outlook, and Gmail. It can help you create whitelists, block senders, and flag and remove spam messages. If you use the Chrome web browser and Gmail, you can add a plug-in to your browser that can help you remove spam email messages.

Surprising way to stop the (annoying!) flood of replies

Parties and holiday get-togethers are fun. Wading through too many emails to organize them is not. When the hostess sends a message, she typically puts everyone's email address in the **To:** field. Then all the recipients receive replies to the whole group that simply say "Thanks!" or "I'll be there!" With a large group, those replies can add up.

Whenever you email a large group — or forward an email to 50 of your closest friends — you should always send it to yourself. It may sound weird, but your friends will thank you for it.

Simply type your own email address in the **To:** field and all your friends' addresses in the **Bcc:** field. Bcc stands for blind carbon copy, and it means when the recipient receives your message, he can't see any other emails on the list. Each person replies only to you and not to everyone in the group. A good way to protect everyone's privacy — and keep your inbox clean.

6 smart ways to avoid the horror of hackers

Hackers love to use email to gather people's private information, like usernames, passwords, credit card numbers, health records, and more. Follow these tips to protect your email account and avoid falling for sophisticated scams.

Use a supercalifragilisticexpialidocious! password. Hackers use super-high-tech software to guess your passwords. To thwart them, you need to choose a long password that includes symbols.

Maybe not as long as Mary Poppins' favorite word, but at least eight to 10 letters. And make it as random as possible. Stringing together your children's names or birth months may be easier to crack than you think.

Never reuse a password. Hackers grab usernames and passwords from online services all the time. The hackers then add these passwords to the dictionaries of password-guessing software. If you use the same username and password for several accounts, you're more vulnerable to being hacked.

Don't save your email password in your browser. Browser-based password tools aren't very secure. They can also make it easy for someone who has physical access to your computer to access your email.

Instead of saving your email password in your browser, use a password manager instead. Two popular password-manager programs are LastPass (*lastpass.com*) and 1Password (*1Password.com*).

For more tips on creating and managing passwords, see *Password protection: How to pick them, remember them, and keep them safe* in the *Online Security* section.

Look for warnings from your email provider. Phishing emails are designed to look like legitimate messages from your email provider, bank, healthcare provider, credit card company, or a friend. With these emails, phishers try to trick you into sharing whatever account information they seek.

Online email programs do a good job of flagging phishing emails for you. If you see a notice from your email provider that a message looks like a scam, don't click any links or respond to the email.

However, phishers are always trying to outsmart email providers, so don't rely on your email service to warn you. If you're ever in doubt, contact your provider with a phone number or email you know is legitimate, and ask whether they sent you the message.

Check whether an email link is safe. Before you click a link in your email, you can check whether it's safe in less than a second. Simply hover your cursor over the link. In the lower left, you'll see the website address that the link points to. If that website address looks suspicious, don't click it. You can always contact the sender first to make sure they sent the link.

Add an extra layer of security. If a hacker gets into your email account, it's a few short steps to reset your password and lock you out. After the hacker gains control of your email, he can use your account to reset your other passwords, locking you out of your bank accounts, credit cards, and other essential services.

Two-factor authentication adds an extra step before you can change your password, which makes it harder for hackers to take over your email account. You can choose to receive a code via text message, phone call, or a special app.

With two-factor authentication turned on, the hacker would need your email login information and access to your phone to success-fully reset your email password.

To set up this extra security feature, look in your account settings — not your email settings. You can often access these settings by clicking your profile picture in the upper right of your email inbox. In AOL, Microsoft, or Google, for example, you'd then look for options for sign-in or security. After you find the option for two-factor authentication, follow the on-screen instructions for setting it up.

Don't let viruses sneak in through attachments

If you see a warning about an email attachment, even if it appears to be from someone you know, don't download it. Online email services have become quite savvy about the sneaky ways viruses travel. They scan your attachments, and if they detect a bug, will block it or post a warning in the message. These scanners work quite well, and most of the time you don't even know they're doing it.

If you're concerned about missing a real message, call or text that person to confirm they really sent you the attachment. If they did, you can let them know your email service found a virus. Ask them to send you a new version of the file that's virus-free.

Give your message pizzazz: Put a picture in your email

Not every photo you email is meant to be kept or printed. Sometimes, you simply want to share the view from your vacation beach house or cheer up your friend with a cute picture of your dog. If that's the case, putting the picture in your email message will make more of an impact.

When you add a photo to an email, you can choose to send it as an inline image or an attachment. An inline image appears inside the message, so your recipient can see it without taking additional steps. If it's an attachment, she'll have to download the photo and open it to view it.

Inline images are sized for online viewing so you don't have to worry about them being too big. When you add the photo to your message, your email program knows you want the image to look good on-screen and reduces the size accordingly — without changing your original file.

> To make a high-quality photo print, the photo file needs to hold a lot of data. That's why digital cameras (even those on most smartphones) create such large files for every image you take. But your photo doesn't need all that data to look good on-screen.

To add an inline photo to your email, look for an icon in the message window toolbar that looks like a picture with mountains in the background. If you're not sure, hover your mouse over the icon, and look for a label like **Insert Photo** or **Insert Pictures Inline**.

Fun ways to express yourself in email messages

Have you ever been writing an email and wished you could show your friend how happy you are about their great news? Or maybe you just want to give them a big hug. Leave it to technology to come up with a way to do it virtually. Emojis and animated GIFs are a great way to have fun and set the tone in your email messages.

Share facial expressions with emojis. Emojis are characters that show pictures instead of letters. Before emojis, people used keyboard characters to make faces called emoticons, such as :) for a smiley face or ;) for a winking face. The facial expressions in your email's emoji tool are basically the same thing, but more colorful and varied.

A smiley, laughing, or shocked face can help convey how you feel about whatever news you want to share in your email message. To insert an emoji, look for a smiley face icon in the window where you type email messages. If you're not sure what an emoji character means, you can look it up on a website called Emojipedia (*https://emojipedia.org*).

Add animated GIFs to your emails. Animated GIFs are short animations that are easily added to an email. Many animated GIFs play over and over, but others stop playing after a certain number of loops.

GIFs are meant to be fun and silly, and you can find hundreds of free ones online. Popular GIFs show animals, babies, celebrities, cartoons, sports moments, and other bits of popular culture.

The most popular place to search for GIFs is a website called GIPHY (*https://giphy.com*). At the top of this website, enter a term that describes the type of GIF you want. For example, if you're sending someone birthday wishes, you might search for "birthday" or "happy birthday."

When you find a GIF you like on the GIPHY website, hover your mouse over the GIF so a link icon appears. Click that icon to copy the link. Then, in your email, click where you want to insert the GIF and use the **Paste** command to insert the link. The GIF will then appear below the link.

Brighten up your inbox with themes

Make the holiday season extra special by decorating your inbox with a special theme. It will put you in the spirit every time you open your email.

Email tips often focus on productivity, but themes let you have a little fun. Depending on your email service, you can find themes that change colors or even add pictures that change automatically throughout the day.

To decorate your email inbox any time of the year, look for a themes option in your email settings. It will usually let you see a preview to decide whether you like it. If it's a thumbs up, click **OK** or **Save** to make your selection stick.

Call and text with ease
Cellphone secrets you need to know

3 tips to pump up the volume on your calls

Do you have trouble hearing people on your phone calls? Don't despair. Here are three cheap and easy remedies that will have your calls coming in clear as a bell.

Turn on your speakerphone. Your phone should have a speaker button that will let you hear the conversation without putting your ear to the phone. The call audio comes from your phone's speaker. You can also use your phone's audio jack or Bluetooth to connect it to an external speaker that will really pump up the volume.

Remember that telling your caller they're on speakerphone is good etiquette, especially if others are around to hear your conversation. On both iPhone and Android phones, you can toggle speaker-phone on or off during a call.

Try out a headset. A traditional headset, or earbuds that fit inside your ear canal, can improve the audio of your calls by cutting out background noise and connecting you more closely to the speaker. They allow for a quieter and more private conversation than a speakerphone. Look for a headset with comfortable earphones and a microphone.

A headset can connect to your phone's audio jack or wirelessly via Bluetooth. If you're an iPhone user, you can test whether this setup helps you hear calls more clearly by using the earbuds that come with your phone. These earbuds typically include a tiny microphone.

If you want to shop for a headset or earbuds, ask about testing products in the store so you can find the best option for your needs. Prices vary, but you can find a good set for anywhere from $15 to $50.

Set up your hearing aids to work with your phone. If you use hearing aids, they may be compatible with your iPhone or Android phone's hearing accessibility features. The settings you choose and how they work depend on your hearing aids and the exact model of your phone.

The basic features include settings that improve the audio when you hold the phone to your ear. Advanced features connect your hearing aids to your smartphone so you can control the tiny devices from your phone. That will allow you to clearly hear phone calls as well as any music or videos you stream.

Your doctor or hearing specialist can help you choose the best options and settings for you.

Save your eyes: Enlarge the text on your smartphone screen

You don't have to live with the small text on your phone. Just like with your computer, you can make the text bigger so it's easier to read.

On an iPhone. Select Settings > Display & Brightness > Text Size. At the bottom of the screen, move the slider until the preview text is the desired size. (See graphic on next page.)

You can also select Settings > General > Accessibility. In this area, you access the same controls for enlarging text by selecting the **Larger Text** option. You can also choose the **Zoom** tool, which lets you magnify your whole smartphone screen.

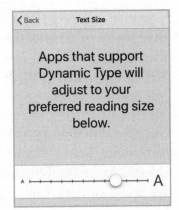

After you enable the Zoom tool, magnify the screen by double-tapping with three fingers. Then use three fingers to move around the screen. To adjust the zoom level, double-tap with three fingers and drag until the zoom reflects your desired magnification.

On an Android phone. You'll find both the display and text accessibility settings by selecting Settings > Accessibility.

To make only the text bigger, select **Font Size**, and use the slider that appears to enlarge the text. To enlarge everything on-screen, select **Display Size**, and move the slider to make the display bigger.

Android accessibility settings also include a magnifying option. After you tap **Magnification**, choose how you want to turn it on — **Magnify with Triple-Tap** or **Magnify with Button**. This turns on magnification whenever you tap the **Accessibility** button and then tap the screen. If you don't see the button option, your phone only supports triple-tap.

When you turn on magnification, you can tap anywhere to enlarge except the keyboard or navigation bar. Then pan around by dragging two fingers across the screen.

To adjust the magnification, pinch or spread your fingers on-screen. To leave the magnified view, triple-tap the screen or tap the **Accessibility** button.

Secret to texting quickly without the keyboard

You can send text messages on your phone without fiddling with that tiny keyboard. With your smartphone's voice-to-text feature, you can text as fast as you speak.

Get the voice assistant's attention. To send a text message with your voice, activate your phone's voice assistant, such as Siri or Google Assistant. On an iPhone, you activate Siri by holding down the home button. On an Android phone, make sure Google Assistant is turned on in Settings. Then you activate it by holding down the home button or saying, "OK Google."

Tell the voice assistant you want to send a text. When the voice assistant is listening, tell it you want to send a text message and to whom. For example, you might say, "Send a text message to George Smith."

Tell it what you want to say. Next, the voice assistant asks you to start speaking your message. That's when you speak the text message you want to send. To add punctuation, say the name of the punctuation mark, like "period" or "question mark." The voice-to-text feature knows to insert the punctuation mark instead of spelling it as a word.

Fix mistakes if needed. Just like humans, the voice-to-text feature sometimes makes mistakes. To fix a word, hold your finger on it until it's selected. Then, tap the microphone icon on your keyboard. At the prompt, speak the word again, and your correction appears in the text message.

When you're done, your smartphone's voice assistant will confirm that you're ready to send the message. By following the prompts, you can even use your voice to send the message on its way.

Create shortcuts for your favorite phrases

How many times do you text someone to tell them you're on your way or you'll call them back soon? If you're like most people, you text certain phrases over and over. With your smartphone's text replacement feature, you can create short-cuts for phrases you use often.

Simply turn "on my way" into "omw" and "call you back soon" into "cubs." As soon as you type the abbreviation, voilà — the entire phrase appears. Think how much time and effort you'll save.

To create a shortcut, open your smartphone's **Keyboard** settings (in iPhone, check under Settings > General) and look for a feature called **Text Replacement** or **Text Correction**. There, you can enter the shortcut and the text you want to appear.

Go ahead and test the shortcut in a text message or new email message on your cellphone. Simply type the shortcut, and watch it expand into your favorite phrase.

Add cool custom keyboards for texting

Custom keyboards can give you a fun way to express yourself with emojis — those cute faces, symbols, foods, animals, and other icons that jazz up your texts. Special keyboards can also add features that make your phone's keyboard easier to use.

Type pictures with the emoji keyboard. This popular custom keyboard is included on most cellphones. To access it, you need to activate it in your smartphone's **Keyboard** settings. On an iPhone, go to Settings > General > Keyboard > Keyboards. Select the keyboard you want to activate and toggle **Allow Full Access** to the on position. On an Android, the emoji keyboard varies by phone manufacturer and may already be activated.

After you turn on the emoji keyboard, look for a button on your regular keyboard that allows you to toggle between letters and emojis.

Look for custom keyboards to add to your smartphone. On an iPhone, tap the globe-shaped icon in the lower left of the keyboard to cycle through your custom keyboards. (See graphic.) On Android, switching keyboards can vary by phone. Typically, the emoji keyboard is available on the standard keyboard by tapping a gear icon and/or a smiley-face icon.

To switch to other keyboards, you typically tap a keyboard icon in the lower right to open a menu of custom keyboards. Select the keyboard you want to use, and your phone switches to that selection.

Choose keyboards with features that make typing easier. Some custom keyboards add practical features like large key sizes or swipe typing. If you want larger keys, you might try the **Big Keys Keyboard** app for iPhones and iPads or the **Big Buttons Keyboard Standard** app for Android phones.

With swipe typing, you drag your finger across the letters you want to type, and the app guesses the word and adds spaces around it. The popular swipe-typing keyboards do a good job of understanding the word you want. Many people prefer this method of typing to tapping individual characters.

Popular swipe-typing apps include **GBoard** and **SwiftKey Keyboard**. An added benefit of these apps is they let you change the keyboard color to increase the contrast. After you download the app, turn on the keyboard in your smartphone's **Keyboard** settings. Then you'll see the keyboard when you're typing on your smartphone or tablet.

10 things you should never do with your cellphone

Just because you can use your cellphone almost anywhere doesn't mean you should. Some bad cellphone habits are dangerous, while others are just downright rude. Plus some can compromise the security on your phone. If you value your life, your family, and friends, you'll avoid these annoying — and possibly even harmful — actions.

Texting while driving. You know this is dangerous. In fact, it's such a factor in traffic accidents that it's now illegal in almost all 50 states. Just don't do it.

Texting while walking. You may not think this is a big deal. But while your feet are moving, your mind is distracted. One study found that pedestrians who crossed an intersection while texting were almost four times more likely to display risky behavior — failing to look both ways, crossing in the middle of an intersection, and disobeying the lights.

Talking while driving. You have a long drive and figure it's the perfect time to catch up with your best friend. But research shows even a hands-free device won't keep you from being distracted by a cellphone call.

Using your phone while dining with others. Wouldn't you be offended if your friend interrupted your lunch date to take a call from her chatty granddaughter? If you absolutely must answer, excuse yourself and step away to have a private conversation.

Talking loudly in public. Try to keep your voice down if you're in a public setting. Nobody wants to hear your half of the conversation.

Leaving your phone on during a performance. Make it a priority to silence your phone whenever you're in a church, theater, or public venue where a call would be distracting — or embarrassing! Be considerate of your fellow patrons.

Checking your phone every five minutes. You swear you're not addicted, but you still can't resist checking to see if you got another picture or cute text from your grandson. One out of five baby boomers can't go 15 minutes without checking their cellphones. Resist the temptation by taking periodic breaks and putting the phone away.

Using only a password to protect your phone. Your cellphone holds much of your personal information as well as info about your family and friends. Don't let thieves steal that private info. With a fingerprint ID, one touch is all you need to stay safe.

- To set it up on an iPhone, go to Settings >Touch ID & Passcode. If you don't have a password set up, you need to add that first by turning on the **Passcode** option and entering the code you want to use. Then select **Add a Fingerprint** and follow the instructions to set up a fingerprint ID. If you ever have a problem using your fingerprint ID, you can use the passcode to access your phone instead.

- On an Android, select Settings > Security & Location. Then look for an **Imprint** option and follow the on-screen prompts to set up your fingerprint ID. If you don't have an alternate password set up, you're asked to add one as a backup option.

Ignoring your phone's software updates. The makers of your phone's software are always testing to make it more secure against hackers and viruses. Typically, your phone shows you a notification when a software update is available. You can also manually check. On an iPhone, select Settings > General > Software Update. On an Android phone, the steps depend on your specific device maker, but try Settings > System > Advanced > System Update.

Allowing text message previews on the lock screen. If someone sends you a message with details they want to keep private, their message will appear to anyone who picks up your phone.

- To hide them on an iPhone lock screen, open Settings and select Notifications > Messages. In the **Alerts** area, clear the **Lock Screen** option. To hide previews from other messaging apps, open Settings and scroll down to the app. After you select the app, you can turn off notifications in the app settings.

- On an Android, the steps might vary depending on the maker of your phone. Generally, try selecting Settings > Lock Screen and Security > Notifications. In the **Show Notifications From** area, you can clear notifications from the **Messages** app and any other app where you receive messages — like Skype or Facebook Messenger.

How to screen your calls (and save your sanity!)

What's that strange number that showed up on caller ID? How can you find out who's calling? Robocalls, which often spoof local numbers, are a huge problem that phone providers and the Federal Communications Commission (FCC) are working to prevent.

Robocalls are automated calls that try to scam people with fake prize offers, crime warnings, credit card schemes, and so on. They often use fake numbers, which makes these calls hard to stop.

A good guideline is to not answer calls from numbers you don't recognize. But what if it's your doctor's office or another authorized caller whose number is not in your contacts list?

To help, you can use a range of tools to identify or stop annoying calls and receive only the calls you want.

Google the number to see if it's legit. Type the mystery phone number into the Google search field, and let the world's No. 1 search engine go to work. It's an easy way to find out who's calling. Google will comb through any information available online, showing you results that might include where the phone is registered and who it's registered to.

Sign up for a robocall-prevention service. Most of the national phone service providers offer an app that helps you identify and report robocalls. Some apps have the ability to learn from your call habits and block robocalls altogether.

After you find out what app your provider users, download it to your phone and follow the instructions for setting it up. The cost for this service depends on your provider, but prices range from free to about $4 per month.

Choose a special ringtone for a contact. Does a certain song bring back memories of your romantic honeymoon? Make it your husband's ringtone, and you'll always know when your sweetheart is calling. Same for your children, parents, or close friends. Give them each a special ringtone, and you'll know whether you want to answer your phone by the sound of the ringer. You don't even have to look at the caller ID.

> Remember, when you select a special ringtone for someone, make sure it's different from your default ringtone. That way, your special ring will stand out as a call from a contact you want to answer.

- On an iPhone or Android phone, open **Contacts** and select the contact that will have the custom ringtone. Tap **Edit**, then **Ringtone**, and select the ringtone you want that person to have. When you're done, tap **Done** or **Save**.

- Some Android phones also let you set a custom ringtone for a group, such as starred contacts or all contacts. Open your **Contacts** and tap the **Groups** option at the top of the screen. Tap and hold the group name until the **Edit Group** option appears, and then select it. On the next screen, you can select a group ringtone.

Sweet trick to only let certain numbers through

Your cellphone has a sneaky setting you don't want to miss. If you don't want to be interrupted while sleeping, driving, or holding an important meeting, Do Not Disturb mode is just the ticket. With this feature turned on, you can block all calls and messages except for those you specify, such as your spouse or children.

Open Settings and look for the **Do Not Disturb** option. For nighttime, you can schedule a beginning and end time for when you're normally sleeping. This is also where you specify which contacts can reach you when the setting is turned on.

To enable the feature any time on an iPhone, go to Settings > Do Not Disturb, and toggle on the **Do Not Disturb** option. You'll see a little half-moon icon at the top of the screen. On an Android phone, swipe down from the top of your screen and tap **Do Not Disturb**. A circle with a horizontal line indicates Do Not Disturb is active.

Locate your lost phone in a flash

Oh no, you lost your phone — or someone stole it. Never fear — you can locate it quickly with a special feature built in to your smartphone.

Set it up while you still have your phone. For this location feature to work, you have to set it up, and you need your phone to complete the process.

- On an iPhone, go to Settings and select your name. Then select iCloud > Find My iPhone. On the screen that appears, you can toggle on **Find My iPhone**. Also include **Send Last Location** so you can see where your phone was if the battery dies.

- On an Android phone, you need to turn on **Find My Device** and share your location. In Settings, tap Security & Location > Find My Device, and make sure the feature is turned on. Then tap Security & Location > Location and turn on the **Location** option.

View its location from your computer. After you activate the find-my-phone feature, you can see where it is on your desktop computer or laptop as long as your phone is turned on and connected to phone service or Wi-Fi. Otherwise, you'll see its last-known location.

- To find your iPhone, go to *icloud.com* in your web browser and log in with your Apple ID. Select **All Devices** and then the device you want to locate. If your phone is online and can be located, it appears on a map. If it's nearby, you can play a sound to help you find it. If your phone can't be located, the last-known location appears for 24 hours. You can also ask the feature to send you an email if and when it finds your phone.

- To locate an Android phone with **Find My Device**, go to *android.com/find* in your web browser and log in with your Google Account. If you have more than one Android phone or tablet, select the one you want to find. If you don't see your lost device, make sure you're logged in to the main Google Account for that device. When you select the lost device, it will receive a notification, and a map will appear showing its approximate location.

> An even easier way to find your lost iPhone is to use the Find My iPhone app on someone else's phone. Simply input your Apple ID and password on your friend's iPhone, and it will track yours down in no time.

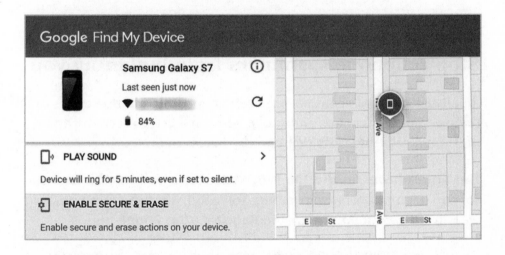

If your phone is nearby, you can play a sound that will alert you to where it's hiding. If you're not so lucky, select the **Lock** option so people will need a password to access your phone. You can also display a message on the lock screen telling anyone who finds the phone to return it to you.

Fix a buggy phone with 1 button

Is your phone or tablet acting up? Turning it off and then back on again may fix the problem right away.

When you turn off your phone, it shuts down the software that runs all your apps and tools. Wait at least 10 to 15 seconds before turning your phone back on again so it has a chance to completely shut down. When you turn it back on, your phone or tablet reboots. During that process, the software restarts everything, which can help it run more smoothly.

This simple tip may help you avoid a time-consuming trip to the repair shop. If it doesn't help, your phone may have a more serious issue that requires a professional touch.

Stop cellphone spammers from bothering you

Telemarketers and spammers are starting to call and text cellphones. With a few tips and tools, you can learn to recognize the unwanted calls and texts and end the harassment.

Put your phone on the Do Not Call list. This is the No. 1 step to stop telemarketers from calling for good. Visit the government website *Donotcall.gov*. Click the **Register Your Phone** option.

To add up to three phone numbers to the list, click the **Register Here** button, enter the phone numbers and an email address, and click **Submit**.

To complete the process, check your email after you submit your phone number, and follow the instructions. If you think you've already registered your phone and want to check, use the verification tool.

Block and report text message spam. Spam text messages try to trick you into engaging with a bot so someone can scam you. These messages may even ask for your personal information. Texting STOP to these text message bots won't help. It may even confirm the bot reached a real number. Try these tools to help you fight these spammers.

Use your phone's Block feature to keep the number from getting through. On most cellphones, you can tap an information icon on a message thread and tap a **Block** option.

Report the spam text to your phone service provider by forwarding it to the number 7726, which spells "spam" on your phone's keypad. AT&T, T-Mobile, Verizon, Sprint, and Bell all use the 7726 service.

- To forward a text message on an iPhone, open the message and tap and hold the message bubble you want to forward. When a menu appears, tap **More**. A round blue check mark appears next to the message bubble, and you can tap the arrow in the lower right to send that text to a new number. Type 7726 in the **To:** field and then send the message.

- Forwarding a text message on an Android phone works similarly. Open the message thread, and tap and hold the message you want to forward. On the menu that appears, tap **Forward**. Then you can enter 7726 in the **To:** field, hit send, and off it will go.

Recognize and stop legitimate messages. All unsolicited texts aren't necessarily bad. If you give your phone number to a company or organization you work with, they may send you updates and reminders by text. You may have seen one from your doctor's office or hairdresser asking you to confirm an appointment. If you don't want to receive these, you can opt out.

A legitimate text message will give you the name of the business or organization and tell you how to stop receiving texts. For example, you'll see a note like "Text STOP to opt out." After you text STOP, it will confirm that you're no longer enrolled in text notifications. Then you'll stop receiving those unwanted messages.

If you're not sure whether a text message is real or spam, don't respond to the text. You can ask any business you work with whether they are texting you. If so, ask them to remove you from their messaging list and only contact you by phone.

4 ways to save big on your cellphone plan

You love your new cellphone, but you don't love the monthly bill. You can find lots of ways to lower it if you know the tricks. In fact, you may even be able to cut it in half. Here are some ways to trim your total expenses.

Find a plan to match the services you use. Here's one simple solution your service provider won't suggest. Check your bill to see how many phone minutes, text messages, and megabytes of data you typically use. Compare this information against the plans your provider offers to see if a cheaper plan will work for you. You can also use this information to comparison shop for a cheaper plan from another provider.

For example, if you send lots of text messages and data, look for an unlimited plan for seniors. You'll get unlimited calls, text messages, and data for a much lower cost than someone who's not on the senior plan. Expect to pay about $35 to $50 per line.

Even better, look for a prepaid option where you pay a small fee for limited services. This works best if you don't use your cellphone much.

T-Mobile, for example, offers a pay-as-you-go plan that includes calls and text messages and starts at only $3 per month. Android users can get unlimited calls and text messages from Republic Wireless for $15 and pay an additional $5 per gigabyte for data. Just be careful about exceeding the limits of your plan because the charges can add up quickly.

Check for extra discounts.
If you're a senior, veteran, or member of an organization like AARP or AAA, you may qualify for extra discounts. Be sure to check whether your provider offers these discounts, and ask about your eligibility.

> Cellphone providers often update their plans without letting current customers know a cheaper option is available. Check your provider's plan offerings regularly to see if a new option would save you money.

Use a wireless network when it's available. When you use Wi-Fi, you don't dip into the allotted data from your data plan. This helps you save those bytes for the times you need them most and avoid extra charges if you go over your max. Look for the Wi-Fi icon in the status bar at the top of your phone to make sure you're connected to Wi-Fi.

Buy an older-model or refurbished phone. An older-model phone is simply a phone that's been discontinued because the manufacturer has released a newer model. A refurbished phone is a used phone that's been wiped of old data and fixed up so all the features work. Using an older-model or refurbished phone can save you hundreds of dollars.

Service providers often promote new phones with high-end features that require expensive data plans. And if you finance it, that's an extra $20 or more on your monthly cellphone bill. But if you just use your phone to call your family or play a few games, an older-model or refurbished phone may have all the features you need.

Timesaving tips for faster calling

It's no fun searching through your Contacts every time you want to call your friends and family. Let your cellphone save you the time and trouble.

Pull up your most recent calls. Did your daughter call a few days ago? To call her back, tap your Phone icon. Tap **Recents** at the bottom of the screen to see all the calls that have recently come in. Simply tap her name or number, and your call will go right through.

Pick your favorites. Get even quicker access to friends and family by putting them in your **Favorites** list. Here's how.

1. Tap the Phone app icon just as you would when making a call.

2. Tap the star-shaped Favorites icon at the bottom of the screen.

3. On the Favorites screen, tap the plus sign in the upper corner.

4. Tap the name of the contact you want as a favorite. If the contact has more than one number, tap the phone number you prefer.

When you want to call a Favorite, tap the phone icon, then **Favorites**. Tap the person's name, and the phone will immediately start dialing.

Video chats
Bring family and friends even closer

Chat with anyone in the world — for free

Don't pay for long distance calls or postage stamps. With a click of a button, you can talk to friends and family almost anywhere in the world — without paying a dime.

All you need is Skype. You may have heard about people "skyping" and wondered what it was. Skype is a popular calling and chatting service that lets you connect with other Skype users for free. Interested? Here's how to get started.

Set up Skype on your computer. To use Skype on your Windows or Mac computer, you need to download and install the software. You'll find Skype for Windows or Skype for Mac at *skype.com/en/get-skype*. After you create an account and log in, you're ready to find contacts and make calls.

To use Skype on your computer, it needs a microphone. To have video chats with your family or friends, you also need a webcam. Most computers today have a built-in mic and webcam, which work great for Skype calls.

Note that your Skype username doesn't need to be your full name. But it will be visible to all Skype users, so choose wisely, especially if you might use Skype for a professional reason.

Find and save Skype contacts. To find other Skype users, type their name or Skype username in the Search box. When you find the person you want to add, click their name in the **Skype Directory**. You can then click the **Wave** button or send them a short message. After the person accepts your message, you're connected via Skype, and the person appears in your contacts list.

If you don't see your contacts, press Alt+2 (Windows) or Command+ Shift+C (Mac), and your contacts list will appear on the left.

Schedule calls in advance. Ready for a long chat with Aunt Becky in Sarasota? Before you jump on Skype, give her a heads up. Skype needs to be open on both your computers to make or receive calls, so it helps to schedule your call in advance. Plus Aunt Becky might like the chance to fix her hair and makeup before making her video debut!

Click the correct icon for a video or audio chat. When you're ready to call, select Aunt Becky's name from your contacts list. On the right, you'll see a panel that shows your call and chat history. In the upper right, click the video camera icon to make a video call, or click the telephone handset icon to make an audio-only call.

If your aunt has Skype open, she'll hear your call and see your name on-screen. To answer your call, she'll click a green button. If you're the one receiving a call, simply click the green button that appears on your screen. Voilà — you're connected.

Profile pointers: Make it easy for friends to find you

Now that you're on Skype, you want your friends and family to connect with you, right? Make it easy for them to find you by personalizing your profile. Here are two ways to let them know who you are and when you're available to chat.

Add your smiling face to your profile. Your profile photo will appear publicly to anyone who uses Skype. When you add a picture, that helps your contacts recognize you, especially when they're trying to connect for the first time.

Your profile photo also helps contacts know it's you when you call them. And if it's an audio group call, they can see your picture when you talk.

To add a profile photo in Skype for Windows or Skype for Mac, click the three dots next to your name in the upper left and select **Settings**. Choose Account & Profile > Profile Picture. Hover your mouse over the profile picture circle, click the **Edit** button, and select an image saved on your computer.

Show contacts when you're available. In the upper left of the Skype window is your profile photo and a little colored dot that shows whether you're available to take a call. If you make it a point to change that icon regularly, it's a great way to show when you are or aren't free to talk.

To change your availability, hover your mouse pointer over the dot. When it turns into a down arrow, click it and choose an option. The availability icon offers three settings — **Active, Do Not Disturb**, and **Invisible**.

- Active is green and indicates you can take a call.

- Do Not Disturb turns the icon red. You don't receive sound notifications about incoming messages in this mode.

- Invisible makes you appear to be offline. You can still use Skype in this mode, but it will mute all call and message notifications.

Take Skype on the go with the mobile app

You're on vacation and want to share your fun times with your grandkids, but your computer is at home. Don't worry — Skype offers a mobile app you can use on a smartphone or tablet. You'll find it in the App Store for iPhones or the Google Play Store for Androids.

If you already set up Skype on a computer, you simply log in with the same account information, and all your contacts appear in the app.

The best thing is you don't need cellular phone service to make calls. With a Wi-Fi connection you can call people on the Skype app for free without using any data. It works whether you're on a smartphone or tablet.

The app has video chat options as well as audio chat. Perfect for taking your family on a tour of your beautiful beach house.

Simple solution: Use your smartphone for video calls

Smartphones offer an easy way to make video calls to someone else with a smartphone. With a camera, microphone, and internet connection, your phone has everything you need to make a video call. The one part that varies is the software that helps you make the video connection.

If you and your contact both have iPhones. You can use FaceTime, which is Apple's video chat feature. Simply open the contact on your phone and tap either the video or FaceTime icon to make a video call.

If you have an iPhone and your friend has an Android phone. Open their contact details, and you'll see a video icon. If you and your contact both have the Skype mobile app or another compatible video-calling app, you can make a video call via that app by tapping the video icon. Or you can open your video-calling app and make the call directly from the app.

If you don't have a compatible app and you tap the video icon, you'll see a screen with information about adding Skype credits, which you need to make a Skype call to a mobile phone or landline. If you use a different video-call app, you may see a help screen from that app instead.

If you have an Android phone. The steps for making a video call depend on your phone model and service provider. Some Android models recently began displaying a video-call option when you open a contact.

For this video-calling option to work, you and/or your contact might need to have the Google Duo app, which is Google's video-calling app. You can also make video calls to another Android or an iPhone via the Skype mobile app.

101

Share the love with a group call — it's easier than you think!

Many people have families spread across the country. When you want to talk to them all at the same time, Skype is the answer. Simply schedule a group audio or video call.

Save a group of contacts you call often. If you regularly call the same set of people, you can save them all as a group. Then you can easily call everyone at once and keep any photos or files you share in a gallery.

To create a group in Skype for Windows or Skype for Mac, click the **Chats** icon at the top of the sidebar on the left. Then click the **+ Chat** button and select **New Group Chat**. (See graphic.) In the window that appears, select the contacts you want to add to the group and click **Done**.

If you want to add people to the group later, select the group in your **Recent Chats** list. (If you don't see it, search for the group by name.) Then in the right-hand pane, click the blue **Invite More People** button.

To call your group, select it and then click the Video Chat or Audio Chat icon in the upper right of the Skype window.

Keep track of who is talking during a call. When you're chatting with a group online, it can be hard to tell who's talking. To help you keep track, Skype has visual cues that help you connect a voice to a face. In an audio-only call, a white border highlights the profile picture of the person who's currently talking. During a video call, you can see each person's webcam view on-screen.

Toggle from video to audio to avoid quality issues. When you have several people in a video chat, your internet connection might struggle to keep up with all those video feeds. If needed, you or other individuals in the chat can toggle off their video camera by clicking the video icon.

For example, you might toggle off your camera while someone else is talking or showing you something special with their camera. Anytime you're ready, you can toggle your video camera back on so others in the group chat can see you again.

Find pictures and other files in the group gallery. Each group has a gallery where you can share photos, other files, and links. To open the gallery, select the group in the **Recent Chats** list. In the pane that opens on the right, click the **Gallery** option in the upper left, and the Gallery opens in a new pane on the far right. Click the plus sign near the top of the Gallery to add a photo or other file saved to your computer.

Poor video quality? 4 ways to fix it now

Video calls are a great way to chat with your grandchildren or see friends and family who live far away. However, because video calls require a lot of data, you may have trouble with the quality of the video or sound. If you're having an issue, these easy tips can help.

Use your Wi-Fi connection instead of cellular data. The better the quality of your internet connection, the better your video call. If you make a video call from your smartphone while you're on the road, you'll use your cellular data. A wireless internet connection can transfer data faster and offers better video quality than a cellular data connection.

Also, the closer you are to your wireless router, the more easily it can handle all that video data. When you're at home, you might find that sitting closer to your router improves the quality of your video chats.

Boost your internet connection speed. You can improve your internet connection's ability to handle video in several ways.

- First, close all the programs on your computer except for Skype or the video-chatting application you use. Most programs connect to the internet and will use space on your internet connection. By closing these programs, you free up that space for Skype video calls.

- If you're still having issues, consider upgrading your internet speed. When you signed up for internet service, you likely chose a connection speed. In most cases, the slower connections are cheaper. If you enjoy frequent video chats, paying an extra $5 to $10 per month for a faster connection may be worth it.

Wear headphones for improved audio. During a video call, your smartphone or computer's built-in microphone is often far from your face. Plus your microphone can pick up the conversation from your speaker, causing more audio problems.

When you use headphones with a built-in microphone, the mic is closer to your face and doesn't pick up the sound coming through your headphones. That makes it easier for you to hear.

Enhance your lighting for a better picture. You can improve the picture in your video chats by adding an extra lamp behind your computer monitor. Or, if you have a laptop, try sitting near a window and facing the natural light.

Super cool way to get help with your computer

Does a friend or family member help you with computer issues? Next time, try showing them what the problem is by sharing your screen via Skype. When someone can see the problem you're having, they can often help you more easily.

To share your screen, open Skype and call your helper. You can make an audio-only or video call. Then share your screen with that person by clicking the Share Screen icon in the lower right. The icon looks like two overlapping rectangles.

When you share your screen, your contact can only see your screen and can't take control of your computer. When your call ends, you stop sharing your screen.

You can also ask someone to show you how a feature works by sharing their screen with you. While they perform a task or use a certain feature, you can watch how they do it in your Skype window. Pretty cool, huh?

Safeguard your privacy on Skype

Concerned about your privacy on Skype? Understanding the personal details Skype shares and how to manage your visibility and privacy settings can help.

Know what's public information. Some Skype profile information is visible to anyone on Skype, whether you use Skype on a computer, smartphone, or tablet. Your Skype profile name and location appear in the Skype Directory. The location shown is typically only your city or country.

Show your profile photo only to contacts. If you add a profile photo, it's visible to all Skype users. However, you can change the settings so that your photo is visible only to your contacts.

Your profile photo helps your friends and family find you in the Skype Directory, but you can share your Skype username with them instead if you're concerned about privacy.

To hide your profile photo, click the three dots next to your name in the upper left of the Skype program. Then select **Settings**. In the window that appears, select Account & Profile > Profile Picture. On the screen that appears, select **Contacts Only**.

Choose how people find you. By default, you appear in search results for your screen name, Skype username, phone number, and email address. Skype may also suggest you as a contact to other Skype users if you have mutual contacts.

To opt out of these features, open the Skype **Settings**. In the window that appears, select Contacts > Manage How People Find You on Skype. In the box that appears, you can toggle off the **Appear in Suggestions** option and the **Appear in Search Results** option.

In the phone number area, you can click **Enabled** and then choose **Disable** so people can't use your number to find you on Skype.

Avoid unwanted calls or messages. Skype isn't known for tele-marketers or robocalls, but if a Skype user is bothering you, a few tools can help.

- If your Skype profile is similar to someone else, you might want to minimize frequent calls from unknown users. Open **Settings** and select **Calling** on the left. Then you can turn on the option **Only Allow Calls from Contacts to Ring on This Device**.

- If a specific Skype user is bothering you, you can block them. Click the **Contacts** icon in the upper left. Then right-click the contact's name and select **View Profile**. At the bottom of the profile window, click the **Block Contact** option.

- If you ever need to unblock someone, open the Skype set-tings and click **Contacts** on the left. Then click **Blocked Contacts** on the right to see a list of people you've blocked. Hover your mouse over the contact and click **Unblock**.

Fine-tune your social media skills

3 fun Facebook features that go beyond the news feed

The Facebook news feed is designed for endless scrolling. But you don't have to be a mindless participant. Facebook has lots of other features that make social media interesting and helps you connect with friends, family, and people who share your interests.

Join groups that reflect your passions. Facebook has groups for every interest, and many users believe groups are the best part of this social media site.

Whether you like crafting, sports, a certain television or book genre, or technology, you can find Facebook groups focused on posts and people who share the same things you enjoy.

To find a group, ask your friends who share your interests for their recommendations. You can also see what Facebook recommends. On the desktop version of Facebook, in the **Explore** section of the left-hand sidebar, click **Groups.** You'll find a similar option in the Facebook app.

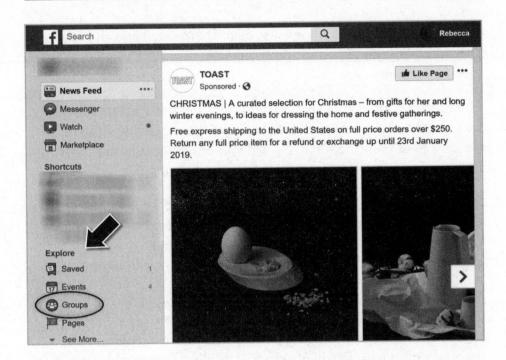

On the Groups page that appears, click the **Discover** tab in the upper left. You'll see categories of groups at the top. Click a category to see related groups. As you browse through the list, you may see whether any of your friends are already a member.

To join a group, click the **Join** button next to the group name. Be sure to read and follow the guidelines. You may want to watch how the group works for a few weeks before you join the conversation.

Keep track of local events. People and organizations use an option called Facebook Events to tell the community what's happening in their area.

Perhaps you saw a local 5K charity race advertised in your Facebook news feed. To find out more, click **Events** in the left-hand sidebar or under the main menu in the Facebook mobile app.

On the Events page that appears, click **Discover**. You can then see events in your area and filter them by time and a more specific location.

To keep track of events that interest you, click the **Interested** button. You can easily find details about the event any time by clicking **Events** in the left-hand sidebar and checking the **Upcoming events** list that appears on the Events page.

Enjoy videos picked especially for you. Facebook Watch is a selection of video channels with shows that are popular with Facebook users. When you select **Watch** in the left-hand sidebar, you can browse videos that Facebook thinks you will like.

The Watch video channels include several cooking and baking shows, *Comeback Kids: Animal Edition*, and *Returning the Favor* by Mike Rowe, which highlights people who make a difference in their communities. It will also include videos from groups you follow. Keep checking back for new and exciting things to watch.

Easy way to hide posts you don't like

If a Facebook friend posts content you don't like, don't just grin and bear it — hide it. In the Facebook news feed, you'll see three dots in the upper right of each post. Click the dots and select **Hide Post** to see fewer posts related to that topic.

You can even take it a step further. If you see a lot of posts about an upcoming event or topic you're not interested in, don't waste time scrolling past them. Click the three dots and select **Snooze for 30 Days** to stop seeing that person or page's posts for the next month.

Helpful hints to find and save your favorite content

Links, posts, videos, and other Facebook content can zoom by quickly. When you want to remember, return, or save a post, these tips can help.

Try searching for what you need. The search bar at the top of the Facebook window is the place to start if you can't find that great dog video you wanted to show your husband. You can type in any terms you remember and see if the results locate what you need.

If you can remember who posted the content you want to find, start your search with the name of the person or page that posted the content and then add your search term.

How to save all those great photos. When someone posts a picture you want to keep, you can save it to your computer. Click the photo in the news feed so it opens in a larger window. Hover your mouse pointer over the photo and click Options > Download in the lower-right corner.

When the photo finishes downloading, you'll find it in your computer's Downloads folder. The file typically has a long name of numbers and letters. To help you find the photo later, rename it with a date and description, and move the photo to a folder with other pictures you've saved to your computer.

Keep your favorite posts and links forever. If you come across a Facebook post you know you want to see again later, click the three dots in the upper left of the post and select **Save Post**. If the post is a link or video, you might see **Save Link** or **Save Video** instead.

To find the saved post later, click the **Saved** option in the Explore section of the left-hand sidebar. If you don't see the post you're looking for right away, try searching for it. On the saved-items page, a search

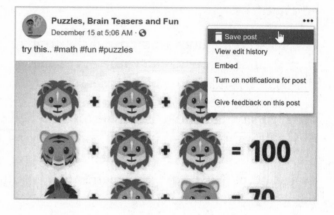

box appears in the upper left where you can type a search term to help you find the post you're looking for.

Organize posts and links into collections. To get even more organized, you can create collections of your saved posts. For example, you can group all your recipes together or create a collection of style tips. Let your imagination run wild.

To add a post to a collection, click the **Add to Collection** option that appears after you save a post. A menu appears where you can select an existing collection (if you've already created one) or create a new collection.

If you select **Create Collection** from the menu, a dialog box appears where you can give the collection a name. When you're ready, click **Create**, and Facebook confirms your post was added to the collection.

Facebook messenger: Your private chat room

Do you know what it means when someone says "PM me" on Facebook? It's no big mystery. It stands for private message, and you can use Facebook Messenger to send one at any time. Messenger is full of great features to help you stay in touch.

Create a group of family or friends. Want to share photos and updates with a small group of Facebook friends or family members? You can create and name a group in Facebook Messenger to share messages, photos, and videos with only that group. To create a group, start by sending everyone you want to include in the group a message. Then you can give the group a meaningful nickname.

To name your group, select your group message in the left-hand list of chats. Then in the upper right, click the gear icon next to the names of everyone in the group message. From the menu that appears, select **Rename**. After you type a descriptive name, click **Done**, and you can use it to find your group chat and send messages to the group.

Leave or mute an overactive group conversation. It was great hearing about your niece's new baby, but the constant flow of congratulations in the chat group is interrupting your work. If you want to stop receiving messages in an active chat, you have two options — mute the conversation or leave it.

To say good-bye to a group conversation in Facebook Messenger, hover your mouse over the list of Messenger chats in the left-hand column. Click the gray gear icon that appears and select **Mute** or **Leave Group**. (See graphic on the next page.)

Make a voice or video call. Although services like Skype are designed for internet voice and video calling, you and your friends might prefer sticking with a single platform like Facebook and Facebook Messenger.

In Messenger, making a voice or video call is free and easy to do. On the desktop version of Facebook, you can open Messenger from the Home screen by clicking **Messenger** in the left-hand sidebar. Next, select the contact you want to call. If you have trouble finding the contact, use the small search box in the upper left, just above your list of Messenger chats.

After you select the contact on the left, you'll see icons for voice and video chats in the upper right. Click the telephone handset icon to start a voice chat or the video camera icon to start a video chat. You'll find similar options in the Messenger mobile app.

Share files in a snap. Messenger is a handy way to share files when you're already communicating with a group in Messenger and want to show them a photo, text document, spreadsheet, or other file.

To attach a file from your computer to a Facebook Messenger chat, click the **Add Files** icon at the bottom of the message area. The icon may look like two rectangles stacked on top of each other, or it may look like a paper clip, depending on your phone.

In the window that opens, navigate to the place on your hard drive where you've saved the file, select it, and click the **Open** button to attach the file.

The file you select appears in the message window. You can type a message to your recipients before you click **Send** to share the file.

To download a file sent to you, click the down arrow that appears next to the file. The file will be saved in your computer's Downloads folder.

Jump on the hashtag bandwagon

Hashtags started out on Twitter, but now you see them on other social media, too. Some people even use them when they speak!

So what is a hashtag? It's a word or phrase without spaces and preceded by the # sign. On Twitter, people add hashtags to show what their tweet is about and to make it easy to find. It's a great way to connect with people who share your interests.

You can find hashtags about almost any topic, including animals (#funnyanimals and #cutepets), books (#amreading and #booklovers), home improvement projects (#diy and #homeimprovement), and so on.

When a tweet that interests you includes a hashtag, you can look for the hashtag using the search box in the upper right. The search results show all the tweets that include that hashtag.

Try using hashtags in your own tweets to add info you can't fit into 280 characters — or even a bit of humor (#tweetingisfun #thanksforreadingthispost).

4 cool ways to use Twitter

Twitter is an online place for real-time conversation. Some chats are tied to a real-life event happening in the moment. Heard about a robbery at the local 7-Eleven? Chances are, someone is tweeting about it. Want to know what that traffic tie-up is up ahead? Twitter will have the answer.

Along with getting up-to-the-moment information, you have the option of dropping in and out of conversations whenever you like. Here are some common ways you can use this popular social media site to connect and keep up to date.

Get to know your favorite celeb. Twitter is a great place to hear more from people you admire. Many authors, actors, journalists, TV personalities, athletes, comedians, businesspeople, and others share their thoughts on news or trends in their fields or in general. Sometimes, public figures host an Ask Me Anything (also called an AMA) where they use Twitter to answer people's questions for a certain period of time.

To see if someone who interests you has a Twitter profile, search for their name in the upper right corner. A blue check mark next to someone's name means that person has verified their profile as real. Click the **Follow** button to see their tweets in your Twitter feed.

Find similar interests in a group chat. In a Twitter chat, people use a hashtag to have a live conversation about a specific topic. A chat is often organized by a leader or organization for a specific day and time. (See the box on page 115 to learn how to use hashtags.)

If you have trouble writing short tweets, good news. Twitter will now allow you to use 280 characters, double what it used to be. Now you have plenty of space to get your message across.

For example, #carechat is a weekly Twitter chat for people who are currently caring for a loved one or have in the past. During this chat, caregivers share their experiences and find support.

Do a search on a topic you're interested in using the appropriate hashtag, and you may find a ton of kindred spirits out there.

Follow live comments about your favorite shows or event. Hashtags are also a great way to find conversations about events and other things going on.

For example, #oscars2019 was most relevant leading up to and during the Academy Awards in 2019. Similarly, you can find hashtags for popular events like the Super Bowl or the Olympics and TV shows. If you're surprised by a plot twist in your favorite show, you can probably find other people talking about it with a Twitter hashtag.

Participate in a challenge. In a Twitter challenge, people with a shared interest take on a project and then share their progress on Twitter, often using a hashtag in their tweet.

Some projects or challenges are ongoing. For example, if you like yoga, you might follow the monthly hashtag from *Yoga with Adriene*, which her followers use to talk about themes such as hope, creativity, or focus. Other challenges have a specific goal, such as working on a project every day for 30 days.

And then there are those crazy challenges like pouring a bucket of ice over your head (#icebucketchallenge) or trying to do activities with a blindfold (#birdboxchallenge). You may want to think twice about one of those, unless it's for a good cause and you won't get hurt doing it.

How to triple your Instagram fun

Instagram is a social media platform that especially appeals to people who love photography and visual arts. The main feed is a stream of photos or illustrations that can be anything from a beautifully photographed sunset to a silly selfie posted by your grandson.

If you like scrolling through photos in your Instagram feed, you may love these other Instagram features, too. They'll give you three times the fun.

Enjoy your connections' stories. Instagram Stories is a feature that creates photo and video sequences. They often show behind-the-scenes looks of the more polished images you see in the main Instagram feed.

A photographer might show how he created a stunning image. A dancer or singer might reveal her daily practice routines or backstage shots. And your friends might highlight the fun trip they took that day or the cute antics of their dog.

To watch stories on the Instagram website, click the circles that appear in the upper right, or click the **Watch All** option to see stories from everyone you follow.

In the Instagram app, stories appear at the top. Be sure to check every day if you don't want to miss anything. The posts in Stories last only 24 hours and then disappear.

Go even further with highlights. Instagram Highlights are posts saved from Instagram Stories. Typically, an Instagram user saves the most interesting stories to their highlights. Although not every Instagram user takes advantage of this feature, artists and public figures often use highlights to showcase their best work and let you know what you can expect from their profile.

To find an Instagram user's highlights, click their profile name to visit their profile page. The highlights are little circles above the square images posted to the main Instagram feed.

Explore Instagram's suggestions. In this area of Instagram, you can browse images posted by an array of Instagram users. Instagram chooses what you see based on the Instagram profiles you already follow. Who knows what new interests you may discover?

To find the Explore area, click the Compass icon in the upper right. In the mobile app, look for the magnifying glass icon at the bottom. If you see an image you like, click to see the full post. You also see which profile posted the image and a link to follow it.

Create your own special story to share with friends

It's fun to see other people's stories. It's even more fun to create your own. Here's how to uniquely share your activities, your vacations — even those fabulous cakes you make — with your friends and family.

1. Tap the camera icon in the top left of your screen.

2. Tap the large circle at the bottom of the screen to take a photo, or tap and hold to record a video. If you'd like to pick a photo from your phone's library or gallery, swipe up from anywhere on the screen.

3. Tap the letter or pencil icons at the top to write or draw something, or the smiley-face icons to add a sticker or filter to your photo.

4. If you'd like to make sure a particular person sees your story, you can tag them. Tap the letter icon, then type @ followed by their username, and select the person from the names that appear. They'll get a notification that you've mentioned them in your story.

5. When you're ready to share, tap **Your Story** in the bottom left.

That's all there is to it. Try it out a few times, and before long you'll be an Instagram story pro.

The magic of streaming
Cheap and easy entertainment at your fingertips

Streaming is the use of technology to bring entertainment — movies, TV shows, music, and more — to any device that can connect to the internet. Once upon a time, you could only stream on computers. But now, with smartphones and internet-connected TVs, you can stream anywhere. All you need is an internet connection to get started. Get a load of these great benefits.

- You don't need to wait for a movie or song to download. You just click "play." The show is transmitted through your internet connection to your screen.

- The content is not "saved" on your device. This allows you to flip from show to show without worrying about running out of room.

- You can stream on any device connected to the internet — a phone, laptop, streaming box, or smart TV. You can also switch between devices without losing your place in your show.

In the last 10 years, cable prices have soared 53 percent. But you don't have to pay hundreds of dollars for entertainment. Streaming has become a popular alternative, from Netflix and Hulu to Amazon Prime and Apple TV. You don't need a cable box anymore to watch your favorite shows!

Who needs cable? Cut the cord fearlessly

Save hundreds a year by ditching cable

Every year, cable prices go up, and your service goes down. Why is this? You can partly blame the networks. They have to pay more for live events, like sports, and deal with increasingly large budgets for their shows. So they turn around and charge the cable companies more money to carry their channels.

Entertainment syndicates also make cable companies bundle less-watched, more expensive channels into their popular channel packages. And who does that cost get passed on to? You.

But it doesn't have to be that way. New developments have made it easier than ever to "cut the cord" and cancel cable. Years ago, you could only watch certain content, and that did not include network shows. Sports weren't available — a huge drawback for any fan looking to save money. And you had to watch on your small phone or laptop screen or mess with a tangle of wires to hook your computer up to your TV.

But now, network shows, blockbuster movies, and even sports are available on your big screen. And often, these streaming options are available for much less than your cable bill. So if you ditch your cable or satellite, you can save money and still watch your favorite shows.

Want to learn how to save hundreds a year on your bill? Follow these three steps to get started.

Make sure you have a strong internet connection. You'll need a good one to get the most out of streaming. You don't need lightning-speed rates, but make sure you have a connection of at least 5Mbps. Many cable companies have websites for you to check your speed.

Find an internet-connected device. Of course, you need a device to stream to. Your phone and laptop are obvious choices, but you can also stream to a smart TV or a streaming box like Apple TV. See the chapters *Get smart with your smart TV* and *Simple gadgets get you streaming like a pro* for tips on setting these up.

Make the call and adjust your plan. Many companies now offer internet-only or internet/phone plans for those who don't want cable. With a simple phone call to your cable or satellite provider, you'll shrink your bill tremendously.

Do the math and see for yourself. Even if you cut just $50 off your $150 per month bill, you'll save $600 in a year. And that's more money in your pocket.

Top 10 reasons to free yourself from cable

The benefits of streaming go beyond just saving money. Here are 10 reasons why you should consider getting rid of your cable package.

You can watch your shows anywhere. If you have a streaming service account, you can watch the same shows across any device. You're not limited to a certain number of cable boxes. Your only limit is how many internet-connected devices you have. So you can watch one episode in your living room and the next in your bedroom. Or you can even watch on your tablet while you sit in your backyard.

Pick and choose to find your favorites. Instead of a cable package filled with channels you never watch, streaming lets you customize your entertainment. Only add the apps that have the shows you want — no bundling required.

Never miss a moment no matter where you go. Say you're going on a trip to visit family, and you're five episodes into a new show at home. If your family has that streaming app, you can sign into your account and find the next episode of the show, right under "Resume Watching."

Say bye-bye to boring commercials. Many streaming services have no commercials at all, although you'll have to pay for that privilege. But, even for services that do have commercials, the breaks are much shorter than on live TV. Instead of four or five commercials in a row, you usually only have to watch one or two before getting back to your show.

Keep your kids safe with kid-friendly content. Streaming services often have a "kid zone" to safely browse family-friendly content. Parental controls can also help restrict access to mature content.

Share your account with family. Typical streaming services allow at least two streams at a time. That means you can share an account with your family, paying one subscription and lowering your cost. Many services allow you to create "profiles," so you can keep your watchlists separate.

PROFILES

Who's Watching?

M   Mom

D   Dad

K   Kids

Say hello to blockbuster shows. Some of the most creative content today is now being produced by streaming services. Companies like Hulu, Amazon, and Netflix are investing millions of dollars into creating amazing shows and movies. Netflix alone recently earned 112 Emmy nominations for its original programming.

Grab a blanket and binge watch. You don't have to wait a week to see the next episode when you're streaming. Streaming services can release the entire season at once, so you can watch at your own pace. And you can catch up on old seasons easily so that you're ready when the newest season premieres.

Navigating channels was never so easy. Never stress about flipping through dozens of strange channels or scanning the guide again. Your favorite shows are all gathered in one place with your watchlist. Looking for something new? Browse the genre sections such as "comedy movies" or "detective dramas."

Enjoy a clear picture every time. Don't worry about a fuzzy picture ruining your next watch party. If you have a strong internet connection, digital streaming delivers crystal-clear video with little to no downtime.

When shouldn't you cut the cord?

Before you decide to pull the plug on paid TV, refer to this checklist of instances when you may want to think twice about it. If more than one of these items applies to you, you may be better off keeping your cable or satellite service.

You're a major live sports fan. You have a lot more options available today for streaming live sports games. But the experience isn't seamless yet, especially if you have a slower internet connection. The last thing you want is a break in programming where you miss seeing the big touchdown catch. Also, streaming services don't always show every game that's available on cable. If you want access to every live game, streaming may not be for you.

You have a poor internet connection. If you live in a rural area, you may have more reliable cable than internet service. And if your connection is poor, you may have to pay additional money to boost your speed to handle streaming. If your internet speed is under 5 Mbps, you should consider sticking with cable.

You watch a wide variety of channels. Every year, streaming services offer more varied programming. But subscribing to all your favorites may come at an additional cost. If you watch many channels, the price per channel may be less if you stick with cable.

You like channel flipping. If you prefer browsing through the guide to see what catches your interest versus following just your favorite shows, streaming may not be for you. While your favorite streaming service may offer viewing recommendations and tips for browsing, you usually need some idea of what you want to watch.

Cord cutting isn't just for millennials anymore

Younger people have embraced the streaming movement. Kids in college can't afford to pay for a pricey cable package — or often even a TV — but they do have a laptop or phone they can watch on. But you don't need to be a tech wizard or even a teenager to be part of the streaming community.

In fact, 33 million U.S. adults are now cord-cutters, meaning they have canceled their traditional pay-TV service. Recent research found that cord-cutters made up 1 in 10 adults across each age group. No difference was found between millennials, generation X, and baby boomers.

Instead of age, income level is usually the common variable among people who cut cable. As cable costs rise, more households don't want to pay the price tag. Thousands of people every year are learning how much they can save by streaming instead.

Breaking up is hard to do — how to win with your cable company

You like the benefits of streaming, and you've considered the pros and cons of sticking with cable. Now, you want to cut the cord. But how?

First, know the terms of your agreement. Some cable contracts have early termination fees if you cancel before your contract is up. If your contract only has a few months left, consider waiting so you can avoid the fees.

Do your research. Before you call the cable company, know these three things — the terms of your contract, the cost of your new streaming options, and the fees you may have to pay to cancel cable. Have these items on hand when you call.

Take the plunge and call. Know that the cancellation department will try to offer you better deals to keep you as a customer. That's why the step above is so important. Weigh the savings of your streaming options with the savings they're offering you to stay with cable. Make sure you're making the most cost-effective choice that still gives you everything you want.

Be prepared so you won't get scared. The cancellation department may also try to scare you with talk about extra fees and lost money. Knowing exactly what your contract states — and what it doesn't — can save you a lot of hassle.

> You may not be ready to pull the plug on cable, but you'd probably love to lower your bill. To get a better rate on your cable, phone, and internet, don't dial customer service. Call the cancellation department. If you say you're planning to take your business elsewhere, they may offer you a great deal — or at least a discount — to keep you from leaving.

Understand the pricing options for internet-only packages or internet-and-phone bundles, so you're not surprised when you call. Also, make sure your internet isn't downgraded to a lower-speed option because you need that speed for streaming. But be aware you may have to pay more for higher speeds.

Bundling — the hidden cost of cable

Streaming has a lot of benefits, but what about cable? Don't you save money by bundling all your services?

The biggest mistake customers make when bundling cable, internet, and phone is not understanding that cable providers are not made equally. A company can have great phone service but terrible cable service. Or perhaps their internet speeds are lightning-fast, but their phone service is patchy.

By bundling, you're forced to take the good with the bad, instead of shopping around for the best providers. That can lead to additional money spent on service calls to fix issues.

Plus, once you're locked into a bundle, those cost savings that brought you there often disappear. Your bill climbs little by little each month, or you're subject to a large increase once a year. The money you saved by bundling is slowly chipped away. The bottom line — bundling may be costlier than you think.

Enjoy fee-free TV with a digital antenna

Check your TV to watch for free

Was your TV manufactured after 2007? Then you're eligible for free viewing. Say good-bye to your cable or satellite bill.

The Telecommunications Act of 1996 ushered in the age of digital broadcasting through "over-the-air" TV. Analog broadcasting was phased out, and networks had to begin transmitting digital signals. After March 2007, all televisions were required to have a digital tuner. This transition allowed for the better video and audio quality seen today.

So if you have a TV made after that time, you can access free TV over the air. Check the back of your television and look for the white sticker. Sometimes you'll find a manufacture date right there. If not, write down your serial number from the sticker and look it up online.

Or you can call your TV manufacturer's help line. The serial number will tell you exactly when your television was made. If yours passes the test, congratulations — you have the option to watch programs for free.

Pay this once and watch TV forever

Forget monthly satellite or cable bills — you're ready to enjoy fee-free TV. There's just one more thing. If your TV has a digital tuner, you need to buy an antenna to access the signal without cable. The good news is, digital antennas cost less than $100.

Get the same access for less money. All major networks broadcast over the air. So you get the same channels you would with cable. How is that possible?

Networks are paid by the advertisers who run the commercials in between shows. You, the viewer, don't pay for the broadcast at all. You pay for access to the broadcast. A digital antenna gives you that access for a lot less money.

No need to worry about finding channels. You'll find even more through a digital antenna, including shows you'd never otherwise see. Each channel now has "sub-channels." These sub-channels are often not offered in typical cable packages, or they are hidden in the higher channels you may not browse often.

Each sub-channel has additional programming beyond what you would find on the normal channel in a cable package. Some have regional content you might find interesting, such as local news.

Other sub-channels have family friendly content or hobby shows, like cooking. Some even play reruns of popular shows. You'll discover a lot of great content with sub-channels.

Enjoy the best-ever picture and sound. Part of the reason the United States switched to digital was because of quality. Digital broadcasting gives you a sharper picture and better sound quality. But you'll often see an even clearer picture if you access over-the-air TV through a digital antenna.

That's because cable providers compress multiple high-definition signals into the same space one analog station used to occupy. Why? To save money, of course. But it ends up having a negative effect on quality. With a digital antenna, you don't have to worry about that compression, leaving you with a much clearer picture.

---

3 simple steps for finding your broadcast towers

Before you buy a digital antenna, you need to figure out where your broadcast towers are. Follow these three simple steps to find the towers near you.

- Go to the FCC's digital TV reception guide at *fcc.gov/media/engineering/dtvmaps* and type in your address.

- The tool will give you a list of towers you can receive signals from. The FCC tool color codes these by signal strength. Green is a strong signal, yellow is moderate, orange is weak, and red is no signal.

- Click on each tower to see how far away it is from you and what direction it is from your house. Look on the map to see if any large natural barriers would interfere with the signal, such as tall trees, mountain ranges, or city buildings.

Once you know the closest tower that will give you the best signal, you can start looking at antennas.

Get the clearest signal with the right antenna

You have two main types of digital antennas to choose from — indoor and outdoor. Once you've found your broadcast towers, you'll need to decide which antenna is best for you.

Indoor antennas have size on their side. They're usually small and easy to position. You also don't have to worry about complicated installation. They are best used when:

- you live close — less than 30 miles — to broadcast towers.

- you live in an apartment or other shared-living space.

- you cannot mount an antenna on your roof.

The downside is that having the antenna inside can affect your signal quality. The signal must go through whatever is between the broadcast tower and the antenna — your walls and furniture. The more material it must cross, the more interference is possible. Some household appliances can also interfere with the signal of an indoor antenna.

Outdoor antennas have the best signal. Because they are larger and usually mounted to your roof, these antennas have a much clearer signal. They usually have fewer obstacles standing between them and the broadcast tower. Plus most outdoor antennas have a much longer range than indoor antennas do. They are best used when:

- you have a roof you can mount on.

- you want a clearer signal.

- you live more than 30 miles away from broadcast towers.

You can also put your outdoor antenna in another location, like your backyard or the side of your house. But keep in mind the signal might not be as clear.

You should always scan for available channels in the area where you are considering placing the antenna before you begin installation. You don't want to move the antenna once you've connected it to your roof. Consult your TV user manual for directions on how to perform a channel scan.

Trees, fences, and other houses can stand in the way if the outdoor antenna is not mounted high up on your house.

Consider direction when choosing. Both outdoor and indoor antennas have two types — directional and omnidirectional (also known as multidirectional).

A directional antenna gives you a more focused signal from the direction you're pointing it in. An omnidirectional antenna loses some of that focus, but it can pick up signals from many directions. If you have broadcast towers close by in multiple directions, you may want to consider an omnidirectional antenna.

Bad reception? 6 easy ways to clear it up

Oh no, your TV reception is fuzzy. What do you do? Here are some things to try if you are not getting a clear signal.

Adjust the direction. Consult your tower map again, and make sure your antenna is pointed exactly at the tower with the clearest signal. Even moving the antenna slightly can affect the signal.

Avoid obstructions. If you have a large tree or building directly in the path of your antenna, consider mounting it in a different location. Although it may not be the most direct path, a clearer path results in a clearer signal.

Inspect your cables. Some cables that connect the antenna to your TV are better suited for digital signals than others. Find out which cable you are using. Most antenna companies recommend using an RG6 cable.

Check for splitters. Splitters, which allow signals to be sent to multiple TVs in the house, can cause a loss of quality. The more ways you are splitting the signal, the more signal you could lose.

Widen the range. You have many different types of digital antennas to choose from, with different ranges. Some antennas only pick up from a 30-50 mile range, while others can pick up a signal from much farther away. If you are not getting the best signal with your current model, consider switching to a long-range antenna.

Boost your signal. If you have tried all of the above and are still having trouble getting a signal, you may want to consider buying an amplifier. An amplifier "boosts" the signal coming in through your antenna.

Be careful with amplifiers. Just like you can blow out your speakers, you can overamplify your digital TV tuner. Consult with an expert to find out which amplifier is right for your TV before buying.

Cheer on your favorite sports team at no cost

Any sports fan knows that lots of channels show sporting events. Some of those channels, like ESPN, are not available with a digital antenna. So if you are an avid college sports fan, you may want to consider another option besides a digital antenna for watching sports, like a streaming box.

But if you usually just watch sports on the major networks (ABC, NBC, CBS, FOX), then a digital antenna is perfect for you. If your antenna picks up that channel, you'll be able to watch the game just as you would normally.

Check the schedule. The NFL and most other sports associations post game schedules online. This schedule will tell you which channel the games for the week will be shown on. Check the schedule and make sure the game you want to watch is showing on a channel you have access to.

Where you live makes a difference. For sports, there are national broadcasts, which are shown in every region, and local broadcasts, which are shown in select regions. Each area will broadcast different local games.

Say you live in Texas. You may only pick up the local game showing in that region, say the Houston Texans game. Meanwhile, someone in New York would pick up a different game at that same time, for example, the NY Jets game. But you can watch the games that are nationally broadcast (usually three per week for the NFL) no matter where you live.

A lot depends on the signal. The station you pick up a signal from determines which local games you will get. If you live in one state, but your closest broadcast tower is in a different region, you may not pick up your favorite local team. Consult a TV guide to know which games you will receive each week.

Get smart with your smart TV

The secret to easy streaming — no hardware required

Why watch streaming video on your computer or tablet screen when you could be watching it on your nice big TV? Here's how — by using a smart TV.

But first, what makes a TV "smart?" A smart TV is any television that can connect to the internet. It does this either with an ethernet cord, like you would use for a desktop computer, or through a Wi-Fi connection.

With this connection to the internet, smart TVs allow you to access content. You do so through different apps (applications) just like you would on your phone. You choose which apps you install on your TV.

Most smart TVs have an app library or app store, where you can look at the apps available and choose the ones right for you.

The age of 4K Blu-ray is here. If you're watching ultra-high-definition content like that, consider using an ethernet cord for a stronger connection. But if your TV isn't near an ethernet port, or you're watching lower-resolution content, it's fine to use Wi-Fi instead.

You can look at the weather, check on news, play workout videos, and watch movies all through apps on your smart TV. Here's an example of what your app screen might look like.

You can also use voice search on many smart TVs. So instead of hunting for the app you want, you can press the voice search button on your remote and say "Netflix" into the microphone. The TV will take you right to the Netflix app, without going through all the screens you would normally have to click through. You can even look up the weather or stock prices.

Some smart TVs can also connect to other devices in your house, like your smartphone. If you have an Android phone, you can easily connect via **Wi-Fi Direct**, which you'll find under **Wi-Fi** in your Settings. If you have an iPhone, you'll need an HDMI cable or, to connect wirelessly, an Apple TV device.

Now you can show pictures from your phone on the big screen or play a video someone just sent you without wearing out your eyes.

4 great reasons to upgrade your TV

Smart TVs come with a lot of great features, but they are more expensive than a regular TV. When is buying a smart TV the right choice for you?

You want access to streaming services without installing another device. A regular TV can still access streaming entertainment by plugging in a streaming box. But if you only want to worry about one device, a smart TV is the way to go. Everything you need to stream is already on the TV. No need to worry about separate remotes and HDMI cables.

You want to stream on a big screen. Of course, you can use the same apps that are on a smart TV on your phone, tablet, or laptop. But the screens are much smaller, and you may miss the cinematic experience of watching on a big screen.

You don't have a good broadcast signal. You might live in an area where you have a good internet connection but a poor broadcast signal. Large obstacles, like mountains or tall buildings, may block your access to broadcast television. Smart TVs allow you to still watch the shows you want to watch, without cable or a poor signal from a digital antenna.

You want high-quality audio and video. Many smart TVs have higher-quality pictures than normal TVs. They also often have audio enhancements. Some have such good speakers that you might not need a separate speaker system for great sound.

Ditch the DVR and watch on demand

Now that you have your smart TV, it's time to start watching. The great benefit of streaming on a smart TV is that you can choose what you watch, any time. You don't need to wait for the show to come on at its scheduled time or flip through endless channels to find your favorites.

Find the app you want to use. The app may already be installed on your TV. If not, you can find it in the app library. Each app offers different shows and movies, depending on their selection.

Search for what you want to watch. Once you've found your app, you need to locate the show or movie you want to watch. If you already have a show in mind, you can use the **Search** feature. If the show is available on that app, it will show up in the search results.

If it doesn't appear in the search results, try looking for it in another app. You may have sworn the show was on Netflix, but it could very well be on Amazon Prime instead.

If you're not sure what to watch, it's easy to browse. Most apps have shows and movies broken into categories like comedy or drama, so you can easily find what you're looking for. You'll also usually find a section of popular or new shows that you can look through.

Take advantage of your watchlist. You can also add certain shows or movies to a watchlist, so you can find them in a snap. Different apps call this feature by different names. Really, it's just a collection of your favorites all in one place. You may not have time to watch the new movie you found right now. But if you add it to your watchlist, you'll know just where to find it later. Here's an example of a watchlist on Netflix.

After you've found your show or movie, select **Play**. For shows, the app will often list all the episodes by season with a brief description. You can start from the first episode or jump around. Don't worry about losing your place. If you must pause or turn off your TV, the app will save your location. Then when you log back in, you can start right where you left off. How easy is that?

Add options galore with the press of a button

So how do you access all these great entertainment options on your smart TV? You get some apps.

Your smart TV usually comes with apps already installed. But you can always add more by checking out the app library. You should have a home page on your smart TV where you can easily access the app selection.

Once you're in the library, you'll notice it's organized by several categories. Looking for an app to watch movies? Check out the **Entertainment** section. Just want to browse around? Look at the **Trending** or **Most Popular** app category to see what others download.

Each app usually comes with a description and a rating, so you know what the app does and what other users think of it. If it looks good, just click the **Install** button, and the app will appear on your TV.

What to do when the streaming stops

Nothing is more frustrating than seeing your streaming video stop or slow down. This usually happens because the show is "buffering," or waiting to download from the server. Before you pull your hair out, consider why it may be happening and what you can do about it.

The connection speed is slow. Sometimes your internet connection may not be fast enough to stream without interruption. You can test your internet speed online through your internet provider's website to see if that's the issue. You can also potentially purchase a plan with faster internet speeds.

The video is too big. If you are trying to watch a show in high definition (HD) or 4K, it may take longer to buffer. That's because the video file that is being transmitted to your TV is much larger than a traditional video file. If possible, try to connect your smart TV through an ethernet port rather than Wi-Fi to give it a boost.

Too many people are watching at once. This rarely occurs in apps and more often on websites. If a video is newly released and many people are trying to access it at once, it can slow the video down. If you're trying to watch a high-demand program, you may want to come back to it later and see if your streaming quality improves.

Take a deep breath and wait. A good rule of thumb when streaming stops and starts is to wait a few minutes. By pausing the video, you give it time to buffer. If enough of the video buffers ahead of time, it won't stop on you again. You can usually tell how much is buffered by pressing pause and looking at the progress bar.

In the example below, the light gray portion to the right of the dot is what has been buffered so far. The dot shows where you've stopped and what you've watched to that point. The rest of the bar shows how much of the video is left. If you see little or no progress in the buffering bar, you need to wait a little longer or turn it off and try again later.

Don't let hackers into your smart TV

Owning a TV that connects to the internet has lots of great benefits. But there is some risk as well. Just like your computer or phone, your smart TV can be vulnerable to hacking or viruses. You want to make sure your TV is protected against threats such as:

- account information theft.

- webcam and microphone hacking.

- remotely controlling the television.

Luckily, there are a number of precautions you can take to protect your smart TV.

Use a wired connection. Wi-Fi can be more convenient, but it is more vulnerable to outside attacks. By using an ethernet cord to connect your TV to the internet, you'll be more protected.

Secure your networks. If you are using a Wi-Fi connection, make sure your password is secure and updated regularly. Consider using a random password generator to increase your password strength. Always password protect your network.

Update frequently. Your smart TV manufacturer releases updates often to address security concerns and make sure your TV is running smoothly. Don't delay on these updates. Make sure you install them as soon as they are released. To check, look under Settings > Support > Software Update, or a similar type of path on your TV.

Be careful with apps. Your TV manufacturer will often monitor for suspicious apps, but you can take some extra steps for your security. Always check the ratings and reviews on apps to make sure they are reputable and do what they say they will do.

Connect with care. Make sure you only connect trusted devices and USB sticks to your smart TV. An infected device could pass on malware to your TV.

Manage your account wisely. You will have logins for your apps on the TV as well as your Wi-Fi login. Make sure to regularly change those passwords. Choose strong passwords, and do not share them with others.

Add another layer of security with a strong gatekeeper

Still worried about security and your smart TV? You can protect yourself more by installing a firewall. A firewall acts as a gatekeeper to your home network. Based on rules that you set, it will block or allow certain actions that involve your internet connection.

A firewall is a great tool not only to protect your smart TV but also other connected devices in your home — computers, phones, tablets, and even printers.

Firewalls come as either software that you can install or as a separate appliance. They will monitor your devices and block "probing" attacks. The firewall blocks access to the network ports except for the devices you allow.

Your TV user manual should have the information you need to make sure your TV is allowed access through the firewall. Often, firewalls can also provide anti-virus software for extra protection.

Simple gadgets get you streaming like a pro

No smart TV? No problem

Maybe you have a perfectly good flat screen TV that isn't "smart," or connected to the internet. Maybe you don't want to be locked into one device and want the option to change streaming devices down the road. Either way, you can still access all the benefits of streaming without a smart TV. You just need some additional hardware.

Why would you choose to buy another device rather than a smart TV? Besides the reasons listed above, streaming hardware is often inexpensive and easy to install. You can carry it over if you decide to buy a new TV.

A streaming device is also portable. You can easily move your streaming device from the living room to the bedroom with just a few simple steps. Many people find streaming devices to be the most convenient way to stream.

Streaming hardware outside of smart TVs and mobile devices typically comes in four forms — a stick, box, gaming console, or computer.

Sticks are the simplest and cheapest option. A streaming stick is a device that plugs into a port connected to your TV. Depending on your TV and system, you can plug the stick directly into the back of your TV or into your audio/visual (AV) system. Sometimes you operate it using your mobile device, which basically acts as an "antenna" to display content from your phone on the big screen. Others have a simple operating system built in. You may prefer this streaming device if:

- you're looking for a low-cost option.

- you have a strong and reliable Wi-Fi connection.

- you're OK with using your phone as a control.

- you don't want to buy and download movies or shows.

- you want the smallest, least-visible device.

A streaming box is the next step up. Boxes tend to be a little pricier, but they also have some additional benefits. They have a larger storage capacity in case you download movies or shows. They can also use a hardwired internet connection, unlike the sticks. Installation is very similar — you plug the box directly into a port on your TV. You may prefer a box if:

- you have an unreliable Wi-Fi connection but a strong ethernet connection.

- you have other devices from the same manufacturer — like Apple — and want to take advantage of cloud services across your devices, for instance.

- you want to buy and download movies or shows.

- you want a small, portable option.

Gaming consoles kill two birds with one stone. Some gaming consoles now offer streaming apps as well. But they are much more expensive than a box or stick. This device may be a good choice if:

- you already have a streaming-enabled gaming console.

- you play video games often.

- you don't want to buy an additional piece of hardware.

Computers are a cost-effective choice. If you already have a laptop, you can connect it directly to your TV using an HDMI cord. This setup tends to be a little bulkier since you have to find a place to set your laptop. It can also be a bit inconvenient since you'll need to unplug your computer regularly to use it. But it could be a good choice for you if:

- you don't mind moving your laptop around.

- you're OK with it taking up additional space.

- you don't want to spend money on another piece of hardware.

Hardware options: Your top 5 choices for streaming

So you've decided you want to stream via a stick or box. What brand should you buy? Below are five of the best streaming hardware options for you to choose from.

Amazon Fire TV. Amazon has several streaming device options, in two categories — streaming sticks and streaming boxes. Both options include voice control with Alexa. The Amazon Fire Cube has additional capabilities, including voice control over your entire AV system and does not require a separate Amazon Echo. These devices are a good choice if you are:

- an Amazon Prime member.

- an Amazon Echo owner.

- someone who likes voice controls and wants a "connected home."

Apple TV. This streaming box works the same way as other Apple devices, such as the iPhone. It has a large app selection and voice control through Siri. If you have other Apple devices, you can connect to iCloud for shared access to photos, videos, and more. The box also has a large storage space for downloaded content. This device is a good choice if you are:

- an Apple user.

- someone who needs storage space for downloaded content.

- someone who stores a lot of content in the cloud.

Chromecast. Google's Chromecast options are all in the streaming stick space. These devices do not use an operating system. Instead you "cast" to the device from your mobile phone over your Wi-Fi network to play the show on your TV. You can also browse the web on TV via your phone. This device is a good choice if you are:

- an Android user.

- comfortable with using your phone as a controller.

- looking for a device with web browser access.

Nvidia. The Nvidia Shield is a mix between a streaming box and a gaming console. Not only can you use it to watch shows and movies through apps, but you can also either play Android games or stream popular PC games. You can buy or rent content from the Google Play store, and it has a large storage space for downloads. This device is a good choice if you are:

- an Android user.

- a video game player.

- looking for a system that can do multiple things.

Roku. Like Amazon, Roku has both streaming stick and box options. Its sticks have a simple operating system and access to thousands of apps. You do not have to stream from your phone, like with Chromecast. Roku is simple and easy to use and has a large app library. This device is a good choice if you are:

- looking for a lot of options to choose from.

- needing something that is easy to use.

- interested in a large app library.

Best places for your streaming box

Let's say you've decided to go with a streaming box for your entertainment. Now the question is — where do you put it?

Remember, your streaming box responds to a signal from your control — either your phone or an actual remote. It needs to have clear access to that signal. So it's not a good idea to tuck it in a drawer or hide it behind something. Make sure that when you're sitting on the couch, you have a clear line from your remote to your box.

And, of course, your box needs to connect to your TV, so your cord will need to reach wherever you've put the box. You can always buy a longer HDMI cord if necessary. If you're using an ethernet connection, you also want to be sure the box is close to your router or that you have a long ethernet cord.

Watch TV anywhere on the go

The great thing about streaming is that you don't even need a TV at all. Whether you need some in-flight entertainment, a road-trip movie, or something to watch while you're outside, you have an option. If you have an internet-connected device — a phone, tablet, or laptop — and an internet connection, you can stream.

If you are watching on a phone or a laptop, you'll stream through apps, just like on a smart TV or streaming device. Go to the phone's app store, select the streaming apps you wish to use, and install them on your phone.

> Be aware of how much storage you have on your device when downloading. Shows and movies often take up a lot of room. If your device has a small amount of storage, you may want to stick to streaming.

Depending on the laptop you have, you may also use an app to watch. But some PCs do not have an app store. In that case, you can access the streaming service through an internet browser. Simply type in the URL, for example *www.hulu.com*, sign in, and you're on your way.

You don't even need an internet connection to watch shows or movies from your apps. Many streaming services allow you to download shows to your mobile device so you can watch without an internet connection. This is a great option if you'll be watching in a place with spotty internet access. You can pick just a few episodes to download or a whole

movie (see graphic). Just remember you'll need an internet connection to download the content.

Never lose your spot with these 2 tricks

The great thing about streaming is you don't have to use just one device. Your account can follow you to whichever device you wish to use at that time. So you can sign in to Netflix on your TV, phone, and laptop all at the same time. Here are two convenient features you'll want to use when switching between devices.

- **Watchlist.** Keep your favorites with you wherever you go. Once you mark a show as a favorite, it will stay in your watchlist for easy access. No more searching for the same show every time you log in. Nice!

- **Resume watching.** Most streaming services also save your progress. Say you're on episode 5 on your TV. When you log in on your phone, episode 5 will show up under **Resume watching**, instead of starting at episode 1. Even if you stop in the middle of an episode, you can pick up right where you left off.

Keep your streaming device safe

Just like your laptop, phone, and other connected devices, your streaming device is at risk for cyberattacks. Password theft, data theft, and remote access are all possible risks. Security is even more important on a streaming device, because you store payment methods to buy apps and content. Luckily, with a few simple steps, you can shrink your security risk.

Use a wired connection when possible. Unfortunately, streaming sticks only work over Wi-Fi networks. But other streaming devices like boxes and laptops can use a wired ethernet connection instead. When possible, consider using the ethernet connection for an extra layer of security.

Choose strong passwords. Make sure your passwords to the device's app store, any cloud applications, and streaming networks are strong and are not the same across your accounts. It can be tempting to use the same, simple password for everything, but it makes your system less secure.

Use 2-step verification. Some apps now offer a 2-step login process. First, you enter your password. Then a code is texted or emailed to you, which you enter into the app. This provides an additional layer of security and makes it harder for someone to log in to your accounts.

Sign out often. While always being signed in is convenient, it can be a risk. Others can purchase items using your account credentials without your permission. Make sure to sign out of your apps every time you finish using them, especially if you've signed in on someone else's device. You can also require your password to be re-entered for any purchases.

3 simple keys to spot a suspicious streaming site

If you stream through your laptop, it may be through an internet browser instead of an app. Unlike an app, which must be approved and rated on the store, a site can be created by anyone. That means you may be at risk for a cyberattack. Make sure you're streaming from a safe site with these three keys.

Use trusted sites. If you stumble on a site you never heard of and it sounds too good to be true — perhaps offering free access to premium cable shows — it probably is. Make sure to only stream from credible providers such as Netflix, Hulu, YouTube, and other sites that are well-known and trusted.

Be careful with downloads. You may see sites that offer "free downloads" of popular shows and movies, maybe even a movie that is still in the theaters. Never download from an unknown site. Often, these downloads will contain malware or viruses that infect your computer.

Look for security indicators. Many browsers display a locked padlock or an "https" before the URL when you are accessing a secure site. Trusted streaming provider sites are always secure. If you don't see the usual indicators, or if your browser warns you that this is an unsafe site, leave the page.

Remember, if it sounds too good to be true — it probably is.

Subscribe and stream
Paid services that are worth the bucks

5 easy steps to setting up streaming subscriptions

Stop paying for cable and still watch your favorite shows. How, you ask? By signing up for a streaming service subscription. Streaming entertainment typically comes in two forms — free streaming (either using a digital antenna or accessing free services online) and paid subscriptions.

While subscription services do cost a monthly fee, you'll be paying a fraction of what you pay for cable. As a bonus, you also get to tailor your entertainment, only paying for the services you want to watch, not what the cable company has decided is most profitable.

Subscription services typically also have a broader range of shows and movies available and include options like watching popular network shows right after they air.

By following these five easy steps, you'll be watching your favorite shows in no time.

Research the offerings. You'll find a lot of streaming subscriptions out there, and they all have different shows and movies available. These services make deals with the networks for the rights to certain shows and movies. So make sure the subscription you're signing up for has the shows you want to watch.

Calculate the costs. Next, figure out the fees. Most paid streaming services use a monthly payment plan, and many have levels within those plans. More expensive plans can include benefits like high-definition video, commercial-free viewing, and watching on multiple screens at once.

Add up exactly how much each of these subscriptions will cost you per month, so you know what your new entertainment bill will be.

Create an account. Once you've decided on your services, it's time to create your accounts. Your streaming account will follow you across your devices, so you won't have to worry about separate ones for your TV, phone, and computer. Make sure to pick a secure password.

Pick your preferences. Many streaming services ask a few questions when you first get started to help make recommendations on what to watch. What genres do you enjoy? What are your favorite shows? These preferences help customize what you see on your home page.

Build your watchlist. The watchlist, which has different names on different streaming services, is your best tool while streaming. Take the time when you first get set up to add favorite shows, movies you'd like to watch, and anything that catches your eye. Not only will it make them easy to find later, it also helps the streaming service provide better recommendations for you.

When to pay the subscription cost

You may be asking yourself, "Why would I pay a subscription fee when I can stream shows for free?" Here are some reasons a paid subscription may be right for you.

You watch a lot of network shows. Many networks, both broadcast and cable, only sell the rights to their shows to subscription services. Remember, they still have to make money, even if you're not paying for cable anymore.

You love premium content. Premium cable channels like HBO, Starz, and SHOWTIME also don't want to lose money by offering their shows for free. While you can watch without a cable package, you still need to pay for a subscription to their service.

You hate commercials. Most free streaming sites have commercials to make money, instead of charging a subscription fee. When you pay for a streaming subscription, you're often paying for the right to watch your shows commercial-free. Although some paid subscriptions also require commercials, you usually only have to sit through one or two per show.

Navigate the 3 streaming giants with ease

You've heard their names — Netflix, Hulu, Amazon Prime Video. But what's the difference between these three streaming giants? And how do you navigate their home pages?

Netflix is the king of original content. Starting as a provider of DVD rentals shipped right to your home, Netflix has expanded to be so much more. Some of your favorite movies and shows can be found on Netflix, and new ones are added all the time.

One of the best parts of Netflix, though, is the original content. Netflix was one of the first streaming services to invest in creating its own shows and movies, instead of just licensing them from the big entertainment companies. Now they have one of the largest libraries of original shows and movies.

Netflix's home page is ordered by rows. The first row is **My List**, your personal watchlist. Below is **Continue Watching**, where you can pick up viewing right where you left off. Other rows include **Popular on Netflix**, **Trending Now**, and **Recently Added**. Finally, you'll see several rows of recommendations.

Hulu is a great option if you love broadcast and cable shows. Hulu has rights to stream most shows that you would normally find in a cable package. New episodes are added every week, usually just hours after they've aired on TV, so you don't have to worry about falling behind.

Keep in mind Hulu does show commercials on the normal plan, but you can pay more for commercial-free watching. It also has a great library of original content, including award-winning shows.

As you'll see, Hulu's home page focuses more on images. **Lineup** includes both shows that you have already watched and options that Hulu thinks you would like. Below is **Keep Watching**. The rest of the home page includes sections for **TV**, **Movies**, **Kids**, and genres and recommendations you might like. There is also a **New on Hulu** section.

Amazon Prime Video comes free with your membership. This is a great perk if you're paying that annual Prime membership fee. Seasons of popular TV shows and beloved movies are all available to members. Many are included with Prime, but some charge an additional fee. It depends on the show or movie. Amazon has original content as well, both series and movies.

Amazon's home page is organized in rows like Netflix. You'll see rows for **Watch Next, Recommended,** and **Popular** as well as genres. There is also a section for **Live Events**, which are included with Prime. If you only want to see content that is available free with your Prime membership, make sure to select **Included with Prime** at the top.

4 amazing apps for watching sports

Many sports organizations now have their own apps, in addition to showing games on streaming services. If you don't want to pay for a live TV subscription, you can still watch your favorite teams.

MLB at Bat. Can't live without baseball? You don't have to. MLB At Bat allows you to either watch the "Game of the Day" for free or unlimited access to out-of-market games for a subscription. They have both a yearly and monthly plan available.

NBA: Official App. You can watch basketball games live or view replays later with the basic NBA app. The NBA League Pass has either a monthly or annual option for additional game access.

NFL App. Watch your favorite local and prime-time football games. The NFL Game Pass subscription allows you to watch games based on your location.

NHL App. This app gives you access to highlights and select hockey games for free, and additional games for a subscription cost with NHL Premium.

Discover your next binge-worthy show

Looking for something new to watch? Streaming services make it easy. Much like online retailers have a "because you bought" section at the bottom to show you other items you might like, so do streaming services. The recommendations are based on the preferences you set in your account, what you have in your watchlist, and what you've watched already.

You can also improve your recommendations by rating shows. For instance, on Netflix, you'll see a thumbs-up/thumbs-down icon you can select to tell Netflix you want more shows like this — or don't.

While every streaming service is different, most recommend by genres. Sometimes these recommendations can get pretty specific, so you shouldn't have any problem finding something you like.

Another way to find a new favorite show or movie is to use the **Browse** or **Explore** feature. These lists are also customized to your tastes. But they include trending items or newly added items. For instance, Hulu's **Lineup** at the top of the home page includes a mix of your favorites and shows Hulu thinks you might like.

Simple trick to spot a paywall

Some networks have a mix of free and "locked" content that lives behind a paywall. So you may get excited when you see your favorite show, only to be disappointed when you realize you must have a cable account to watch it.

These shows are often right on the home page to catch your attention and hopefully get you to pay the extra money. How can you tell which is which? Use this simple trick.

Apps typically use a padlock icon for shows that are behind the paywall. Check out the graphic. See the padlocks under the show names? That tells you right away the content is locked to users at your level.

Make sure to glance at the corner of the image for every show, and you'll know right away which ones you have access to.

Network apps: Bringing home all your favorites

While the streaming giants provide a wide range of entertainment, they're not your only options for watching broadcast and cable shows. Most networks now offer their own apps. Some of these apps are subscription-only, while others offer a mix of free and paid content. If most of your favorite shows are only on one or two networks, this can be a great option.

The major broadcast networks are all in. ABC, CBS, Fox, and NBC now have apps you can install on most streaming devices. These apps have most on-air shows available episode by episode, available right after the live broadcast.

Unlike the streaming giants, the networks usually only have the current season available to watch. Shows are typically divided by normal commercial breaks, although the breaks are shorter — typically two to three commercials. Cable networks like FX, AMC, Bravo, and others also have apps available.

> Cable isn't the only answer. Many network apps now treat live TV subscriptions, like YouTube TV and Sling TV, as cable providers. So you can access that locked paywall content by signing in to your live TV account.

The downside? You may need a cable account. Unfortunately, some of the network shows are only available by signing in with a cable provider. Check your app to be sure.

Some networks have an "all access" subscription you can buy, where you don't need a cable subscription. Others have a mix of free content and content behind the "paywall," allowing cord-cutters access to some of the content without a subscription. See the box *Simple trick to spot a paywall* to learn how to tell the difference between the two.

Popular live events are right at your fingertips. Do you love award shows and sporting events? If they'll be shown on your local network, you can watch them on the app.

Say you want to watch the Oscars. Log in to the ABC app, and the live broadcast will be right there for your viewing pleasure. No need to worry about finding a place outside your home to watch Hollywood's biggest night. And the next day you can catch all the red carpet glamour on your favorite morning news show.

Check out premium cable networks as well. HBO, Starz, and SHOWTIME all have at least two options — an app for its cable subscribers and an app for those who don't have a premium cable package but still want to watch. The second type of app is subscription-based, just like the streaming giants. The best part? You don't have to worry about commercials.

Don't miss out on live TV with these options

Streaming isn't just for watching replays. You can now watch a lot of networks live, too. These options tend to be a bit more expensive than traditional streaming subscriptions. But with that extra cost you get more of a "traditional" cable experience. Multiple channels, live browsing, and local content are all available with live TV subscriptions.

You also have access to the live TV guide, which looks just like the one on your TV. You can see what's on now and what's coming up. And for those of you who can't stay up past 10 p.m.,

Location, location, location. Many of these live options are different depending on where you live. Just like watching network TV, some live options, particularly sports, are only available in certain markets.

some providers will let you record shows on a virtual DVR (digital video recorder). Check out some of the most popular live TV streaming options.

DirecTV Now. You don't need a cable subscription anymore to get DirecTV. By signing up for a monthly subscription, you can access hundreds of channels live on your streaming device. Sports, news, and your favorite cable shows are right at your fingertips, with multiple plan levels.

Hulu Live TV. For an additional fee, you can add live TV access to your Hulu account. Hulu Live TV offers access to sports, news, and live events from a wide range of channels.

Sling TV. Sling TV's monthly subscription offers a couple of different packages with your favorite channels. It also offers a "Cloud DVR" service for an additional fee, so you can record shows you might otherwise miss.

YouTube TV. YouTube now has a live TV option as well, with many of your favorite sports, news, and entertainment networks. You also get a DVR option for free with the package.

Make streaming safe for your family

Streaming services know that it's not just you watching. That's why they offer plenty of ways to make streaming safe and fun for the whole family.

Many streaming services now have a **Kids** portal, which is easy to find. These portals offer family friendly content, without the worry that mature content will show up. Favorite movies, shows, and channels are all right there for your family to watch. Perfect for your next movie night with the grandkids.

Experts also recommend that you create a separate kids profile within your account. This makes it easier to provide age-appropriate entertainment and limit access to mature content.

You can put limits on the shows they can watch — for example, "for little kids only" — or put in their age, depending on the streaming service. This will make sure mature shows and movies aren't recommended to this profile.

Finally, just like your normal TV, streaming services offer parental controls. You decide what rated content is available for your family. That way, you don't have to worry about the latest gory murder movie popping up right next to the newest animated show.

You control the level and which profiles are affected. You can even block certain titles. Some services use the age on the profile to limit content, while others have a **Parental Controls** option in settings.

Movies, TV, sports, and more
Watch your favorites for free

Stream your favorite shows without the cost

Knowing this secret could save you a lot of money — you don't need a paid subscription to stream entertainment. If you have a streaming box or stick, you'll find many apps that now provide content for free. How do they do it?

Advertisers pay for the cost. Much like the lower-cost subscription services, many free streaming services show commercials. Free services still have to pay for the rights to show their content. By showing ads, they pass that cost onto their advertisers instead of you. Ads are often shorter and less frequent than ads on cable.

Your favorite movie may not stick around. Another way these apps reduce costs is by rotating shows and movies on a regular basis. This means you trade off availability for new variety.

If you like discovering new shows and movies, free streaming services are a great choice. Look for those that show only "public domain" content, and you won't have to watch any ads. These videos are usually older films and shows that are past their copyright.

They give access to some content. A lot of news organizations and other entertainment apps offer smaller snippets of free content in addition to their paid content. A "paywall" limits the content you watch to what's available for free, unless you decide to pay the subscription. So you can still watch sports highlights, news broadcasts, and selected shows for free without moving past the paywall.

Netflix steals the spotlight, but these free streaming services may give you everything you need. Which ones are right for you?

- Crackle — watch shows like *Seinfeld* and *Married with Children* as well as popular movies and original content.

- Viki — find older favorites like *The Lone Ranger* and *Ozzie and Harriet*.

- Rewinder — enjoy classic movies and TV like Alfred Hitchcock's *The Man Who Knew Too Much* and *The Lucy Show*.

- Pluto TV — watch live TV without the cable bill, with access to hundreds of channels like BBC America and Bloomberg. It even has a guide for easy browsing.

- Tubi TV — access over 7,000 movies and TV shows, without the Netflix subscription cost.

Stay up to date with streaming news

One of the main reasons people are hesitant to cut the cord is the fear of losing live content, like news. The last chapter covered the subscription options available. But you can also watch the news for free.

- **News section.** Depending on your streaming device, you may have a news app that displays top stories of the day. These are usually a mix of written stories and video, and they're a great way to quickly browse the highlights.

- **Network apps.** Many network apps also offer news clips or full news shows for free (with ads).

- **Free news apps.** Check out your streaming device's app library to see what news apps are available for free. Some, like Bloomberg, offer specific content like business news. Others, like Newsy, offer their own news instead of broadcast news shows.

- **Local news sites.** If you miss your local news, you can still watch through the web. NewsON broadcasts offer many local news stations from around the country. Or you can find your local news station's website and see if it offers a live stream. You may have to access this through your computer or phone if your streaming setup doesn't allow for web browsing.

---

4 ways to speed up your streaming

Are your videos stopping and starting often, or do they take a long time to load? You may be experiencing "lag," a slow response from your internet-connected device. Here are a few tips to speed up your streaming.

Close out other apps. Even though you may not be using other apps while you're streaming, they often run in the background. Close out all other apps when streaming.

Pause at the beginning. Give your video time to load or "buffer" by pausing for a minute or two before you watch.

Stay updated. If an update is needed, your streaming device may run slower than it should. Always install updates to your device as soon as they are available.

Use a wired connection. When possible, go wired instead of wireless. The internet connection is typically stronger through an ethernet cord than over Wi-Fi.

Find the answer to anything on YouTube

Need to know how to put together that new bookshelf you just bought? Or do you want to learn how to make the perfect spaghetti sauce? You can learn how to do practically anything from skilled experts — for free. Simply go online to *youtube.com*.

YouTube is the most popular video platform around today, and it's free to watch, upload, and browse entertainment. Much like other free streaming services, it uses advertising as a way to make money, although it also has a paid, ad-free version called YouTube Premium.

The great part about YouTube is that the content isn't dominated by a few networks. It's open to anyone who wants to create videos. Here are just a few of the video topics available.

- **How-to's.** From putting on makeup to tying a tie, if you're looking for how to do something, there's probably a video on YouTube for it. Don't worry about struggling through instruction manuals. Instead, watch how it's done from an expert.

- **Music.** Most artists today post their music videos to YouTube, so you can listen to the latest songs for free. You'll even find playlists you can listen to with the same theme.

- **Clips.** Popular clips from late night shows, talk shows, and more can all be found on YouTube.

- **Workouts.** Whether you're looking for a soothing yoga workout or an upbeat dance routine, Youtube can bring the personal trainer to you.

- **Miscellaneous.** YouTube's search makes it easy to find a video for any topic you're looking for. You'll also see recommendations on the home page similar to videos you've already watched.

Never miss a video again with these 3 simple steps

Let's say you've found a favorite musician or a workout video series that you love. How can you make sure you never miss a video? Good news — YouTube lets you subscribe to your favorite channels.

Subscribing is free. You'll be notified when new videos are posted, and your subscriptions will appear for easy access on your home screen. Follow these three steps to start subscribing.

Find the name of the channel. It's typically directly below the video you're watching, right underneath the title.

Go to the channel page. Click on the name, and you'll be taken to the channel page with all that channel's videos.

Click subscribe and select notifications. At the top, look for a red button that says **Subscribe**. Once you've clicked on that, an alarm bell will appear to the right. Click the bell to turn on notifications for videos from that channel.

Binge your favorite videos whenever you want

YouTube makes it easy to continue watching videos of the same type, so you don't have to keep searching for new ones. The **Playlist** feature allows you to collect your favorite videos in one place. In a playlist, the videos play one right after the other, except for some ad breaks in between.

Say you love watching dog videos and want a place to keep all
your favorites together. Here's how to save to a playlist.

Find the save button underneath the title. It's the button with
three horizontal lines with a plus sign.

Choose a playlist. If you already have a playlist created, you can
select that playlist.

Create a new playlist. You'll also have the option to create a new
playlist. Click **+ Create New Playlist**.

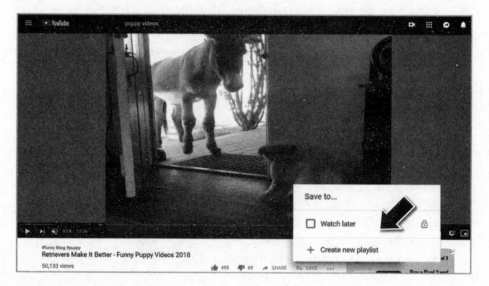

Name your playlist. Next, you'll be asked to name your playlist.
Type in a name that's easy to remember and best fits the collection
of videos.

Select your privacy options. You'll have three choices — **Public,
Unlisted**, and **Private**. Public means anyone can see the video on
your channel. Private means only you and the people you share
the video with can see it. Unlisted means that only you can see it.

Once you've created a playlist, it will appear on your Youtube
home page. You can also watch public playlists made by other
channels. Simply go to that channel's page and click **Playlists**.

Your digital library
Entertainment to buy, watch, and keep forever

Build a fantastic digital library in 5 easy steps

Is it worth keeping cable TV — or a premium channel — for just one favorite show? Not when you know this trick. It doesn't require Netflix, Amazon, or any other non-cable subscription service.

Simply buy episodes or entire seasons of shows directly through your streaming device. Most devices typically have a "store" where you can do this.

It's like buying a season on DVD, only you get all the episodes in a digital format. And because you paid for them, your shows are always available through supported devices.

Even better, your shows follow you from device to device. You can watch one episode on your TV and the next on your phone. You just need to download the episodes you want. So how do you get started building your digital library?

Go to your streaming device's store. Apple TV has two store options, one for **Movies** and one for **TV Shows**. Amazon Prime has a **Rent or Buy** section, and devices like Roku and Chromecast use the Google Play store.

Find your show. Use the search function to find the show you're looking for. Once you find it, you'll typically be taken to the show's page, where all the available seasons and episodes will appear.

Pick your season (or seasons). The great thing about digital content is you can buy as much or as little as you want. Make sure you're only buying the seasons you want to watch.

Decide what quality your prefer. Some stores offer you the option to choose between high-definition (HD) and standard definition (SD). While HD is obviously higher quality, it costs more.

Purchase and download. If you buy content on a streaming device, your selection may automatically download once you hit the **Buy** button. But if you're trying to watch on a phone or tablet, you can usually choose which episodes to download.

Only watch your favorite episodes with this nifty trick

You don't have to commit to buying a whole season if you only want to watch a few shows. Most stores will also let you buy individual episodes. This is a great option if you just have a few that you love re-watching.

To buy an episode, click on the show, but instead of clicking **Buy Season**, scroll down. Beneath the header where they describe the show — and usually encourage you to buy the whole season — you'll see a list of episodes. Find the episode you want, and click the **Buy** button.

The same rules for video quality apply to episodes as they do to seasons. Standard definition videos will be cheaper than high definition.

Rent videos without leaving your home

Buying isn't your only option when you watch digital content. You can rent movies through the streaming store options as well. Rentals are usually for 24 hours, and unlike purchases, are not stored forever on your account. Instead, if you want to watch the movie again, you will either have to rent it again or buy it.

Rentals are a great option for new releases you're not sure you'll love enough to watch again. They are priced much lower than purchases. Some movies are available to rent for less than a dollar, much cheaper than a movie ticket.

How do you know if a movie is available for rent? Select the movie in the store and see if there is a **Rent** option next to the **Buy** option.

Sometimes, movies are available for purchase-only for a few weeks before you can rent them. In that case, a date will appear to let you know when the movie will be available for rent.

Don't worry if you have to pause the movie or stop it for a time, too. As long as you are within the 24-hour rental period, you can come back to the movie at any time. So don't stress if you need to take a popcorn break.

Take your library with you wherever you go

One of the main benefits of buying digital content is that it's not restricted to one disc or device. Your content is tied to your account, and it lives in the cloud. To get a selection on your phone, tablet, or laptop, you usually need to pull it from the cloud to your device.

To download it, go to the store's app on your mobile device, or the website if you are on your computer. You'll usually find your purchases in a section called **Purchases**, **Library**, or something similar. Don't be surprised to see every item you have ever bought with your account, no matter which device it came from.

Pick the episodes you want, and click the download button, which may be in picture form. In the graphic, for example, the download button is a cloud with an arrow pointing down.

While it may seem inconvenient, this process is actually a good thing. TV episodes and movies are huge files and can quickly eat up your phone's memory, leaving you less room for pictures, messages, and other items you store on your phone. By only downloading the

episodes you want to watch, you can make sure you're getting the most out of your phone's memory.

Save money by sharing with your family

Don't you just love sharing your favorite movies with your family? With a digital library, it's so easy to do. Many stores offer family accounts, where multiple households can share one overall account.

Your billing information stays separate, but the digital content you purchase can be accessed by anyone in the household. That means books, movies, TV shows, music, and more can be enjoyed by everyone, without having to pay for them multiple times.

> Some digital library services allow you to easily "family share" other content you have in the cloud, like photos. You can even share calendars for important appointments.

When you set up a household, make sure you have a device that can access that store. For instance, if your family all has Apple TVs and iPhones, you may want to consider creating an Apple family plan. But if you have a mix of Android or Amazon devices, you may want to set up a Google or Amazon family plan instead.

There are usually limits to how many family members you can add. Accounts for kids don't have purchase rights so you don't have to worry about spending sprees. And you can set parental controls on what they can watch.

Sharing your digital library is a great way for your family to save money, especially if you all have similar tastes in movies and shows.

Turn up the tunes
Stream music you love anywhere, any time

Choose the music service that's right for you

Streaming isn't just for TV, movies, and videos. You can also stream music. And just like videos, you can access a lot of different content without having to pay the extra money for CDs or satellite radio.

How would you like to listen to your favorite artists on demand, find stations that play the music you love, and build your own playlists from millions of available songs? Sound good? Then you're ready for a streaming music service. Here are a few things to think about when making your choice.

Ads or no ads? Some streaming music services like Google Play Music, iHeartRadio, and Pandora have free versions. But those free versions come at the usual cost — you'll have to listen to some advertisements. One good thing — the ad breaks typically are much shorter and less frequent than listening to standard radio.

Their radio experience or your own? Music services have different approaches to how they present their content. With Pandora, for instance, you select a station, and songs will play randomly from within that station, just like on the radio. This can be a nice option if you don't want the fuss of searching for the music you like to listen to.

Others, like Spotify, weigh more heavily toward building your own playlists or listening to playlists that others have built. This is a great option for music lovers who want to control what they listen to, versus leaving it to chance.

Related video account? If you have a family video streaming account, you may want to consider using the music service that goes along with it. That way you can share the cost of the subscription with your family, and you can all enjoy.

Not sure where to begin? Check out some of the top names in streaming music services — Pandora, Spotify, iTunes, Amazon Music Unlimited, iHeartRadio, Tidal, Google Play, Slacker Radio, YouTube Premium, and Soundcloud. Search on the name to find its website.

Streaming services like Amazon Prime provide a music option as well as video. If you have an Amazon Prime account, you automatically qualify for its free music service.

Prefer high quality or standard? Some music services, like Tidal, pride themselves on delivering the highest-quality sound. If you are passionate about your audio quality, look for a service that has higher streaming rates for better sound.

4 fast tips for discovering new artists

Now that you've got your streaming service set up and you've found your favorites, it's time to find some new artists to listen to. Streaming music services are a great way to widen your musical repertoire. Use these four tips to find your next favorite artist.

Check the expert's suggestions. Just like with videos, music services use what you've already listened to so they can find more of the same. Look for a **Recommendations** section where you can find artists like those you already enjoy.

Seek out genre playlists or stations. Search and you'll find a ton of stations dedicated to genres you love. By listening to some different stations, you may find new artists within that genre.

Hit the discover button. Streaming music services want to help you find new music to listen to and promote new or lesser-known artists. Many services have a **Discover** section, with featured artists and playlists that you may never have heard before.

See what friends are listening to. Some music services, like Spotify, allow you to connect to your social media accounts and see what your friends are listening to. Your new favorite song may be on your friend's latest playlist.

Having a party? Find a station for any occasion

Streaming services don't just have stations based on genres or artists. They also have stations built around moods, themes, or occasions.

Looking for a Christmas music channel for the holidays? Or do you need some quiet background music to play while you read? Find a station that best fits your needs, press play, and let the DJs do the work for you.

You can find these stations either by looking for a section like **Genres & Moods** shown on the next page in Spotify, or by browsing your home page. Your home page will often suggest broadcasts based on the season, what you like to listen to, and even the day. You can even find channels specifically designed for entertaining or working out.

Theme stations take the stress out of searching for music and give you exactly what you're looking for, any time of day.

3 creative ways to share your favorites

That new reggae station you found brings back fond memories of the Caribbean vacation you took with your sister. You just know she'd love to bask in those special memories, too. Guess what? She can. Streaming music services allow you to share your favorite music with your friends and family. Here's how.

Use a family account. Most family accounts tied to popular stores like Amazon, Apple, and Google have the capability to share music as well. You can share one streaming music subscription across your family so you can all enjoy listening to your favorites.

Multiply users. Even if the streaming service doesn't have a "household" option, you can often add multiple users to one account. Just like video, there are usually limits for how many users can listen at one time. But this is a great way to get more enjoyment out of one account and build your favorite stations together.

Connect on social media. If you have a social media account, sometimes you can connect it to your streaming music account. That lets you share what you're listening to with others on social media and gives your friends access to playlists you make public.

For example, on Amazon Music you can go to **Playlists**, tap the three vertical dots next to your selection, tap **Share Playlist**, and pick the social media site you want to send it to.

If you use Instagram, Spotify makes it even easier. It has created a **Share to Instagram story** option in its **Share** menu so you can instantly stream what you're listening to.

Sharing playlists among friends is a great way to discover new music and enjoy classic favorites.

Online security
Expert help to battle internet threats

Everyone has to be careful when they're online, but as a senior, you may need to exercise extra caution. Why? Your generation has unique qualities that may make you an easier target for online scams.

In general, seniors are likely to be more trusting than younger generations. This could be a disadvantage in the cyber world.

- You may think you're a great judge of character and know when someone is being truthful. But if you haven't spent a lot of time online, you may not have the skills to assess the character of people and companies you deal with over the internet.

- Many seniors are so used to trusting official-looking material that they don't question it, which makes them more apt to fall for scams.

- Older adults tend to be more worried about ruining their good name. If someone claims your information has a problem, you immediately want to take care of it.

Scammers tailor their cons specifically to exploit older internet users. Instead of touting trips to Disney World, they'll offer you discount drugs and low-cost insurance. Email scams will target you with "bank notices" or official-looking "government documents."

Today, nearly 2 out of 3 Americans over 65 are internet users, according to a Pew Research Center survey. And, like most Americans, they fail to take the safety measures necessary to protect their online data. The biggest lapse is in the area of passwords and smartphone security.

Don't let yourself be swindled by cyber thieves. Read on to find out how you can stay safe and secure online.

Protect your good name
How to fight fraud and stop identity theft

Stop ID thieves dead in their tracks

Identity theft is no joke. When thieves steal your identity, they can apply for a credit card, take out a loan, obtain a cellphone, and more — all in your good name. They can even claim your tax refund or steal government benefits. Here are 10 simple steps you can take to foil these fraudsters.

Don't click that link. ID thieves often send fake emails that look like they're from a bank, store, or the government to trick you into providing personal information. The links in these message usually lead to a false website designed to rob you of your private data, or they install malware on your machine.

Encrypt your email. Some email programs let you encrypt sensitive outgoing messages — like messages that contain personal information. Encrypting your emails can prevent ID thieves from intercepting your info.

Inoculate your system. Some ID thieves operate by infecting your computer with malware that scans your system for sensitive data. To stop this, safeguard your setup with anti-virus software.

Build that wall. Installing special software called a "firewall" can prevent intruders from accessing your system and sniffing out your personal information.

Pick an impenetrable password. Picking a poor password is like placing a welcome mat on your system — it practically begs identity thieves to come inside. To protect yourself, pick a password that no one else can guess.

Double your security. You can set up most types of accounts to require two-factor authentication — your password plus some other proof that you are who you say you are, like a code sent to your cellphone. Two-factor authentication makes it twice as hard for thieves to steal your ID.

Watch out on Wi-Fi. Many public Wi-Fi networks lack even basic security. Stay off these public networks if you can — especially to bank or shop.

Check your score. Often, the first sign of identity theft is a change in your credit score. Spot this sooner rather than later by regularly checking in with the three major credit-reporting services — Experian (*experian.com*), Equifax (*equifax.com*), and TransUnion (*transunion.com*).

Freeze your credit. If you know you won't be applying for any new credit cards or loans, freeze your credit. You will also do that through the credit bureaus. That will prevent someone else from applying for credit in your name.

Monitor your identity. Sign up for an ID-monitoring service like Complete ID (*completeid.com*), LifeLock (*lifelock.com*), or PrivacyGuard (*privacyguard.com*). These services flag signs of identity theft, like unauthorized use of your Social Security number.

Guard these 2 pieces of information at all costs

For identity thieves, not all personal data is created equal. Sure, thieves can do a bit of damage with your name, address, and phone number. But they can do way more with your Social Security number and date of birth — including opening a credit card account in your name and racking up charges. And leaving you to deal with the payment.

You already know better than to hand out your Social Security number to strangers. That's why you take steps to secure your data from malware and hackers and to steer clear of scams.

Your date of birth is another story. Heck, you've probably shared that information on purpose — for example, on social media sites like Facebook, or even on retail sites to receive coupons on your big day. If so, you'll want to remove it from those sites right away.

Suspicious email? 3 easy ways to prove it's legit

Scam artists often send phony emails that appear to be from a bank, a store, the government, or some other organization. These emails — which can be quite convincing — might claim your account has been compromised or you owe money to the IRS. Or they could scare you by saying a security breach has occurred that requires your immediate attention.

But clicking the link in the email directs you to a fake website meant to mine your personal info. It can also download malware that scans your system for sensitive data or triggers some other harmful process. This tactic is called "phishing."

You can block the bulk of phishing emails by setting up your email program to divert suspicious messages into a separate junk mail folder. In case any suspicious messages slip through, here are three easy ways to see if they're real.

Check the sender's email address. If the domain in the sender's email address (the part after the @ sign) doesn't match the name of the organization the email claims to be from, the message is likely a fake.

Verify the link's URL. In most email programs, you can hover your mouse pointer over a link in a message to reveal its URL. If this URL look suspicious — for example, its domain (the part after the *http://*, *https://*, or *www*) doesn't match up with the alleged sender, or it contains strings of random numbers or letters — don't click it.

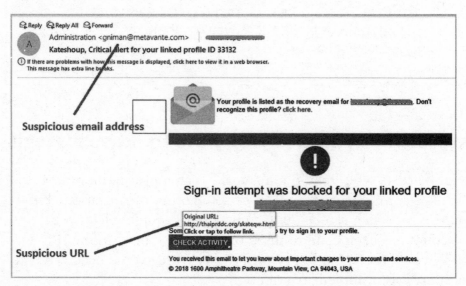

Manually enter the site's address in your browser. Suppose you get an alarming message claiming to be from your bank. Instead of clicking the link in the message, type your bank's URL into your web browser, and then log in to your account. If there really is a problem, the bank's site will alert you.

If you receive a phishing email, forward the message to the Federal Trade Commission at *spam@uce.gov* to report it.

Scam alert! How to safeguard your Social Security number

Your Social Security number is the bedrock of your identity. It's no wonder scammers constantly dream up new ways to rob you of this vital information. Beware of these three scams and keep your Social Security number — and your identity — safe.

Watch out for phone scams. Identity thieves posing as employees of the Internal Revenue Service (IRS) frequently phone unsuspecting victims and ask them to confirm their Social Security number for administrative purposes or to resolve some sort of tax issue. Often, the scammer even fakes the caller ID to make it appear as though the call truly is coming from a government office.

Don't be reeled in by "phishing." In this scam, thieves again pose as employees of the IRS. But this time, they send a phony phishing email message that instructs you to update your info with the IRS. Clicking the accompanying link directs you to a website that looks official but is in fact a front for scammers seeking to strip you of your personal information.

Ignore offers that are too good to be true. Who wouldn't want to find a little extra money in their mailbox? That's why this scam is so effective. In this case, scammers send a letter by mail that promises you an extra Social Security check. All you need to do is pay a small fee and submit some private information — including your Social Security number. Needless to say, no extra check ever arrives.

Want to make sure your Social Security number is safe from scammers? Here are some things you should never do.

Never provide your Social Security number to any caller. Generally speaking, no government agency will contact you by phone and ask you to provide your Social Security number. If you receive such a call, hang up.

Never click the link. If you receive a suspicious email, don't click the accompanying link — even if the message appears to be from an official source. Follow the steps in the previous story to verify the sender.

Never assume that a mail offer that asks for your personal information is legitimate. Be skeptical. Like the old saying goes, if something seems too good to be true, it probably is.

To verify the legitimacy of phone calls, text messages, or emails that request your Social Security number, call the Social Security Administration at 800-772-1213. You can report attempted scams to the SSA's fraud hotline at 800-269-0271.

Check for leaks: Prevent sites from broadcasting your personal info

Millions of internet users share their private information online — without even knowing it. This is because countless websites peddle user data — personal information, online purchases, browsing history, and more — to entities called "data brokers."

These brokers then sell this user data to businesses, who in turn use it to target their marketing efforts. Now you know why you keep seeing ads for those hiking boots you researched last week every time you're online.

Want to find out if a website is profiting off your personal information? You have two ways to do it.

Read the terms of service when you sign up with a site. Let's face it, nobody reads the terms of service. But buried deep in that legalese you'll find out what, if anything, that site does with your user data.

Peruse the privacy policy. Reputable sites spell out their privacy policy, and some even let you change your privacy settings to protect your user data. Read this policy to find out if your private data will stay private.

One way to stop data brokers from distributing your data is to use an online service that specializes in removing your information, such as DeleteMe (*abine.com/deleteme*) or Safe Shepherd (*safeshepherd.com*). If you don't want to pay for the service and are willing to put in the time, check out *stopdatamining.me* for a list of data broker opt-out links.

Take these 4 steps to 'disappear' online

Maybe you're worried your personal information is being stolen online. Or maybe you're just freaked out by how easy it is for people to find you. Either way, here are four ways to "disappear" on the internet — or at least reduce your online footprint.

Go dark on social media. Shut down your Facebook, Twitter, Pinterest, LinkedIn, and other social media accounts.

Delete other online accounts. If you shop or bank online, chat in online forums, or even check Yelp for restaurant reviews, odds are these sites know your real name and other personal information. If your aim is to vanish from online view, you should close these accounts. For help, you can turn to services like Account Killer (*accountkiller.com*) and Just Delete Me (*backgroundchecks.org/ justdeleteme*).

Do a search of yourself. Google your name and see what comes up. Then contact any sites that feature content by or about you and ask them to take it down.

Dummy it down. Suppose you want to disappear online but still enjoy the internet. Here's a handy workaround. Use a fake name to create dummy accounts — including a phony email account. You can't shop or bank with these fake accounts, but you can use them to do just about anything else that doesn't involve a financial transaction.

The one document you should never store on your computer

It's not enough to draw up a will. You should also create a simple list of your financial accounts, life insurance policies, assets, personal items (including anything you keep in storage), the names of your financial and tax advisors, and login information for any digital accounts you maintain.

That way, you ensure that you and your heirs don't lose track of valuable assets. But for the love of Pete, do not store this document on your computer. Even if you password-protect it, there's always a chance a motivated thief could crack the code. Far better to print it out and place it in a safe-deposit box. Just don't forget to tell your heirs where it is.

Beyond the grave: Smart ways to protect the dearly departed

For ID thieves, nothing is sacred — not even the dead. These soulless swindlers steal the identities of millions of deceased Americans each year, a practice called (wait for it) ghosting.

You aren't on the hook for charges if identity thieves ghost a loved one. But you might lose out if they collect a tax refund using that person's ID. To prevent this, take these four simple steps.

Edit the obit. Omit your loved one's birthdate, mother's maiden name, and home address from the obituary. This also blocks bandits from burgling your loved one's home during the funeral service. Sadly, this often happens.

Notify credit-reporting services. Ask the three main credit-reporting services — Experian, Equifax, and TransUnion — to place a deceased alert on your loved one's credit report. And ask for a copy of the report so you'll know what accounts need closing.

Alert account holders. Send a copy of the death certificate via certified mail — with return receipt — to every bank, store, and other business where your loved one held an account, and ask them to close it.

Inform government agencies. Report your loved one's death to the Social Security office and the department of motor vehicles.

Password protection: How to pick them, remember them, and keep them safe

Most Americans maintain dozens of online accounts — each requiring a password that is strong, memorable, and unique. That's a tall order. Here's what you need to know to keep your accounts safe online.

Give serious thought to picking a password. Each password should be at least eight characters — preferably longer, to make it harder to crack. And make sure you mix it up. Use a combination of uppercase letters, lowercase letters, numbers, and symbols.

Want an example of a strong password? How about 1<3R&R, spa.10itjb? You're probably saying, OK, but how the heck do you remember it? Believe it or not, this one's easy. The foundation of this password is a famous song lyric by Joan Jett. It's the sentence

"I love rock and roll so put another dime in the jukebox baby," with the following changes:

- the numeral 1 replaces the word I.

- a sideways heart (<3) replaces the word love.

- an ampersand (&) is used in place of the word and.

- the word dime is replaced by .10.

- each remaining word is replaced by its first letter.

- the Rs in rock and roll are capitalized.

You can take a similar approach, using a favorite lyric or quote, or just an easy-to-remember sentence, as the basis for your password.

One easy change gives you a multitude of passwords. You might be tempted to use this one strong and memorable password for all your accounts. Don't. If an online thief decodes it, they'll have access not just to one of your accounts, but to all of them. Instead, modify this password for each account.

For example, you could add the first three letters of a site's name to the password — so your Amazon password could be AMA1<3R &R,spa.10itjb, your Facebook password could be FAC1<3R&R, spa.10itjb, and so on.

Leave the decision — and management — up to the experts. If you'd rather pick wildly different passwords for each of your accounts, you certainly can. In that case, you might need help managing them all. That's where a password manager app comes in.

With this helpful app, you only need to remember one password — the one you use to access the app. The app "remembers" the rest for you. And if you don't want the pressure of coming up with creative passwords, your manager will create them for you.

Popular password manager apps include Dashlane (*dashlane.com*), LastPass (*lastpass.com*), Sticky Password (*stickypassword.com*), RoboForm (*roboform.com*), and Keeper (*keepersecurity.com*). These apps are safe, secure, and easy. Never forget an online password again.

Smart ways to protect personal files and emails

You probably store at least a few files on your computer that you'd rather keep confidential — for example, spreadsheets with financial information, a copy of your will, or even a personal journal. Password-protecting these files makes them private, so only you can open them. Of course, the standard rules for setting strong, memorable, and unique passwords apply.

To password-protect an iWork file on a Mac (a file generated using Pages, Numbers, or Keynote), click the **File** menu and choose **Set Password**. Then, in the dialog box that opens, type a password for the file, type it a second time to confirm it, and click **Set Password**.

To password-protect an Office file in Windows 10 (a file generated using Word, Excel, PowerPoint, Outlook, Publisher, or Access), click the **File** tab in the ribbon. Then, on the Info page, click **Protect Document** and select **Encrypt with Password**. Finally, type the password in the dialog box that appears, and click **OK**.

If you want to share a password-protected file with someone via email, you can — you just need to provide

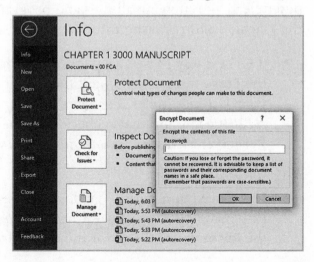

the recipient with the password. But what if a hacker or thief intercepts the email containing the password? In that case — or anytime you're concerned about a private email being made public — you can encrypt the email.

As long as the recipient of the encrypted email has the "key" needed to open it, they can do so. For more on encryption, check your email program's help information.

When 'Delete' doesn't do it: How to wipe private info off your computer for good

You've upgraded to a new computer and you want to sell, donate, or recycle your old one. So how do you make sure whoever ends up with your old machine doesn't have access to your files?

Simply deleting all your files won't solve your dilemma. Deleted files aren't really gone, they're just floating around in your system until they get overwritten by new data. If that hasn't happened yet, it's still possible to retrieve them.

To remove your files from your computer for good, you need to erase your hard drive and reset it. This feature wipes your computer clean — removing all files and programs you've installed on the machine and restoring it to its original state.

- The best way to restore your Mac to factory settings is to use the **Erase** feature that you'll find in the Disk Utility app in your Utilities folder. For help, visit *support.apple.com/en-us/HT201065*. You can also check out a helpful tool called Permanent Eraser at *edenwaith.com/products/permanent%20eraser*.

- If you need to restore a Windows PC, see *support.microsoft.com/en-us/help/17085/windows-8-restore-refresh-reset-pc* and click the **Reset your PC** link for more details.

I've been hit! Do these 6 things ASAP if thieves steal your identity

It happened — thieves stole your identity. What now? Here are six simple steps you can take to diminish the damage.

Lock down compromised accounts. For each affected account, call the company's fraud department, tell them your identity has been stolen, and ask them to freeze the account or shut it down.

Place a fraud alert on your credit report. This informs lenders that they should contact you before extending new credit in your name. Later, you'll also want to take the appropriate steps to fix your credit.

File a report with the FTC. Visit *identitytheft.gov* to report the theft. This site also offers resources for formulating a personal recovery plan to fix your credit and putting that plan into action.

Report the theft to your local police. Filing a police report offers you certain protections, including protection from companies that attempt to collect debts resulting from your identity theft.

Shut down accounts opened in your name. Review your credit report to see if anyone opened any new accounts in your name. If so, contact each company's fraud department, tell them you're a victim of ID theft, and ask them to shut the account down.

Check for bogus charges. If thieves rack up charges on your account, you'll once again want to contact the company's fraud department — this time to ask them to remove the unauthorized charges.

Smart defense against spyware, viruses, and other malware

Viruses, worms, and Trojans (oh my!) — malware secrets you need to know

Malware is just what it sounds like — malicious software. This software has one purpose — to damage or exploit a computer, server, or network. Maybe the programmer behind the malware just wants to have some fun — the digital equivalent of vandalism. More often, malware is the product of a criminal enterprise whose aim is to steal your identity or other valuable information.

Malware is no malarkey. Yes, some types of malware, like the kind that repeatedly displays ads — called adware — are merely annoying. But other sorts can wreak serious havoc on your system — deleting files, corrupting your hard drive, and worse.

- One variety of malware, called spyware, scans your system for personal information, tracks your internet activity, or intercepts your keyboard input — like when you enter your login info to access financial accounts.

- Another type of malware creates a backdoor into your system, which a hacker can use to gain access to your machine.

It can also take it over completely — for example, to send spam, spread illegal content, mine cryptocurrency, or attack other computers.

- Maybe the worst of all is malware that hackers install to lock down your system and hold it hostage until you pay a "ransom." Can you guess what it's called? That's right, ransomware.

Security experts generally categorize malware by how it spreads from machine to machine. They identify three main categories. Get to know these "tech-wreckers" and how they work, and you'll be more alert to their threats.

Viruses — computer programs that "infect" other files. These malicious little programs attach themselves to other programs or files on your computer. When you run the infected file, the virus makes a copy of itself, or "self-replicates," and infects another program or file. When you run that one, the virus spreads again, and so on, until your computer is crippled.

If an infected computer is connected to a network, like the internet, the virus can spread to other computers by exploiting security holes in the target computer's operating system, programs, or plug-ins.

Worms self-replicate and spread like viruses do. But unlike viruses, which require a user to run a program or file to spread, worms can spread all on their own.

Trojan horses pose as harmless or even useful programs. Just as the famous Trojan horse of Greek myth was stuffed with soldiers, this program carries killer cargo inside — damaging code, called the "payload."

Trojans generally don't self-replicate, like viruses or worms do. Instead, hackers typically spread Trojans by tricking users into installing them, either by sending phishing emails with malicious links or attachments or by embedding these links in pop-up windows in your web browser.

Some hackers take an even more aggressive approach — booby-trapping a website with a tool called an "exploit kit." When you visit the site, the exploit kit automatically scans for security holes in your system and uses them to install the payload on your machine.

Here's a scary thought. Hackers generate hundreds of millions of pieces of malware each year. Yikes! Fortunately, you can take plenty of steps to secure your system against malware. That's what this chapter is all about.

You can see how important it is to be careful online. Malware is everywhere, and scammers are constantly thinking up tricky new ways to access your computer. Read on to find out how you can stop them.

'Mal' cop: 8 easy ways to guard against malware

Worried about hackers stealing your identity or nasty viruses destroying your expensive computer? Relax and rest easy with these easy-to-follow simple security tips.

Install anti-malware software. Sometimes called anti-virus software, this type of program vaccinates against nasty viruses and other malware. It works by standing sentry on your system to stop malware from sneaking in. It also scans your system to expose and erase any known types of malware that might slip through.

With anti-malware software, protecting your computer, identity, and information is fast, easy, and in some cases, free. Installing a reputable anti-malware program — and keeping it up to date — is the single best thing you can do to protect your system.

Turn on automatic updates. When software makers discover security holes in their products, they release "patches" to plug them. By turning on automatic updates for your operating system and other programs on your computer you ensure your system puts these patches in place the minute they become available.

It's especially important to enable automatic updates for your anti-malware software so it can detect and defuse new types of malware as they emerge. Here's an example of what your update options might look like.

Install a firewall. A firewall acts as a barrier between your computer and the internet. It monitors traffic to and from your system and permits or blocks it based on a set of security rules.

For example, a firewall might block traffic from a site known to distribute malware.

Hop on pop (ups). Every web browser has one secret setting that can help keep you from accidentally downloading a virus — the Block Pop-ups setting. Different browsers call it different things, but enabling this setting prevents websites from displaying pop-up windows, which often contain harmful links.

Click attachments with care. Phishing emails containing malicious links are the top attack method for hackers. If you get an email you think might be a phishing attempt, don't click the link. The same goes for pop-up windows in web browsers. You can't be too careful.

Just say no to unsafe downloads. Only download from trusted sites. If you're not 100 percent sure a program — or anything else — is safe to download, follow former first lady Nancy Reagan's advice and "just say no."

Beware problematic plug-ins. A plug-in is a wee bit of software that adds functionality to some other program, like a web browser. Some plug-ins are great. You can use them to block pop-up ads, detect "fake news," and even send encrypted messages. By all means, install them. But other plug-ins are designed to damage. Don't install a plug-in unless you know it's on the up-and-up.

Back up your system. In case your efforts to prevent a malware attack fall short, you should set up your system to back up your files on a regular basis.

Don't forget to store the backup on an external hard drive or on the cloud. That way, if you fall victim to a virus or other type of malware, you can use the backup to restore your system to its pre-infected state.

7 warning signs your system might be infected

With some types of malware, like ransomware, it will be extremely obvious your system has been infected — like you might not even be able to log on. With other types, the clues are less clear. Here are seven subtle signs your system might be infected.

- Your computer is slow or takes a while to start up.

- You're subject to constant pop-ups.

- Your computer keeps crashing, or you regularly see the dreaded "blue screen of death."

- Your operating system mysteriously informs you that you're running out of disk space.

- Your internet home page suddenly changes — even though you know you didn't switch it.

- Programs keep opening or closing automatically with no input from you.

- You see strange new icons or toolbars on your web browser or desktop.

While none of these signs offer absolute proof your system is under attack, they might indicate a problem — especially if you notice more than one.

Anti-malware programs to keep your system safe

Luckily, Windows 10 and macOS both contain built-in tools to protect against malware. But for maximum protection, it's wise to double up by installing additional anti-malware software on your system.

For best results, it pays to purchase comprehensive anti-malware software from a reputable security company, like one of the following.

- Bitdefender (*bitdefender.com*)

- Kaspersky Lab (*usa.kaspersky.com*)

- McAfee (*mcafee.com/en-us/index.html*)

- Norton (*us.norton.com*)

- Webroot (*webroot.com/us/en*)

These firms provide packages that shield your system from all types of malware, including viruses, worms, ransomware, spyware, and so on. Perhaps more importantly, they quickly update their software to combat new malware threats as they emerge.

> Most anti-malware programs run regular scans to make sure your system hasn't been infected with malware. But if you suspect some malicious software might have slipped through, you can run a manual scan. To check using Norton, for example, launch the Norton window, click **Security**, and click the **Quick Scan** link.

If cost is an issue, something is always better than nothing. Fortunately, you can find lots of free anti-malware programs that will help keep your system safe. Here are a few options.

- Avast Free Anti-virus for Windows and Mac (*avast.com*)

- AVG Anti-virus for Windows and Mac (*avg.com*)

- Avira Free Security Suite for Windows (*avira.com*)

- Kaspersky Free for Windows (*usa.kaspersky.com*)

- Panda Free Anti-virus for Windows (*pandasecurity.com*)

- ZoneAlarm Free Anti-virus for Windows (*zonealarm.com*)

But watch out — some diabolical hackers package malware as free anti-malware software. In other words, downloading this software doesn't protect your machine, it infects it. As long as you stick with software from upright providers like the ones listed here, you should be in good shape.

Beware ransomware: 2 ways to reclaim your hijacked system

Ransomware is a particularly destructive form of malware. It locks down your files or system and holds them hostage until you pay some sort of ransom. Scammers usually demand a form of cryptocurrency like Bitcoin because it's harder to trace than a credit card payment. Here are the two main types of ransomware to look out for.

- **Crypto-malware.** This type of ransomware encrypts files on your computer to prevent you from accessing them. To obtain the key needed to decrypt them, you must pay a ransom.

- **Screen lockers.** This ransomware locks you out of your computer completely. Forget about accessing certain files, you can't even boot up your machine. To add to your anxiety, screen lockers typically display an official-looking message that claims the FBI or some other law-enforcement agency has detected illegal activity on your computer. It demands you pay a fine to restore access. Here's a tip — that's a good way to tell it's ransomware. If the FBI were really after you, that isn't how you'd find out!

So if a hacker manages to slip some strain of ransomware onto your system — usually by way of a Trojan horse — you'll know it.

You'll be unable to access your system and/or your files, and you'll likely get a menacing message, too. The question is, what should you do?

First off, don't pay the ransom. Doing so just encourages hackers to launch more ransomware attacks. Besides, there's no guarantee your system will be restored. Remember, these are criminals you're dealing with.

Beyond that, here are two steps you can take to reclaim your system.

Fight back with an antidote. Depending on what strain of ransomware your system has contracted, there might be an antidote, called a decryptor.

To find out, use a free tool called Bitdefender Ransomware Recognition Tool at *abs.bitdefender.com/2017/09/bitdefender-ransomware-recognition-tool* to identify what strain of ransomware you're dealing with. Then check online to see if any decryptors for that strain exist. Here's a good place to start — *www.nomoreransom. org/en/decryption-tools.html*.

Roll it back to its previous state. Bad news — you've found no decryptor for your strain of ransomware. That means you'll have to roll back your system to a "pre-infection" state.

If you can't access your files but you can boot up your system, you're in luck. Both PCs and Macs create regular backups, called "Restore Points" or "Time Machine backups," respectively. Simply roll back your system to the most recent of these backups before the infection. If you don't know how, check the Microsoft or Apple websites for instructions.

If you're unable to boot up, you'll have to wipe your system clean to get rid of the ransomware. Then, assuming you've set up your system to automatically back up your files to an external hard drive or to the cloud — and you have, right? — just copy the files back onto your clean machine.

Here's an example of how to do a System Restore on a Windows computer.

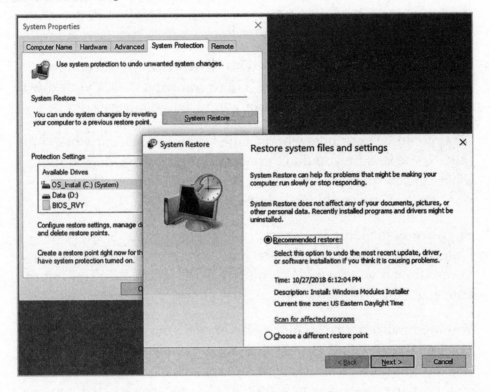

The spy who bugged me: Shut down spyware with free programs

Hackers use a kind of malicious software called spyware to secretly harvest data from your computer. Passwords, PINs, credit-card numbers — spyware puts it all at risk.

Spyware can also intercept your keyboard input (this type is called a keylogger), track your internet activity, change your security settings, or simply slow your system.

How it sneaks onto your machine. Spyware usually gets in through a security hole in your computer's operating system, programs, or plug-ins. Or it might be the payload in a Trojan horse.

In some cases, you might even install spyware by downloading a legit free program without reading the fine print first. Spyware is not just sneaky. It's crafty, too — so crafty that some varieties can even outsmart attempts to remove it.

Hackers aren't the only ones who distribute spyware. Some "legitimate" companies do, too. These companies track your every move online, building a profile of you to sell to advertisers.

Or it could be your boss who installed spyware on your work computer to make sure you don't goof off online during work hours. There's even spyware software to surveil your spouse. (You may want to think twice about that one.)

Spyware is difficult to detect. Like any good snoop, spyware blends into the background. Once it's on your system, you might never know it was there. Your only real clue could be a slowing of your machine.

You might also notice strange behaviors in your web browser. For example, it could display a seemingly endless parade of pop-up windows or redirect you to sites unexpectedly. Or you could discover a strange new toolbar in your browser that you never installed.

Use these super tools to fight back. The internet is riddled with spyware. Fortunately, if you discover your system is under surveillance, you can remove this sneaky software from your computer. Most anti-malware programs also battle spyware. Or you can specifically target spyware with these free programs.

- SUPERAntiSpyware (*superantispyware.com/free-edition.html*)

- SpywareBlaster (*brightfort.com/spywareblaster*)

- Spybot Search & Destroy (*safer-networking.org/products/spybot-free-edition*)

Watch out for RATS in your computer

You're sick. Like, really sick. There's no way you can go to work. And considering that you're almost definitely contagious, your colleagues would probably also prefer you stay home.

Just one problem — you're in the middle of a big project and you need to do a few things today to keep it on track. Fortunately, your company's IT guy set up a remote access tool (RAT) on your computer.

That means you can access it from home via the internet. When you do, it's just like you're sitting at your desk at work. You can open all your files, change settings, run or install programs, whatever you need to do.

So you drag yourself to your home computer, connect to your work machine, and check in on your project before crawling back under the covers.

Clearly, RATs are great. Except when they're not. Hackers can use the same type of software to gain control of your computer. When they do, they can operate your system just like you can — opening files, changing settings, running or installing programs, and so on. They can even activate your computer's webcam and microphone to spy on your offline activities. Yikes!

> If you want to ensure your privacy, cover your webcam when you're not using it, just in case. A small piece of electrical tape should do. Just try to keep the sticky part off the lens to avoid gumming it up.

Sometimes hackers use a RAT that they've installed on your system, usually via Trojan horse. Other times they use a RAT that's already there. The RAT that comes pre-installed on some Windows machines, called Remote Desktop, is a notorious target.

Your anti-malware program should take care of most RATs. But if you run a version of Windows that supports Remote Desktop (not all of them do), you should shut it down any time you're not using it.

To shut down Remote Desktop in Windows 10, open the Control Panel, click **System and Security**, and select **Systems**. In the left side of the window, click **Remote Settings**. The System Properties dialog box opens with the Remote tab displayed. Under Remote Desktop, select the **Don't Allow Remote Connections to This Computer** checkbox, and click **OK**.

Ugh, these ads are annoying! How to easily block pop-ups

Remember that old arcade game "Whac-a-Mole"? It had a large box with holes in the top. When you played the game, little plastic moles randomly popped up through the holes, and you used a mallet to "whack" them back down.

Dealing with ads that pop up in your browser window, called "pop-ups," can feel a bit like playing that game — but way less fun. As soon as you close one down, another one pops back up.

Lots of pop-ups are just advertisements. They're annoying but basically harmless. But some pop-ups are more than merely annoying — they're dangerous. Clicking the link in these pop-ups can install hazardous malware on your computer.

Don't panic if you encounter a hostile pop-up. To persuade you to click, some pop-ups disguise themselves as a Windows or Mac dialog box that informs you of some kind of "problem."

Other pop-ups, called scareware, might claim to have detected malware on your system and demand payment to clean it up. Sometimes they try to intimidate you by blasting loud sounds and flashing lights from your computer. Who wouldn't be scared?

What to do if you see a "problem" message. If a pop-up presents itself on your screen, don't click the window — not even its Close button (the one that looks like an X in the upper-right corner). Instead, close the window by pressing Ctrl+W (Windows) or Command+W (Mac) on your keyboard.

Sometimes the pop-ups are not closable, and if you restart the browser it takes you right back to where you were — pop-ups and all. Try holding down the shift key while re-launching the browser to start the browser in safe mode.

This allows you to change the browser settings to open with a blank page or a specific home page and not where you last were. Or you can disable the malicious extension or plug-in you installed.

Better yet, block pop-ups altogether by doing either, or both, of the following.

- Install a pop-up blocker plug-in. Free browser plug-ins like AdBlock Plus (*adblockplus.org*), Adfender (*adfender.com*), and Ad Muncher (*admuncher.com*) make blocking pop-ups easy. All three work on a variety of browsers, although Adfender and Ad Muncher only run on Windows computers.

- Change your browser settings. Every web browser has a Block Pop-ups setting, although it might go by a different name. Turn this setting on to protect yourself from pop-up advertising.

Don't be afraid of all pop-ups. Sometimes you actually want them. For example, some legitimate sites use pop-ups to provide additional information or to prompt you to fill out a form. Pop-ups are especially prevalent on banking sites. Go figure.

Fortunately, you can tell your browser and most anti-pop-up plug-ins to make exceptions for certain sites. For example, to do this in Google Chrome, open the Customize menu, choose **Settings**, and click **Advanced** at the bottom of the page.

Then select **Content Settings**, choose **Pop-Ups and Redirects**, and, in the Allow section, click **Add a site**. Finally, enter the URL for the site you want to allow, and click **Add**.

Which is safer — Mac or PC?

It used to be that malware affected PCs but not Macs. In fact, if you have a Mac-using friend, you've probably heard him brag about never having to worry about viruses.

It's not because Macs were so much more secure than PCs, it's that PCs dominated the market. It just wasn't worth a hacker's time to make malware for Macs.

But nowadays, hackers do target Macs, although still not as aggressively as PCs. So whether you're a Mac groupie or a PC pro, you'll want to take steps to secure your system against malware.

Caution ahead! Protect yourself by avoiding dangerous sites

Unfortunate, but true. You could visit any website — even one that's 100 percent legit — and find yourself at risk of downloading malware. For example, in early 2018, hackers distributed malware by advertising on major websites, including *The New York Times* and *The Atlantic*.

Still, some websites are markedly more dangerous than others. To limit your chances of encountering malware, steer clear of these particular types of websites.

Torrent sites. These websites, like The Pirate Bay and others, enable you to quickly download large files. They work by chopping the file into a gazillion little pieces and harnessing dozens — maybe even hundreds — of computers to send a small scrap of the file at once.

Are there legitimate uses for torrent sites? Maybe. But mostly they're used to distribute pirated movies, music, and other copyrighted files. No surprise — they're also a haven for malware.

To avoid malware — not to mention prosecution for violating copyright laws — stay away from torrent sites.

The "dark web." Sounds like the name of a scary movie. It's actually a shady corner of the internet where online communications are completely anonymous.

The dark web does have some legitimate uses. It's often home to journalists and freedom fighters who operate in repressive countries. But it mostly traffics in illegal drugs, weapons, stolen data, fake IDs, malicious software, and so on. This is not a part of the internet where you want to hang out.

Fortunately, you can't really stumble onto the dark web by accident. It takes special software, like a Tor browser, to get there.

Whenever you surf to a new website, think carefully about the type of material it deals with and whether it's a likely place for hackers to do their dirty work. The more aware you are, the less likely you'll get caught.

Safe shopping and banking
Guard your green from online swindlers

Smart shopping strategy: Be careful how you pay

In recent years more and more Americans have abandoned brick-and-mortar stores in favor of online shopping. In fact, nearly 80 percent of U.S. consumers — some 217.1 million people — shop online at least some of the time.

It's easy to see why — online shopping is way convenient. (You can do it in your PJs!) Plus there's more variety online, and often, better prices.

Like most things, online shopping has a downside. Specifically, it opens you up to fraud and theft. After all, most internet shopping transactions require you to submit your credit card information online. This means thieves could intercept it — unless the internet storefront has proper security in place.

Make security your top priority. To find out whether it's safe to hand over your credit card number to an online store, check for these two security indicators.

- HTTPS in the address line. When a website supports secure transactions, its URL starts with the letters HTTPS (for example, *https://www.amazon.com*) rather than the usual

HTTP. This proves the site uses a security protocol called Secure Sockets Layer (SSL) to scramble data sent to and from the site. If this S is missing from the site's URL — especially on its checkout page — skip that sale.

- A lock icon. Most web browsers, such as Google Chrome, show that a site is secure by displaying a small padlock next to the address bar. (See graphic.) If Chrome determines a site is not secure, the icon changes to a red triangle with an exclamation mark, meaning "danger." Or if Chrome isn't sure, it shows a white circle with a small letter "i," as in "more information needed." No matter which icon appears, you can click it to see more information about the website's security.

Think twice about which card you use. Even if you think a site is secure, there's one time you should never pay with plastic — when that plastic is your debit card.

Debit cards offer less protection than credit cards if the card or number is stolen. With a credit card, you have zero liability in the case of fraud.

But with a debit card, you might find yourself responsible for all fraudulent charges, depending on how quickly you report the theft. And if that debit card is attached to your savings account, it could cost you your life's savings.

Even if your bank does reimburse you for charges made with your debit card, it might not be right away — meaning you could find yourself with a serious cash-flow problem. Definitely not worth the risk.

Save email receipts from online purchases

You need to save your online receipts, just like you would paper receipts. That way, if you run into a problem — like your package is mysteriously delayed or disappears en route — you'll have all the info you need to follow up.

One easy way to do this is to create a special "Receipts" folder in your email program to store them. Or if you want to get fancy, try using the Slice mobile app (*slice.com*).

This app, available for download on iPhone and Android devices, automatically scans your email inbox for online shopping receipts and stores them in one easy-to-access place. Slice also tracks shipments of online orders. It's like having your own personal shopping assistant.

4 tips to spot shady shopping sites

It's safest to shop on sites you know are on the up-and-up. Look for the online arm of a reputable brick-and-mortar store or an established internet-only outlet like Amazon.

But what if you find the exact thing you've been looking for on a site you've never heard of? In that case, it's best to do a bit of investigating before you click the **Buy** button. Here are four tips to test a site's trustworthiness.

Check the security indicators. You've already learned what to look for. When you direct your web browser to a secure site, a small lock icon appears near the browser's address bar, and the site's URL starts with HTTPS instead of just HTTP. If the site you're evaluating contains these indicators, that's a good sign.

Confirm that you can get hold of them. Most reputable shopping sites want you to contact them. That's why they include contact info, like a physical address, phone number, and/or email link. If a site is missing this validating info, it might be an indication that it's more shifty than safe.

Examine their policies. In addition to contact info, a reputable shopping site should also spell out various policies, such as its privacy policy and its return policy. Having these available on the website is another thumb's up.

Read the reviews. Before you drop your dough on some untested site, take a minute (or 10) to read reviews. Skip the ones on the site itself, though. Some seedier websites delete negative reviews and even post fake ones.

Instead, enter the site's name and the string **+ review** in a search engine like Google or Bing and see what pops up. Or try searching review sites like the Better Business Bureau (*bbb.org*), Trustpilot (*trustpilot.com*), and SiteJabber (*sitejabber.com*). If reviews of the site are sub-stellar, it's best to steer clear.

10 sly scams you need to watch out for

Emails that claim to be from a bank or store that ask you to provide personal information are obvious attempts to relieve you of your identity, drain your bank account, or both. But some scams are subtler — and that makes them even more dangerous.

Here are 10 top scams in the United States. No. 2 will really surprise you — in a bad way. To find out about even more scams, check out the Federal Trade Commission's "Scam Alert" web page at *consumer.ftc.gov/features/scam-alerts*.

Tech-support trickery. This is when a scammer informs you that cybercriminals have hacked your computer. He tricks you into providing sensitive information or even allowing him remote access into your system to "fix" the problem — for a fee of course.

Donation deceptions. After a natural disaster or some other type of catastrophe, scammers inevitably pose as charity workers seeking donations. What they're really after is your credit card number.

These scammers are particularly shameful. They don't just rob you of your identity or your money, they deprive the victims of these tragedies of desperately needed help.

Seizing's greetings. Someone sent you an e-card. How sweet. Not so fast. Yes, some e-cards bear good tidings. But more often they bring bad news, when they open your machine up to malware.

Dishonest daters. Millions of people use online dating services to meet their mate. But some scammers scour these sites to meet their mark. These scoundrels profess to be interested in you romantically. But what they're really after is your private information or your money.

Fakes on a plane. Suppose an official-looking email message promising you two free airline tickets lands in your inbox. All you have to do is click a link and fill out some sort of survey, and you'll be halfway to Hawaii. The truth is, there is no free trip for you. But you can kiss your private information goodbye.

Lies on the prize. OMG you won the lottery or some other amazing cash prize! You just need to click the link in this notification email and provide your bank account info to claim your prize. Hate to burst your bubble, but this is definitely a scam.

Access "grant"ed. This scheme works like the lottery scam. But this time your prize is a free government grant. Don't fall for it.

Career criminals. You found the perfect job. It lets you work from home and pays twice what your old job did. You provide the requested personal info for processing purposes, including your Social Security number and bank info. Then — nothing. Soon it dawns on you. There was no job — but scammers have done a job on you.

Over and out. Suppose you post something for sale online. A buyer overpays you for the item — by a lot. They contact you to tell you they made a mistake and ask you to refund the overpayment. You're a nice person, so you do it, and ship the item, too.

Then you find out the initial payment was fraudulent. To summarize — the buyer keeps the initial payment, the refund, and your item, and you get bupkis.

Tax traps. You know by now that scammers often call and pose as an employee of the Internal Revenue Service (IRS) to relieve you of your Social Security number. They usually accomplish this by telling you they need to update your records or straighten out a tax problem.

To quote Admiral Ackbar from *Star Wars*, "It's a trap!" The IRS will never contact you in this way.

Be a savvy online banker: 4 ways to keep your money safe

Online banking can be a huge timesaver. You can monitor your accounts, track your transactions, transfer funds, and pay bills — without setting foot in your local branch.

There are just two troubling downsides. First, you don't get a lollipop when you make a deposit. (So disappointing!) And second, as with online shopping, online banking opens you up to theft and fraud.

Following are four easy measures you can take to keep your online banking experience 100 percent fraud-free. As for the lollipop, sorry, you're on your own.

Go incognito and keep your sessions private. By default, when you go online, your web browser keeps track of sites you visit and other information. If your internet session involves a visit to your bank's website, this information could include sensitive data like your account number, balance, statement, and so on.

Even after you close your browser, this data could remain on your machine — which means if a hacker or thief compromises your computer, they may be able to capture it.

Fortunately, most web browsers have a special feature that lets you browse anonymously, usually called Private Browsing or Incognito Mode. When you use this feature, the browser still tracks your browsing activity but wipes it from your system when you end your browsing session. You don't want to bank online until you activate this important security feature.

Do a two-step for double the protection. Some financial institutions support the use of two-step verification for online banking. This means that rather than simply entering your username and password to log into your account, you must enter this information plus something else — usually a "token" or code sent to your mobile device. If your online bank allows for two-step verification, you should absolutely, positively, definitely use it.

View your statements online. Financial statements contain all sorts of personal info, including your home address, account number, account balance, and more. This makes them particularly attractive to thieves who want to steal your identity.

That's why robbers raid mailboxes and even trash cans or dumpsters for paper statements. To foil these fraudsters, you can cancel mail delivery of paper statements and view them online instead.

Opt out of credit card offers delivered by mail. In addition to paper statements, crafty crooks also look for pre-approved credit card offers delivered by mail. If thieves intercept a pre-approved offer addressed to you, they could easily apply for the card and have it sent to themselves.

Assuming the application goes through, these thieves might well rack up thousands in charges — ruining your credit in the process — as quick as you can lick a stamp.

To prevent this, you can opt out of these offers by calling 888-5-OPT-OUT or visiting *optout prescreen.com/selection*.

> Most banks let you sign up to receive text alerts any time funds are withdrawn from your account. Enabling this feature is a no-brainer. The next time some crook tries to refurnish his living room using your debit card number, you'll be glad you did.

Safety dance: Nimble steps to shop and bank securely

You eat right, exercise, get adequate sleep, and floss (you do floss, right?) — all to keep your body healthy. Likewise, you should take certain steps to maintain your computer's health (not to mention your identity's and your bank account's) while shopping and banking online. Here are six simple tips to get your started.

Be suspicious of messages. If you receive an email message from a store or bank claiming your account has been compromised, or that some type of security breach has occurred that requires your immediate attention, be wary. It's entirely possible it's a phishing email that contains malicious links.

Play favorites with your accounts. Bookmark your internet banking site and any online shops you like to visit. That way, you can simply click the bookmark — also called a "favorite" — to access the site. This prevents you from mistyping the URL and landing on the wrong (read: dangerous) page by accident.

Call on the "P" manager. It's a good practice to set unique passwords for each of your online shopping and banking accounts. To keep track of them all, try using a password manager.

For more on setting strong passwords and on using a password manager, see *Password protection: How to pick them, remember them, and keep them safe* in the chapter *Protect your good name: How to fight fraud and stop identity theft.*

Play it cool on public Wi-Fi and computers. Most public Wi-Fi networks offer little, if anything, in the way of security. If you use one of these networks to bank or shop online, hackers lurking on these unsecure sites could intercept your login information and use it to take over your accounts.

On a related note, it's wise to avoid using public computers, like the ones found in hotels or your local library, to shop or bank online, for similar reasons.

Beware of that cute (shoulder) surfer. A hacker doesn't necessarily need sophisticated skills or tools to steal your login info. All he really needs is physical proximity and at least one functioning eyeball.

That is, he can simply watch you type this info in — a practice called "shoulder surfing." Beware of shoulder surfers in crowded spaces like airports, hotel lobbies, or internet cafes.

Remember to log out. When you're finished shopping or banking online, it's a good practice to log out of the site. That way you know for sure no one else can access it from your machine. This is especially important if you ignored the advice about not shopping or banking using public computers!

Savvy surfing
Your easy guide to internet safety

Safe searching: 4 web browser tweaks you need to make

When you surf the web, you use a special application called a web browser to move from site to site. You may be familiar with several popular browsers, like Microsoft Internet Explorer, Apple Safari, Google Chrome, or Mozilla Firefox.

Different browsers offer different security tools and settings to head off cyberattacks. For example, Internet Explorer identifies "security zones." Choosing to operate only in the most secure zone limits your exposure to internet dangers. But guess what? This also limits what sites you can visit — sometimes preventing access to legitimate sites by mistake.

Although other browsers don't take this specific approach, they do support other common security settings. Here's what you need to do to stay safe on your favorite browser.

Toss your cookies. When you visit some websites, they deposit a small file called a "cookie" on your computer. The site might then use this cookie to verify your identity the next time you visit, or even track your other activities online.

Cookies are potentially dangerous for two reasons — they may violate your privacy, and they can be intercepted by hackers, who can then use them to assume your identity online. To prevent this, change your browser's settings to delete and disable cookies.

You may have to search your Settings to figure out where to do it. On Google Chrome, for example, you would go to Settings > Advanced > Privacy and security > Content settings > Cookies. Look for a similar path on other browsers.

> A web browser acts as a portal between you and the internet. So if your web browser isn't secure, it provides an entry point for attackers into your system. That's why it's so important to check your browser's settings and make sure they're protecting your computer.

Disable pop-ups. You've probably visited plenty of sites that use pop-ups — small windows that "pop up" on the screen. Pop-ups aren't just annoying, they may also be harmful. For example, some pop-ups can install malicious software on your computer. To avoid this, you'll need to disable the pop-up setting.

Undo auto-fill. Some browsers automatically fill in your personal info on sites that request it. While this auto-fill feature is super convenient, it may also be super dangerous.

That's because some sketchy sites hide info boxes on their web pages. When your browser detects these boxes, it fills them with your information automatically — without your knowledge. To prevent this, simply deactivate your browser's auto-fill feature.

Hide location information. Most browsers track geolocation information. On the pro side, this makes it easier for your browser to offer location-specific features, like restaurant recommendations and local movie times.

On the con side, well, your browser always knows where you are — and can even reveal your location to others. Yikes! Fortunately, you can easily disable your browser's geolocation settings to prevent it from tracking you.

Strengthen your web browser with these 3 simple steps

The weaker your web browser's security, the more attractive it is to a hacker or other attacker. To protect your browser from hackers, take these three simple steps.

Keep your browser up to date. When the company behind your web browser digs up a security hole, it releases a patch to fix it. By keeping your browser up to date, you ensure it has all the latest patches.

Use anti-virus software. This not only blocks malware designed to affect your browser, it also defends against malicious programs you might accidentally download using your browser.

Install security plug-ins. A browser plug-in is a tiny add-on application that helps your web browser in some way. HTTPS Everywhere (*www.eff.org/https-everywhere*) is a plug-in that encrypts communication with major websites to make them more secure. Another, Web of Trust (*mywot.com*), flags unsafe sites.

Shhh! How to keep your browsing a secret

Most web browsers make it a practice to track your browsing history and compile a list of pages you visit. Sometimes this is a good thing. For example, if you can't quite remember the URL for that cool site you landed on last week, you can check your browser's history to track it down.

Other times, you might prefer to hide your browsing activity, like if you're planning a surprise party for your spouse. If that's the case, you can easily cover your tracks online. Look for one or all of these features on your favorite browser.

Clear your browsing data.
All web browsers let you delete your browsing history, download history, cookies, and more, sometimes in one fell swoop. (See graphic.)

Browse on the down-low.
Most web browsers have a special feature that lets you browse anonymously. Internet Explorer calls it InPrivate Browsing, Safari and Firefox call it Private Browsing, and Chrome calls it Incognito Mode.

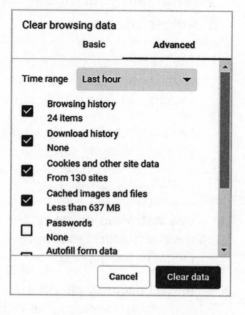

When you use this feature, the browser still tracks your browsing and download history but wipes this information from your system when you close your browsing session.

Set up your search engine to not save searches. Google, Bing, and other top search engines save searches by default. They then use this information to make suggestions when you search later on. This is handy if you frequently search for the same thing, like "stock market news" or "dinner recipes."

But if you're planning a surprise anniversary trip with your spouse, you probably don't want him to find your recent search for "Florida destinations" when he searches for "florists in town."

Fortunately, you can easily disable this feature.

Switch to a private search engine. Some search engines are designed with privacy in mind. These private search engines don't track your searches or collect your private information. Popular examples include DuckDuckGo (*duckduckgo.com*) and StartPage (*startpage.com*).

You may have heard of a Tor browser, which can hide your identity online. But it can also expose you to some shady sites and services. Think twice before exploring this option.

Simple rules to steer clear of sketchy sites

Ah, the internet. Home to pretty much all the world's information ever — plus cat videos! It's hard to believe such a force for good could also host sketchy sites designed to relieve you of your identity, your money, or both. Fortunately, you have plenty of ways to steer clear of the darker corners of the online world.

Heed the warnings. Many standard anti-virus programs flag dangerous websites. So do browser plug-ins like Web of Trust (*mywot.com*). Even some search engines and web browsers have built-in tools to detect problem pages or hide them from view altogether. Although these tools may occasionally flag legitimate sites in error, it's generally wise to heed these warnings.

Don't guess the address. Unless you're 100 percent sure of a site's address, don't type it right into your web browser's address bar. Whole scam empires are built on sites whose URLs are one letter off from the address of a more popular page — or, say, end in .com instead of .gov.

Instead, type the name of the website you seek into a search engine, and then click the site's link in the search results. That way, you can guarantee you land on the right site. Even better — bookmark your favorite sites for easier access.

Check the link. Suppose you're on a web page, and you see a link to a site that looks interesting. Before you click the link, it pays to verify where it will take you.

To do so, simply hover your mouse pointer over the link. The associated URL should appear in the bottom-left corner of your browser window. If the URL looks shady — for example, it contains a suspicious domain — don't click the link.

Do some research. If you want to be absolutely, positively certain a site is safe, run its address through a website safety checker like Google Safe Browsing (*transparencyreport.google.com/safe-browsing/search*) or VirusTotal (*virustotal.com/#/home/upload*).

These tools troll servers looking for dangerous sites and can tell you if the URL you entered is one of them.

Public Wi-Fi: Smart tricks to avoid hackers and scammers

Picture this. You're at the airport for a work trip, and your boss asks you to email her an important spreadsheet that contains sensitive financial information before you board your plane. "No problem!" you say.

You flip open your laptop, connect to the airport's free Wi-Fi network, and send the file. While you're at it, you log on to your bank's website to make sure your paycheck was deposited. Mission(s) accomplished.

Just one problem — that public Wi-Fi network likely has zero security. That means any hackers eavesdropping on that network could have intercepted your sensitive spreadsheet — not to mention your bank login information.

The fact that most public Wi-Fi networks lack even basic security is bad enough. What's worse is that cybercriminals often set up fake networks to intercept what you send or even install malware on your system.

The best thing is to avoid Wi-Fi networks that don't require a password whenever possible. It's just not worth the risk. But if that's not an option, and you absolutely, positively must use a public network, then take these four steps to stay safe.

Make sure it's the right network. To avoid accidentally connecting to a fake network, carefully check the spelling of the name. These phony networks often have names that are similar to a legitimate Wi-Fi connection — say, "LaGardia Airport Wi-Fi" instead of "LaGuardia Airport Wi-Fi" — to dupe you into connecting.

Don't bank or shop on public Wi-Fi. Do your personal browsing at home where your network is password-protected. Otherwise, you might expose your login information to hackers, who can use it to take over your accounts.

Disable file sharing. Some operating systems let you share selected files with others via a network connection — for example, to collaborate with colleagues on a work project. When you're on a secure network, this is great.

But when you're on public Wi-Fi with zero security, then not so much. To prevent hackers from seeing files you've selected for sharing, you should disable file sharing any time you use public Wi-Fi.

Use a virtual private network (VPN). A VPN allows you to "tunnel" through a public Wi-Fi network to connect to a secure private network somewhere else. This secure network then acts as your gateway to the internet.

VPNs also help hide your identity by blocking your location and encrypting your transmissions, which makes it even safer to search and browse online.

To use a VPN, you must create an account with a VPN provider and install special software on your computer. Top VPN providers include NordVPN (*nordvpn.com*), Private Internet Access (*privateinternetaccess.com*), and TunnelBear (*tunnelbear.com*).

Make life easier — double up on browsers

Obviously, taking steps to protect your privacy and stay safe online is a good idea. But it also makes using the internet, well, kind of a pain.

Let's face it — sometimes it's nice when your web browser recognizes you, remembers where you've been, and knows where you are. It just makes searching and browsing online easier.

One way around this is to use not one, but two, web browsers. On one browser — say, Internet Explorer — you can apply the strictest possible security settings. You can then use this browser for more sensitive tasks, like online banking and shopping.

On the other browser — it could be Safari, Chrome, Mozilla, whatever — opt for looser security settings. The defaults should work fine. You'll use this browser for more casual web activities, like checking the news or goofing around on Facebook.

Avoid the privacy pitfalls of social media

5 tacks to hack-proof your social media accounts

Social media lets you easily connect with friends and family members, no matter where they live. You can also use social media to make new friends, follow your favorite celebrities, and keep up with current events.

It's no wonder more than two-thirds of American adults maintain an account on the most popular social media site — Facebook. It claims over 2 billion users a month. And more than a billion social media fans check out both YouTube and Instagram each month.

Of course, when you gather that many people onto one site, it naturally piques the interest of hackers and other bad actors. So you need to be extra cautious on social media. Here are a few basic ways to stay safe.

Set solid passwords. Just like any other account, you need to set solid passwords for all your social media accounts. And don't use the same one, as tempting as it may be.

Lock down your privacy. All social media sites let you apply privacy settings to limit who sees what you post. Accessing these settings is easy.

For example, on Facebook, simply click the down-arrow in the top-right corner of any page and choose **Settings** from the menu that appears. Then, click the **Privacy** option on the left side of the Settings page, and make your changes in the pane on the right.

Keep your personal info to yourself. Thieves look for five main things on Facebook — your date of birth, your child's date of birth, your mother's maiden name, your address, and any travel plans you have. Don't reveal this personal information!

You may think that's just common sense and you would never do it. Maybe not consciously. But what about when you wish your son a happy 35th birthday on Facebook? Or thank everyone for their good wishes as you turn 60? It won't take anyone very long to do the math and figure out your exact birth dates.

Beware of "likejackers." You've probably seen Facebook posts that promise you'll win a free iPad or some other cool prize if you "like" the post. Ignore these. Clicking the **Like** button simply diverts you to some other page that tells you to enter all your personal info to claim your prize — which is Hackerese for "surrender your identity."

Don't take that quiz. Obviously, when Facebook presents you with a quiz to find out "Which *Gilligan's Island* Character Are You?" it's hard to resist. (OMG I got Mary Ann!)

More often than not, these quizzes are simply vehicles for shady data-collection firms or even hackers to access your private Facebook info or expose your computer to malware.

Can your boss check your social media accounts?

If your friends and family see a regrettable post on your social media, that's bad. But it's even worse if the post comes to the attention of your boss. Like, you-could-lose-your-job worse — especially if the post reflects poorly on your boss, your workplace, or your work performance.

Of course, one way to avoid this sad outcome is to lock down your privacy settings on social media. That way only friends and family can see your posts.

But depending on where you live, your boss might be legally entitled to demand access to your social media accounts. The same goes for prospective employers. In that case, you have little choice but to comply if you want to keep your job.

To find out whether your state allows this practice, visit the National Conference of State Legislatures website at *ncsl.org*, and search for "state social media privacy laws."

How to tell if your account has been hacked — and what to do next

If a bunch of spammy or inflammatory posts not written by you mysteriously appear on your Facebook wall or other social media page, it can only mean one thing — your account has been hacked.

Some social media platforms, such as Facebook, can notify you of a suspected breach even before you unwittingly broadcast that amazing (read: fake) deal on sunglasses or vitamins or whatever to all your friends.

How? By flagging unusual login locations. For example, suppose you normally log in to Facebook from your desktop computer in Peoria. If someone logs in to your account from somewhere else — say, Russia or China or that island in *Castaway* — Facebook can flag it.

To enable this feature, open the Settings page, click **Security and Login** in the left pane, and click the **Edit** button next to the **Get Alerts About Unrecognized Logins** entry in the **Setting Up Extra Security** section. Then select how you want to receive these notifications, click **Save Changes**, and click **Close**. (See example below.)

Regardless of how you find out, if you discover a social media account has indeed been hacked, there's only one thing to do — change the account password pronto.

Setting Up Extra Security

🔔 **Get alerts about unrecognized logins**
On • We'll let you know if anyone logs in from a device or browser you don't usually use   [Close]

    Get an alert when anyone logs into your account from an unrecognized device or browser.

    🅕 **Notifications**
      ⦿ Get notifications
      ◯ Don't get notifications

    💬 **Messenger**
      ◯ Get notifications
      ⦿ Don't get notifications

    ✉ **Email**
      ◯ Email login alerts to kateshoup@live.com, kateshoup@att.net
      ⦿ Don't get email alerts

    Add another email or mobile number

    [Save Changes]

👥 **Choose 3 to 5 friends to contact if you get locked out**
On • Your trusted contacts can send a code and URL from Facebook to help you log back   [Edit]

Avoid the TMI syndrome — take care when you share

You know how people say, "Nothing lasts forever"? They're right — mostly. While it's true that life is fleeting, love is ephemeral, and so on, one thing will indeed endure for all time — that opinion/photo/meme you really wish you hadn't posted on social media.

Sure, you can delete the post, but even then, there's no guarantee it won't linger. If someone captured a screenshot of the post, they could reignite your regret by resharing it.

Given the permanent nature of social media, it's extra-important that you ponder before you post and avoid giving out too much information (TMI).

The surest way to avoid post-posting penitence. Always keep things positive. It's like Thumper says in *Bambi*, "If you can't say something nice, don't say nothin' at all." Or put another way, post about others as you would have them post about you. Think of this as the silicon rule — like the golden rule, but for social media.

The bottom line — if you wouldn't email something to your boss, distribute it in your church bulletin, or say it out loud in front of your grandkids, don't post it online.

It's not enough to watch what you post on social media. You also need to watch what others post about you. You might be smart enough not to post a photo that shows you doing something you'd rather keep private — like your wild New Year's Eve dance moves. But your friends might not be.

If someone posts a photo of you that you'd prefer stayed offline, ask them to delete it, or at the very least untag you.

Review posts you're tagged in before they go public. If you really want to take control, set up your Facebook account to approve any photos you're tagged in before they're posted on your timeline.

To do this, click on the arrow in the top-right corner of your Facebook page and click on **Settings**. Click on **Timeline and Tagging**. Under **Review**, turn on the suggestions you want to add.

5 ways to dodge problem people and keep your site serene

You'd like to think people would behave themselves on social media. Sadly, you'd be wrong. In fact, people often show their worst side on social media — especially on sites like Twitter, where online interactions often involve strangers.

Fortunately, you have a few easy ways to shield yourself from hostile online exchanges. Follow these tips for Facebook, and look for similar options on other social media sites.

Be selective in who you follow — and in who follows you. With some things — cake comes to mind — more is definitely better. Social media is different. Interacting with too many people, especially when you don't really know them, often makes things worse. Limit yourself to communicating only with people who make your day better or more interesting.

Hit the reject button on strangers. Suppose you get a Facebook friend request from someone you don't recognize. Of course, it could be that you did know the person at one time in your life but have long since forgotten them. Or it could be the person is a scammer in search of a mark. Either way, it's best to reject Facebook friend requests from people you don't know.

Share a post only with your closest friends. Sometimes you might want to post something on social media, but you want to limit who sees it. Facebook lets you do this directly from the post itself.

Simply click the **Friends** button next to the **News Feed** entry under your post, and choose **Friends Except** or **Specific Friends**. Then specify the friends you want to prevent or allow access to the post.

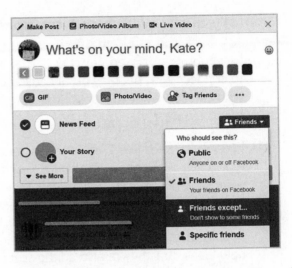

Take a break from a bothersome buddy. Maybe you have a Facebook friend who you like, but who's driving you a little crazy just now. You can "unfollow" that person but still remain friends.

Simply click the **Following** button on that person's page and choose **Unfollow** on the menu that appears. When you're ready to reconnect, just reverse the operation.

Permanently delete an unfriendly face. If a Facebook friend gets to be too much, you can kick them off your news feed by unfriending them. Just click the **Friends** button on the person's page and select **Unfriend** from the menu that appears.

Or you can go one step further and block them. When you block someone on a social media site, that person can no longer see your posts or attempt to friend, follow, or otherwise engage with you on the site.

To get this done, open the Facebook Settings page, click **Blocking** in the left pane, type the name of the person you want to block in the **Block Users** box, and click the **Block** button.

Safety alert! Watch out on 'open' social media sites

Facebook is a "closed network." That is, you generally use it to connect with people you already know. You also control who can see what you post by issuing, accepting, or rejecting friend requests.

In contrast, sites like Twitter and Instagram are open networks. On these sites, by default, you can follow anyone you want, and anyone can follow you.

Open networks are great. You can use them to meet new people who share your interests and to open your mind to new ideas. But they're also a little scary, because, well, you're basically interacting with a bunch of strangers online.

To stay safe on open networks, consider using a fake name and keeping your location private. And be especially careful about getting together in person with any pals you meet. Let someone else know where you'll be, and with whom, in case it turns out your "friend" isn't quite who they said they were.

Alternative facts — how to spot fake news and bots

According to a recent survey by Pew Research Center, about two-thirds of American adults get at least some of their news on social media. The problem? A lot of that news is "fake."

Indeed, a recent study published in *Science* magazine revealed that falsehoods traveled "farther, faster, deeper, and more broadly" than the truth in all categories of information — especially when they pertain to politics.

How does misinformation spread? Usually, when someone shares "fake news" on social media, they do it unknowingly. That is, they believe the information they're sharing is true.

But there are also "bots" — fake social media accounts that automatically generate messages pretending to be real people. These bots are programmed to spread misinformation on purpose, often to benefit some nefarious cause.

For example, after the school shooting in Parkland, Florida in 2018, millions of Russian bots flooded Twitter to spread falsehoods about the shooter and victims to stoke division among Americans.

Investigators also believe Russian bots were used to influence the outcome of American elections in 2016 and 2018 and the 2016 Brexit campaign.

How do you know if a story on social media is true or false? One way to verify a story is to research it using various online fact-checking resources, such as FactCheck.org (*factcheck.org*), PolitiFact (*politifact.com*), and Snopes (*snopes.com*).

You can also research the source of the story to determine whether it has a known bias. For a handy media-bias chart, visit *adfontes media.com/intro-to-the-media-bias-chart*.

Finally, you can install browser plug-ins designed to flag fake news, such as the B.S. Detector plug-in at *bsdetector.tech*.

Do your homework before you pass along a social media story, and you'll avoid contributing to the "fake news" syndrome.

Secure your smartphone
Stop hackers in their tracks

7 best ways to sink malicious phone pirates

Got a smartphone? Did you realize it can be hacked — in some cases more easily than your home computer? It's true. Here's how to keep hackers out of your smartphone to protect your privacy, your security, and even your bank account.

Raise your (anti-) malware-ness. Your computer isn't the only machine that can benefit from anti-malware software. Your smartphone can, too. Fortunately, several third-party vendors offer anti-malware for mobile devices, including Norton (*us.norton.com/ norton-mobile-security*), McAfee (*mcafeemobilesecurity.com*), and Avast (*avast.com/en-us/mobile*).

Pay attention to patches. Remember how hackers often use security holes in your computer's operating system to gain access? The same goes for smartphones. When a phone manufacturer discovers a security hole in its operating system, it releases a "patch" to plug it.

To ensure your phone has all the latest patches, set it up to automatically install all operating system updates the minute they become available.

Do your 'appy' dance at the right store. Most smartphone apps are perfectly safe. But some are designed with one purpose in mind — to compromise your device. To steer clear of these, only download apps from your phone-maker's store — for example, the App Store (iPhone) or Google Play (Android).

Check the app's ratings and read any reviews, too. Still not sure? Try using a special tool called the Zscaler Application Profiler (ZAP). Just direct your web browser to *zap.zscaler.com*, type the app's name in the box, and click **Search App**.

Set up your lock screen for quick and easy security. Your smartphone isn't just at risk of being hacked from afar. It's also in danger of being nicked from close by — like by the guy sitting next to you at Starbucks or standing behind you on the subway.

That's why you should set up your phone to display a lock screen after it's been inactive for a short while — say, one minute or five minutes. That way, if a thief pinches your phone, they'll need your password, passcode, face, or fingerprint — depending on what unlock mechanism you choose — to use it.

Encrypt your files to keep them safe. If your smartphone contains files, photos, or videos that you want to keep private, you can use an app like Folder Lock at *newsoftwares.net/folderlock/iphone* or *newsoftwares.net/folderlock/android* to encrypt them. Even if someone manages to bypass your phone's lock screen, they won't be able to open the encrypted files.

Track your phone in the field. The bad news — your smartphone's gone AWOL. The good news — you wisely enabled the Find iPhone (iPhone) or Find My Device (Android) feature before the device disappeared.

This feature — which may go by different names on other mobile devices — transforms your smartphone into a beacon so you can track its location. To do so, simply direct your web browser to the Find My Phone page on iCloud (*icloud.com/#find*) or the Find My Device web page (*google.com/android/find*).

The final stage — erase your data. Having navigated the five stages of grief, you've accepted that your phone is gone forever. But to truly move on, there's one thing you must do — erase its contents.

If the device is an iPhone and you enabled the Find iPhone feature, you can do this by using iCloud to erase the phone. After you pull up a map showing its location, click the green dot that represents the phone, then click the Information icon. In the dialog box that appears, click **Erase Phone**, and choose **Erase**.

Even better — before you lose your phone, set it up to erase automatically after 10 unsuccessful attempts to enter the passcode. Tap the Settings icon and choose **Touch ID & Passcode** or **Face ID & Passcode**, depending on which model iPhone you have. Then enter your passcode and toggle the **Erase Data** setting to on.

Safety net: 3 tricks to block nefarious networks

You know public Wi-Fi networks offer nothing in the way of security. To prevent hackers lurking on these networks from intercepting your personal information, it's best to avoid logging on in the first place. Want your smartphone to be even more secure when you're out and about? Try these three tricks.

Deactivate the Wi-Fi setting on your phone. Your phone will automatically connect to wireless networks it's joined before. So if you've previously jumped on Wi-Fi while waiting for your plane to depart, your phone will happily reconnect every time you're at the airport.

The best thing is to turn off Wi-Fi before you leave home. But be sure to re-enable the setting when you get back if you have your own secure Wi-Fi router. You don't want to burn through your cellular data plan.

Disable Bluetooth anytime you're not using it. Any Bluetooth device, such as a smartphone, is vulnerable to so-called "BlueBorne" attacks. A hacker in close physical proximity of your smartphone — within 30 feet, give or take — can use Bluetooth to gain access to your device and any sensitive data it might contain. It can then infect it with malware or even hijack it completely.

Turn off location services when you don't need them. While these services can be useful — enabling you to search for movie theaters nearby, "check in" at your favorite restaurant, or map out a route to the nearest cupcake shop (oops, gym) — they also track you everywhere you go.

This isn't just alarming in a general "Big Brother" sense. It's also scary from the standpoint that anyone could hack into your location history and use this information to pinpoint places where you're likely to turn up in the future.

Disabling location services prevents this from happening, and as an added bonus, prolongs your phone's battery life. If you can't bring yourself to turn off location services for all apps on your phone, at least disable it on less critical ones.

241

1 thing you MUST *do before selling or donating* *your phone*

Personal information, text messages, and more are hiding on your old smartphone — even if you've deleted them. Before you sell or donate your phone, you should wipe them out for good.

First, you need to back up the phone. Once that's done, you're ready to wipe the phone clean.

- If it's an iPhone, tap the Settings icon, tap **General**, choose **Reset**, and select **Erase All Contents and Settings**. When you erase your content, Find My iPhone and the activation lock should turn off. To be sure, turn off the features before you wipe the phone. Otherwise, whoever buys your phone can't activate it without your iCloud password.

- The steps for an Android device are similar. Tap **Settings**, choose **System**, and select **Reset** or **Backup and Reset** (depending on what model Android you have). Then tap **Factory Data Reset** and **Reset Phone**. Again, it's a good idea to turn off security features first.

Safety-conscious apps keep your messages private

Most of the text messages you send and receive are probably pretty tame — like the one you just sent your brother about that upcoming family reunion, or the text you received from your granddaughter about her new kitten.

So the fact that the technology behind text messages, called short message service (SMS), isn't terribly secure might not worry you much.

Some messages, however, might be more personal or private in nature — say, a message to a friend about her upcoming surgery or to your son about his precarious financial situation. For these types of messages, security probably is a concern.

Fortunately, you can find several apps that allow you to send and receive secure messages. These apps offer end-to-end encryption, meaning only you and the message's sender or recipient can read it.

Here are three apps that not only offer encrypted messaging, but are available free of charge. Just remember, for these apps to work, both parties in the conversation must use them.

iMessage *(support.apple.com/explore/messages)*. If you have an iPhone, you already have iMessage. It's the default messaging app on all iPhones. Messages sent to other iPhone users are always encrypted and appear in blue text bubbles. Messages to users of Androids or other devices will be sent via SMS and appear in green text bubbles on your device. These are not encrypted.

WhatsApp *(whatsapp.com)*. It's said that WhatsApp is a popular choice for criminals because its security is so tough to crack. Not even the FBI can decode it. What's more, the app includes a feature to verify the identity of the person on the other end of the exchange.

And it's not just for text messages, either. You can also use WhatsApp to make voice and even video calls. This popular app, which was bought by Facebook in 2014, boasts more than a billion users.

Some text-messaging apps allow you to not only delete messages but to "vaporize" them — leaving no trace behind. If you truly want them to remain private, you need to take advantage of this feature. Search the app for "disappearing messages."

Signal *(signal.org).* Some people are not comfortable with WhatsApp's connection with Facebook because of privacy concerns. Enter Signal. This open-source app operates in much the same way as WhatsApp. In fact, it shares much of the same code. But some people say Signal is even more secure than its more popular counterpart.

Mobile misery — signs your smartphone has been hacked

Is your smartphone suddenly slow as a sloth? Does it hemorrhage data? Do mysterious charges appear on your bill — like expensive phone calls overseas? These are all signs your smartphone may have been hacked. But they're not the only symptoms of an infected device. Other clues include:

- a battery that dies faster than a minor villain in a shoot-'em-up movie.

- the sudden appearance of annoying pop-ups.

- weird apps on your phone that you definitely didn't install.

- attempts by your phone's browser to direct you to unsavory sites.

- strange service interruptions.

If you notice any of these indicators, install an anti-malware app on your mobile device ASAP.

Google software
The free suite that does it all

Gone are the days when you had to spend hundreds of dollars every few years on software. From Chrome to Docs to Gmail and more, Google software does most of what Microsoft Office can, and Google software is both free and far more convenient.

Simply open a Google account and log in once, and you can use it all. There's no need for further logins or registration. What's more, Google's software lives in the cloud. That means you can use it and get your files on any device — PC or Mac, Android or iPhone and iPad.

And it's all integrated with Google Drive, your own free hard drive in the cloud. There, you can store and share photos, videos, songs, and all types of files.

Along with the world's most powerful search engine, here are some of Google's most popular features.

- Chrome internet browser

- Gmail, a user-friendly email system

- Drive, convenient and secure storage in the cloud

- Docs, a free word processor program

- Sheets, a spreadsheet program for numbers and data

- Slides, for presentations

- Calendar, for planning across all devices

- Maps, your GPS navigation lifeline

The ease, convenience, and free availability of Google software has made it a favorite at schools, businesses, and homes around the world. If you're not using it, it's time to step into the future and discover all this powerful software has to offer.

Top-notch tricks for polishing Google Chrome

Cruise the internet with the speediest browser

Why drive an old clunker around the internet when you can zip about in a Maserati?

Speed is the reason Google Chrome beat out Internet Explorer so quickly as the world's most-popular browser. Since it was introduced in 2008, Chrome has grabbed more than 69 percent of the global browser market, almost seven times more than Firefox's share and 11 times more than Internet Explorer's.

Get lightning-fast information while working in Chrome. Hit Ctrl+n (Apple users, Cmd+n) and immediately type what you want — don't touch the mouse. Chrome will open a new page with the cursor already in the address/search bar. Presto, your results appear the moment you hit **Enter**.

Give Chrome a test drive and feel the speed. Skip reading about speed tests and try it for yourself. Download Chrome (*google.com/chrome*) and compare. Open browser windows and click on links. While Firefox and Microsoft's new Edge have caught up some, Chrome's surging popularity has left them in its dust. And while speed is a plus, Chrome offers a whole lot more, too.

Search from the address bar for even more speed. One slick trick Google added to Chrome was the ability to both search and type web addresses in the address bar. The browser recognizes addresses (URLs), and when it sees one will whisk you there. If it doesn't recognize it as a web address, it delivers Google's array of search results.

Try it and get ready to be impressed. In Chrome's address bar, type *nasa.gov*, and you'll find yourself dazzled by the official NASA website. Type just NASA and you'll get enough search results to write a research paper.

4 easy ways to make Chrome your own

People praise Chrome for its simple, uncluttered feel, but that doesn't mean you can't jazz it up. In fact, when it comes to customizing, Chrome has features other browsers do not.

Make yourself feel at home. Chrome lets you choose a background image for your home and startup page. Just click the gear icon, bottom right, to customize the page. Choose either a free Chrome background or **Upload an image from your computer**.

Set your favorite website as your home page. Do you like to check your email every few minutes, or perhaps the stock market? As with other browsers, you can set Chrome to open websites as your home/startup page.

- Click the Menu icon (three vertical dots) in the top right-hand corner.

- In the drop-down menu that appears, choose **Settings**.

- Under **Appearance**, find **Show home button.**

- Click the on/off icon to the right.

- There, the second line offers a space to paste or type a web address.

While here, you can also choose a Chrome theme, which will change the background and look of your browser, as well as font size, page zoom and more.

Simplify life with your bookmarks bar. The Appearance settings also let you show or hide your bookmarks toolbar. Definitely turn it on. Your bookmarks toolbar sits along the top of your browser, putting your favorite websites at a click's distance. To add bookmarks:

- go to a favorite website.

- click the Star icon on the right of the address bar.

- under **Folder**, choose **Bookmarks toolbar** or a folder on it.

To save real estate on this key toolbar, give your bookmarks shorter names as you create them. For example, make American Heritage Dictionary just AHD. You can also create folders of bookmarks, say, Sports, Music, or Cooking.

Control your shortcuts — they're doors to the world. On your home/startup page, Chrome automatically creates up to 10 short-cuts to the websites you visit the most. They appear in circles under the search bar. You'll see them on your tablet and phone as well.

See the example on the next page. It also shows the locations of your settings, bookmarks, and background. To change a shortcut, move your cursor over it and click the Menu icon that appears top right.

How to magically update all your devices

If only your many clocks could sync their settings when daylight savings time hits. With Chrome, it's possible. Just make one change and all your devices will update like magic.

Save your Chrome bookmarks, history, passwords, etc., so they will appear on any computer or device. To manage what you share, log in to your Google account on a trusted computer, then:

- click on the Settings icon. On a Mac, you'll need to click on the three vertical dots in the upper right, then click on **Settings**.

- under People, click **Sync**.

- click the on/off icons for each feature you want to sync.

You can also manage these settings from the Settings menu in Chrome on mobile devices.

Security alert — don't turn on Sync when you're using someone else's computer or mobile device. If you sync to the device, you'll be leaving behind passwords, browsing history and other data. If you do want to share bookmarks, be sure to turn off other features in the Sync settings.

Want to import your bookmarks? It's easy as pie

Do you already have a collection of, say, recipe websites that you've bookmarked on another browser? No problem. Importing them to Chrome is a piece of cake.

- Click on the Menu icon.

- In the tab that appears, choose **Bookmarks**.

- In the expanded tab, click **Import Bookmarks and Settings**.

- Choose the browser (Firefox, Chrome, Edge) to import from.

- Make your choices and hit **Import**.

And now you're cooking.

Tabs — easy ways to organize your windows

If you're like most people, you end up with a ton of windows open on your desktop every time you sit down at your computer. And you get tired of going from one to another searching for something you know is open somewhere.

So use tabs. As with other browsers, Chrome lets you set up work spaces in tabs and offers keyboard shortcuts to make tab browsing easy. All you have to do is click the plus sign next to the row of tabs at the top of your browser, and another tab will appear. Or use one of the shortcuts shown below.

Now when you want to find that recipe you opened 10 minutes ago you simply glance through your tabs instead of opening countless windows. And remember this trick — you can drag a tab out into its own window any time you want.

On Windows, use the following keyboard shortcuts to browse like a pro. On a Mac, substitute the Cmd key for Ctrl.

Action	Shortcut
Open a new window	Ctrl+n
Open a new tab, and jump to it	Ctrl+t
Reopen the last closed tab, and jump to it	Ctrl+Shift+t
Jump to the next open tab	Ctrl+Tab
Jump to the previous tab	Ctrl+Shift+Tab
Jump to a specific tab	Ctrl+1 through Ctrl+9
Close current tab	Ctrl+w
Close current window	Ctrl+Shift+w

Make Chrome's hidden features work for you

Ever feel like you're being watched? On the internet, you are, and that can be good and bad.

Your browsing history works for you. Your browser records every page you visit. With Chrome, if Sync is turned on, that includes activity on your phone and/or tablets as well.

To access your history, click the Settings icon and then in the drop-down menu, click **History**. Your History page lets you search and view where you've been, making it easy to find that funny article or useful video you saw last week.

Cover your tracks to stay safe. It's a good idea to delete your Google search history every once in a while before the information is used without your permission. That will help keep your computer secure.

Browsers record more than just pages you visit. They also collect cookies, which are small files that record data about your visits to websites, as well as passwords and other things.

To clear your history in Chrome, go to your History page, and click **Clear browser data**. Then you can choose whether to erase browsing history, cookies, and images your browser stores. This is also handy if you use a shared family computer to do your Christmas shopping and want the gifts to be surprises.

Don't get buried in bookmarks. If you get into the habit of bookmarking every cool web page you come across, pretty soon you have piles of bookmarks to sort through, and you won't be able to find anything. Your browser's Bookmarks manager is the place to fix this problem.

On the Settings drop-down menu, select **Bookmarks**, then **Bookmarks manager**. This tool lets you drag items to rearrange them, rename bookmarks, and open new folders. To edit, click the three vertical dots to the right of the bookmark. To add a new bookmark or folder, right-click the space between the bookmarks and folders.

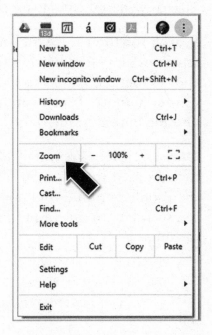

Control your view and give your eyes a rest. Tired of having to use reading glasses and a magnifying glass to read tiny fonts on web pages? Well, take control. Click open Chrome's Settings menu. Halfway down you have the option to zoom in (+) and out (-), as well as go full-screen, which hides the bookmarks and address bars. (See the graphic on the previous page.) And remember, to exit full screen with Chrome, you hit F11 instead of Esc, as you do in other software.

Want an even easier way to control your screen? Simply click Ctrl + or Cmd + to enlarge it. To make the page smaller, use the same keys with the minus sign (-). This shortcut will work in all browsers.

Add the power of Chrome extensions

Internet pop-up ads can be a pain. But popping open a calculator, dictionary, or other handy tool right in your browser? That's a huge plus. Chrome extensions are the answer to both.

Let Google extensions work their magic. You can easily install ad-blockers and all sorts of tools by visiting the Chrome web store at *chrome.google.com/webstore*. Here you will find thousands of extensions as well as themes that personalize your browser even more.

Search for the tools you want. Go to the search bar, top left, and type in what you're looking for. You'll be presented with top choices, but check for the **More extensions** button, top right, to view even more. When you find one you like, click the **Add to Chrome** button to the right.

Once extensions are installed, you can open them by clicking on their icons at the top right of your Chrome browser, just left of the Profile button. From pop-up blockers to drawing tools, you can spend more time exploring Chrome extensions than you do the internet.

Go incognito when searching the web

If you're worried about internet privacy, you should be. Remember, when you use Chrome or most free Google software, you can't expect total privacy. This is true of other web browsers as well.

Cool solution gives you peace of mind. As with other browsers, you can use private windows in Chrome. Google calls them incognito windows. Just hop up to the Settings icon and choose **New incognito window**, or use the keyboard shortcut Ctrl+Shift+n (Windows) or Cmd+Shift+n (Mac).

Good way to protect your information. These hidden search windows keep your data safe because they don't save your browsing history, cookies and website data, and any information you enter in forms. For example, if you're using someone else's computer for online banking, private windows add a layer of protection against passwords and user data being automatically stored.

They're also super handy when you're gift shopping. If you do a regular search for flowers or jewelry, that search can pull up ads for these items on your computer. When you're incognito, Chrome won't save your browsing history or cookies, so advertisers can't ruin the surprise.

You still don't have total privacy. As Chrome's incognito windows inform you when they open, you're not completely invisible. Your activity may still be visible to websites you visit, your employer or school, and your internet service provider.

Search smarter, better, and faster with Google

Google more effectively — how to find exactly what you're looking for

Getting a product name into the dictionary is the Holy Grail in the tech world. Most famous is the verb google, which entered Merriam-Webster's in 2006. (As a verb, you can lowercase the word, by the way.)

Google has dominated the search market for decades, and for good reason. It has indexed more pages, offers the most-relevant results, and has led other search engines in adding features — not to mention dealing well with user typos and misspellings.

Google Search also offers tricks and tools that instantly turn anyone into a professional researcher.

Search by category to narrow your results. Search the internet for the types of results you want by choosing different search categories. Google has led the way in promoting and enhancing these. The company currently offers nine categories, compared with Bing's six.

- All
- News
- Flights
- Image
- Shopping
- Finance
- Videos
- Books
- Personal

256

Mix and match to expand your search. Just because you're looking to buy something doesn't mean you have to search only in Google Shopping. Try also searching for items in Google Images, which will return way more images per page. Many will link you to Amazon, eBay, Walmart, or other retailers.

Likewise, if you're looking for a recipe, try an image search instead of an internet (All) search. You'll find hundreds of images of the food or dish, many of which lead to recipes.

Search engines used to brag about how many millions of web pages they indexed. Google has stopped doing that, but its most recent report said it indexed 130 trillion web pages. That's a lot of reading!

Take advantage of Google's suggestions. Google moves categories around and puts tools where you need them. If you do an **All** search, the results page will come with the categories most likely to help you.

Search on something that sounds like a restaurant name, say, Joe's Seafood, and **Maps** will be the first category across the top of your results page. Meanwhile, search on winter coat, and **Shopping** will come first. And if you google George Washington, **Images** is the first category shown, followed by **Books**, **News**, **Videos**, and **More**, all the things Google thinks you'll most want to see.

Google	george washington		🎤 🔍
All	Images	Books	News	Videos	More	Settings	Tools

About 871,000,000 results (0.87 seconds)

Maps

Shopping

George Washington - Wikipedia
https://en.wikipedia.org/wiki/George_Washington
Flights
George Washington was one of the Founding Fathers of Finance ...tes of America and served as the nation's first president (1789–1797). In the American ... Personal
Vice President: John Adams   Rest...... ....shington Family Tomb, Mount ...
Years of service: 1752–58 (British Militia); 177...   **Commands**: Virginia Colony's regiment; Conti...

Hit the jackpot with these handy search tricks

You don't need to go to Vegas to hit the jackpot. Google offers a treasure trove of search tips that will enrich your internet experience.

Use quotation marks (" ") for exact phrases. Let's say you want to find examples of how the phrase "hit the jackpot" is used. Search on the phrase in Google News without quotes, and you'll get many examples that contain just jackpot. But add the quote marks and your results will have the exact phrase.

Use the minus sign (-) to exclude a word. For example, if you want to learn about pumas, or cougars, a search on puma will teach you more about Pumas, the shoes. But try "puma -shoes," and many of the footwear results will disappear. You can also search on "puma cat."

Use an asterisk (*) for an unknown or variable word. This is useful if you're trying to remember a song lyric, such as the opening line of "Summertime." Type "the * is easy" and you'll see the lyric, "the living is easy," as well as other examples, such as "the first step is easy," and "predicting the future is easy."

Use "site" to search within a website. You hear from a friend that flaxseed helps fight cholesterol and is a tasty ingredient in many foods. So you go to your favorite recipe website and search within it — "site:allrecipes.com flax." The results will include web pages, videos, and images from the website.

Use "dictionary" to get instant definitions. How often have you come across words or phrases that make you ask, "Is that correct?" With Google Search and Chrome, definitions have never been easier.

Imagine you see the phrase "hit the jackpot" and wonder if it's used correctly. Type Ctrl+n or Cmd+n, then "hit the jackpot definition" and you'll see instantly a full definition (1. win a jackpot and 2. have great success) and links to the phrase in popular online dictionaries.

Stop to have some fun. Google has always had a sense of humor. Search Pacman and the top result is a playable Pacman game. It's known as a Google doodle, which is a type of art shown on the Google home page. Do an Image search on Atari Breakout, and the first result turns all the results into a game of Breakout.

Check out more Google doodles. Browse the Google doodle page (*google.com/doodles*) and see all the artwork the search giant has put on its search pages over the years.

Find old friends anywhere in the country

Are you looking for an old friend from school or that fun boss you used to work for? Google is a good place to start. Type in a person's name — in quotes — and search. Then begin to narrow your search. Add the city the person might live in or the name of the school or company.

Numerous sites collect information on people, including addresses, phone numbers, and email addresses. Your Google search will likely include results from reputable sites like Facebook, LinkedIn, Twitter, and Spokeo. Some of the information is free, although several sites that come up may charge for help.

You can also try an image search. You just have to hope your old friend hasn't changed too much.

---

11 amazing things Google can help you do every day

Google isn't just for searching the web. It wants to be your go-to tool for everything. Here are some fun things you can do with Google that you never suspected.

Make math easy. Need a calculator? Google can help out. Click Ctrl+n or Cmd+n to open a new window and search on an equation, for example, 9 * 9 (with spaces). That returns an answer and a calculator to go with it.

Decipher the metric system. Running a 5K and trying to figure out how far that is? Do a search on "5 kilometers to miles." You'll find out you're running 3.1 miles. And if you want to check out the 10K, the handy conversion calculator is right there.

Convert currencies. If you're traveling abroad — Japan, for example — and need to understand prices, simply search on dollars to yen. You can also enter an amount, like 500 yen to dollars. You'll get exchange rates and a currency-conversion calculator.

Check the market. Get stock prices and charts by simply searching on a stock ticker. For instance, search on AAPL and get market prices and charts for Apple. You can also type just a company name with "stock price."

> Google doesn't just lead in the internet search market. It dominates. Google enjoys 73 percent of the global search market. Its closest competitors, Yahoo and Bing, hold only 7.91 percent and 3.9 percent.

Calculate tips like a pro. Tired of figuring out tips in your head? Just type the bill amount like this: "tip $34.80." Don't forget the dollar sign. This is especially helpful when you're splitting the tip. A calculator figures up the tip and allows you to customize according to the amount of the bill, tip percentage, and number of people.

Watch the weather. When you travel, you have to know what to pack. Type "weather" and a place name and you'll get detailed information on how hot or cold it is and whether you need to bring an umbrella.

Keep up with flights. Search on a flight number such as UA100 to get instant flight status. You'll also get links to websites where you can watch the flight's progress via radar. You'll be amazed at just how many planes are in the air at any one time.

Set a timer. Just tell Google how much time you need. Your search will look something like "10 minute timer." If it doesn't kick off automatically, select **Start** to begin the visual countdown. An alarm sounds when time runs out. You can stop, reset, and even make it full-screen.

Learn how to habla español. Search something like "translate how are you to Spanish." You have options such as translate by voice, listen, and swap languages as well as a choice of 90 languages. Or you can go straight to *translate.google.com*.

Track your packages. Never lose a package again. Enter your tracking number, click **Search**, and see exactly where that store item is. Whether it's en route or hanging out at the post office, you'll know when to expect it.

Name that tune. If you can't remember the words to your favorite songs, just search on the song name and "lyrics." It's perfect for karaoke.

The magic of Images — when a picture is worth 1,000 words

Have you ever searched online for a hotel and been impressed by pictures of the huge room and amazing swimming pool? Then you got there and discovered it wasn't nearly as beautiful as it looked? Next time, do a quick image search on Google, and you'll spare yourself the disappointment.

Google Images is useful for more than just finding pretty pictures. You can use it for shopping, research — and, yes, checking out a hotel before booking. Here's how to get the most out of this handy feature.

Use Google Images' suggestions. When you do an image search, the results come with related or suggested searches across the top. For example, an **Images** search on New York will pull up suggestions including Times Square, Manhattan, Central Park, and Christmas.

Take advantage of Images search tools. Search for images by size, color, usage rights, type, and time. These options appear above results once you do an initial search. (You may have to click on **Tools** first.)

You can choose sizes ranging from icons to huge. The **Color** tool lets you pick a predominant color. **Usage rights** labels show you images you can reuse for free and even edit. And with **Type**, you can search for Face, Photo, Clip art, Line drawing, and Animated.

Easily save pictures to your computer. Click on images that interest you. When a larger version appears, right-click, then click on **Save image as** to make a copy on your computer. But first, check out the related images to the right to see if you like any of those better.

Find diagrams and more. You can find a lot more than just photos and clipart in image searches. Let's say you're buying new living room furniture. A search on "living room furniture" will show all kinds, but not different ways to arrange it. But add the word "diagram" and you'll get a ton of ideas on how to set up your new furniture.

Remember — maps are images too. If you're traveling to Boston on vacation, you'll probably want a sightseeing map. Instead of searching scores of tourist websites to find a good one, do an image search. A search on "Boston tourist sights" will give you mostly photos, but add the word "map" and you'll get hundreds of Boston maps.

Use a picture to track down similar ones. Most people do a search by typing key words into the search bar. You can also speak your words by using the microphone option on the right side of the bar.

Google Images offers you a third way to search — by image. Next to the microphone, you'll see a camera icon. Use this to upload an image from your computer and search for similar ones.

Have a picture of a sweater you love, but don't know what store it's from? Google will show you comparable pictures until you find the right one. Want to identify a strange plant that's growing in your yard? Upload a picture, and Google will clear up the confusion in no time.

Get all the news you want — for free

The internet gives you so many news sources, it's hard to know where to begin. With Google News, you can go beyond a standard news search and get stories from everywhere, tailored to your interests. On your computer, go to *news.google.com*, and download Google's free news apps for your phone and tablet.

Get to know how it works. You'll see the main menu in the left panel. It arranges content from everywhere and presents it like a traditional newspaper. You can browse topics of

Google Finance offers information on stocks and markets alongside market news. Planning to buy stock? It's a good place to start finding financial and other data on publicly traded companies. But it lacks the wealth of analyst reports and research you can get on trading websites like eTrade.

interest, such as business, technology, sports, and entertainment. Find stories presented "for you," and check your favorites and saved searches.

Share and save favorite stories. Move your cursor over a headline, and underneath you'll see icons allowing you to share the story, save it for later in your favorites, view full coverage, and go to the website that published it.

Save topics and searches you want to view later. Save your searches by clicking **Save** to the right of the search results. Then you're one click away from getting the latest on the topic in **Saved searches** on the left panel.

Read the news anywhere with the mobile app. At the core of the Google News mobile app are four categories along the screen's bottom — **For You, Headlines, Favorite,** and **Newsstand.** The last one lets you choose the news sources you prefer by tapping the stars to the right.

The layout and features of the mobile app depend on the phone or tablet. Google has been making changes to its news apps and news website in recent years. But for the most part, it's easy to learn your way around.

Surprising way Google can help you stay healthier

Let's say you're trying to decide between pizza and a bacon cheeseburger for dinner, and you want to know which is healthier. Or less unhealthy, anyway. Why not google it?

Compare nutrition and ingredients. Use "vs" to compare nutrition, calories and even taste. Results will include quick answers, related questions, and links to more information.

For instance, a standard search on "rice vs quinoa" and "hamburger vs pizza" will call up calorie and fat comparisons. Not surprisingly, a search on "Big Mac vs Whopper" may return a review focused more on which tastes better rather than which is healthier.

Get exact information on nutrition. Thirsty for a nice cold glass of lemonade? If you're worried about all the sugar, search on "How many calories are in lemonade" to help you make a decision. You can choose the type of lemonade and the serving size that meets your requirements.

On the right side of the window, you'll see a host of nutritional facts along with a glass of lemonade that is sure to make you thirstier. Of course, the calorie and nutritional info may quench your thirst faster than the drink does.

Secret to keeping your browsing safe

You may not know it, but when you use the Google search engine, you've got someone watching your back. In a good way.

Each week, Google's Safe Browsing technology finds and blacklists thousands of websites that contain malware. The system keeps you safe by issuing warnings when you try to visit malicious sites. It also alerts webmasters if their sites have problems.

This feature is part of the Google Chrome, Mozilla Firefox, and Apple Safari browsers as well as some others. But Google can't stay on top of everything. That's why you should still use additional security software to protect your computer.

2 great reasons to go armchair shopping with Google

Whether you're searching for shoes or a flight to the Caribbean, Google can help you out. Sit back in your chair, log on to your computer, and enjoy the ease and convenience of online shopping.

Search every market with Google Shopping. You need a winter coat so you spend hours looking through all your favorite store sites to find the best deal. Why go from site to site when you can view them all together at once?

A Google search on "winter coat" will bring you results from LL Bean, Macy's, Nordstrom, REI, and other major retailers, and sometimes compare prices at multiple stores.

Check out the left-hand panel on the results page. It will let you search on price, color, brand, material, size and seller. What more could you ask for?

Google Flights solves your travel problems. The first headache of taking a long journey is booking flights. You want to be an expert traveler so you spend hours poring over airline and travel websites to find the best deals.

Google Flights solves that problem. Compare routes, prices, airlines and times all from one place. With built-in maps, Flights makes the rough journey of buying plane tickets more like armchair travel.

The power of Gmail
Surprising hints and hacks you need to know

Uncomplicate your life — let Gmail handle all your email

So you changed your email address once or twice, and maybe set an account for work. Then your internet provider gave you an address that might have important messages. Pretty soon, checking your email means logging on to AOL, Yahoo Mail, Comcast, and Outlook.

One solution is to use a complicated email "client" that can bring you mail from different accounts in one place. But you may have to take a college course to learn how to. A far easier fix is to use Gmail. It lets you receive all your mail together and check it on any device, and you don't have to pass Computer Science 101 with a C or better first.

Keep using your old addresses right in Gmail. Google doesn't have a "me only" mentality. Gmail can serve as an email program for

> Don't lose mail. If you move an old email address into Gmail, check your Gmail Spam folder regularly, since Gmail's spam filter is more aggressive than those of other email services. Also check different Gmail categories to make sure nothing gets lost.

multiple email accounts. The messages come in right alongside your Gmail.

To add email addresses, start by opening Gmail's settings. Click the gear icon on the right above your emails, and choose **Settings**.

Now the first thing many people do when they first see Gmail's settings is panic. Don't do that. There's a lot of information, because it's a powerful program, but most settings have a friendly **Learn more** link that pulls up easy instructions.

How to pull in email from other addresses. Along the top of the settings page is a line of tabs such as **General, Labels, Inbox**, etc.

1. Choose **Accounts and Import**.

2. Halfway down the page, find **Check mail from other accounts**.

3. Click on **Add a mail account**.

4. Type in the email address and click on **Next**.

5. Choose **Link accounts with Gmailify** to get the most features.

6. Type in the email account's password if asked.

7. Agree to giving Gmail access if asked.

That's all there is to it. Now you can manage your other email account(s) from Gmail.

Send email as another address. When you send messages from Gmail, they can be labeled as coming from your Gmail address or other addresses.

1. Choose **Accounts and Imports** from the Settings menu.

2. Find **Send mail as**.

3. Click **Add another email address**.

4. Type in the address.

5. In the next box, choose **Send through Gmail**.

6. Here, Gmail wants to send a verification email to the address you're adding. Click **Send verification**.

7. Open the verification message in the other account, and type the Confirmation code into the Gmail box.

Now when sending a new message from Gmail, you'll be able to choose to send it from different addresses. Open a new message, put your cursor next to **To**, and a down arrow will appear underneath offering a choice of addresses.

4 creative ways to make the program your own

If you spend a lot of time reading email, you might as well decorate your email program the way you like it. You can also create a custom signature that will appear at the bottom of your emails.

Pick out a theme. Go to the gear icon, top right. In the drop-down menu you'll be able to choose a theme and background photo, either one of Google's or one uploaded from your computer. You can also configure your Inbox.

> When Gmail came along in 2004, you could join by invitation only. Hotmail and Yahoo Mail were the leading email services then. Fourteen years later, Google boasted 1.5 billion Gmail accounts. That's equal to 4.5 email addresses for every person in the United States!

Create an email signature. Do you want to add contact information, a logo, or maybe a slogan at the bottom of each email? Click the gear icon, and then choose **Settings**. In the **General** tab, scroll down to **Signature**. Here you'll find a text box where you can type and format your signature, and even add images.

Choose your email font. Also in the **General** tab, you can choose a typeface for your email as well as type color.

Let people know you're away. The first thing you get to enjoy when going on vacation is setting up an auto response to all messages that will arrive while you're away.

Look for **Vacation responder** at the bottom of the **General** tab. There, you can type the beginning and end date as well as a custom message, like "I'm out of the office and relaxing on the beach until Monday."

The email address you'll never have to change

Changing your email address is a huge hassle, but many email services have gone out of business, been acquired, or stopped offering decent support. Today, AOL, Hotmail, even Yahoo mail can be filled with ads and other distractions.

But Gmail is powerful and will be around for a long time. Given Google's size and range of products, a Gmail address is one you'll be able to use forever.

Check email from everywhere — instantly

You've come a long way from having to dial up your internet service to check email when you got home each evening. Nowadays you can read email on your smartwatch while sitting on a beach watching Dick Tracy cartoons.

Check and send from any device. One great feature of Gmail and other web-based email is that you can use it on any computer or device. If you have company email or use an email program at home, getting it on your phone can be difficult. That's why many businesses are turning to Gmail.

Choose the app or the website. You'll get the best mobile Gmail experience by downloading the free Gmail app on your phone or tablet. Just go to the App Store or Play Store to get it.

Get your email on other people's devices. If you want to check your email on someone else's device, you can do it without the app. Just open a browser and go to *mail.google.com* to log in.

Easily find important emails

Your daily email probably includes spam, promotions, social media alerts, e-bills, and reminders that you'll get a discount if you "jump to Grubhub." You find yourself really wishing you could just see the important stuff. You can. Save yourself from getting lost in piles of email with Gmail's organizing features.

Avoid email overload. Save time sorting through mounds of mail with Gmail's Priority Inbox. This feature in Gmail finds messages that are important to you, based on the emails you read and reply to. These important messages are labeled with a yellow arrow on the left and copied into your Important Inbox.

Narrow down your message search. Gmail tries to sort your email for you into categories to help you find messages more easily.

Under the mailboxes in the left-hand panel you'll see Categories, with labels like Social, Updates, and Promotions. Do a quick check there to find similar messages grouped together.

Master the power of Gmail's advanced features

Gmail might seem complex, but so does that fancy new microwave oven your neighbor bought. A bit of complexity means a lot of power. One of Gmail's advanced features includes labels. Put these labeling tricks to work to make your email life even easier.

Use labels instead of folders for better organization. For years you've organized email in folders. With Gmail you can use labels instead. Labels are similar to folders but with a key advantage — you can apply multiple labels to one email. With labels, you can:

- search mail by labels.

- open labels in the left panel.

- put labels inside of labels (sub-labels).

- have Gmail add labels automatically to incoming email.

Improve sorting with your own labels. Label messages anything you want — "Important," "Waste of time," even "I hate e-bills." Here's how.

1. Click the gear icon, top right.

2. Select **Settings**.

3. Click the **Labels** tab.

4. Scroll down to **Labels** and click **Create new label**.

5. Name your label and check **Nest label under** if you want it to be under another label.

6. Click on **Create**.

You can also create labels from inside an email. Click the Labels icon along the top. Choose **Create new label**.

Apply labels to any email. To add labels to an email, simply take the following steps.

1. Open your Inbox.

2. Check the boxes to the left of email you want to label.

3. Click the Labels icon along the top.

4. Check the boxes for the labels you want to add.

5. Click **Apply** at the bottom of the drop-down menu.

Make it even simpler with colors. Feeling artistic? Organize your email world with colors.

1. Put your cursor over a label in the left-hand panel.

2. Click the more icon (three vertical dots) to its right.

3. In the drop-down menu that appears, select **Label color** and make your selections for text and background colors.

4. Click **Apply**.

Easily move email around. Use your labels in the left-hand panel the same way you use folders — just drag email into them.

Filter your incoming email. You can easily filter incoming email, making Gmail automatically label it and more. Let's say you want to label all messages from your Aunt Betty.

> Remember, you can manage, delete, hide, show, and edit labels and filters in Gmail's settings.

1. Click the down arrow on the right of the Gmail search bar.

2. Enter Aunt Betty's address in the **To** field.

3. Click **Create filter**.

4. In the new menu, check the box to the left of **Apply the label**.

5. On the right of **Apply the label**, choose a label for your Aunt Betty.

6. Click **Create filter**.

┌─ **Timesaving tricks you need to know** ─────────────

Want to make an important message stand out so you can find it later? You can mark it as important by clicking the star next to it in the Inbox, or at the top side in an open email.

And wouldn't it be nice to instantly save or delete a message? Gmail lets you do that, too. In your Inbox, just move your cursor over an email. On the right you'll see icons allowing you to archive the message, delete it, mark it as read, or "snooze" it, which will save it for later.

Super handy tools you can use right in Gmail

Who'd have thought you could make a phone call from your email program? Or take notes, or automatically put an event in your calendar? Surprise — Gmail lets you do all these things, plus a host of others.

Get organized in a snap. Your email on any given day might include an invitation to lunch, a concert recommendation, or a promotion for a big sale at your favorite store. That makes your own calendar a great tool to have on hand.

On a computer, in Gmail's right-hand panel toward the top, are icons for your Google Calendar, Keep (notes), and Tasks (to-do lists). Click any one of them to expand the panel. (See graphic.)

- Calendar shows your saved events and other data right in Gmail.

- Click the Keep icon and then **Take a note** to create a new note.

- Click the Tasks icon and add tasks to create your own to-do list.

Extend your suite of Gmail tools. Below the tasks icon is a plus sign. Click this to explore the many extensions available for Gmail. Here you'll find a host of tools for business, education, productivity, and more. For example, get professional templates for your email, promotions, invitations, greeting cards, and other uses.

Use your email to make a phone call. If you can check your email on your phone, shouldn't you be able to make a phone call from your email? Gmail lets you. At the very bottom of Gmail's left-hand panel are icons for using Google's Hangouts social media site, along with one that allows you to make phone calls.

Of course you'll need to have a microphone set up. Better yet, get a webcam if you don't have one. Google software gives you opportunities to make video calls as well.

Google Drive
Sync, store, and share your files in the cloud

Use the ultimate backup — Google's cloud service

How many times have you lost photos, videos, or other files because of a hard drive failure or a mistaken move of the mouse? Well, you'll be on cloud nine with Google Drive, which will make sure that never happens again.

"The cloud" sounds like some mystical, magical technology for businesses, but in fact it's basically just a server (a computer and storage) that is not sitting in your home or office.

As soon as you open a Google account, you already have Drive, Google's cloud service. Just go to *drive.google.com.* Log in and in the left-hand panel you'll find a list of folders on your Drive, similar to the left panel in Windows Explorer (or File Explorer) and Gmail. (See the graphic on the next page for a view of Drive's start page.)

> Here's a slick trick. Open a Gmail message with an attachment (for example, a Word doc), move your cursor over the attachment icon, and you'll get an option to save it directly to Drive. You can also edit or download it.

Enjoy lots of free storage. In terms of free storage, Google Drive is quite generous compared with other cloud storage services. Drive offers 15 GB of free storage, while the popular Dropbox offers only 2 GB and Microsoft's OneDrive gives you 5 GB. As with other services, Drive offers more space for a price.

Upload your files to Drive. Get that cloud nine feeling of security by backing up your files into the cloud. Google's security and backup technology makes sure nothing will ever be lost.

To get started, click the large, friendly **New** icon, top left and then **File upload** or **Folder upload**. These allow you to select items to upload from your computer. You'll get the same drop-down menu by right-clicking in the main work area (not the left or right panels).

Upload from your phone. Sharing is good. Really. Move files to Drive from your phone or tablet the same way you would share a photo with your cousin Bob. Install the Drive app on your phone, open, say, a photo, and tap its share or download icon. Drive will be one of the options.

Simply drag files into Drive. Feeling lazy? Or ambitious? A far simpler way to move files and folders onto Drive is to drag them directly from open windows on your PC to Drive in a browser.

Store any types of file. Drive is not just about dull documents and spreadsheets. Move your music, movies, and photos into the cloud as well. That includes documents, PDFs, photos, songs, and kitty videos. Drive secures them and makes them easy to use and share.

Store — and use — Office documents. Free yourself from the clutches of MS Office, and work on its files on Drive as well. For example, move a Word document onto Drive, click it to open, and you'll get a preview. At the top, you'll have the option to open and edit it in Docs, or in non-Google choices, like Zoho Writer.

G Suite software — powerful (and free!)

Remember the bad ol' days when Microsoft controlled your life with its pricey Office suite — Word, Excel, and PowerPoint? Well, Google came to the rescue with its Google apps — Docs, Sheets, and Slides — which are just as powerful and, more importantly, free.

In 2016 Google renamed this software from "Google Apps" to "G Suite," along with Gmail, Calendar, and other products. And Google Drive is what drives most of it. When you open files in Sheets and Slides, for example, they live on Drive, as does your Gmail.

This makes Google Drive a powerful workbench where you can manage, share, and open all types of files in the correct software, all from one screen. The best part? You don't have to shell out more money every time an updated version comes out.

Access your files from any device

One great thing about cloud storage is you can get at your files — and edit and share them — from any device. And Google Drive makes it all far less cloudy than competitors.

For the best experience on smartphones and tablets, download Google's Drive app from the device's app store.

If you're using someone else's phone or tablet, no app is needed. Simply open a browser, go to *drive.google.com*, sign in and do what you need in the browser.

Now you're all set. You can show people your vacation photos, listen to your favorite song, or watch the latest kitty video anywhere, even on your aunt's $40 cellphone.

Need to collaborate? Group sharing is a snap

Let's say you're planning a holiday dinner for 30 and want a few relatives to check your shopping list and add anything you've forgotten. You save the file, attach it to several emails, and then hope they all have the pricey word processor program you used. When they receive it, they'll have to open it, save it, edit it, and reattach it to emails.

You can make all this tremendously easier using Google's Drive and G Suite software.

Work together in real time. One of the features that has made Drive and other Google software so popular is the ability to share and work together on files — even at the same time. Here's how to share a file from your computer.

1. Open a browser and go to Google Drive (or Docs, Sheets, or Slides).

2. Choose a file or folder and click on the Share icon (person with +) that will appear upper right. (See graphic on next page.) You can also right-click on a file and select **Share** from the drop-down menu.

3. Type the names or email addresses of people you want to share it with.

279

4. Click the pencil icon to choose what access to give people (**Can edit**, **Can comment**, **Can view**).

5. Add a note if you'd like.

6. Click on **Send**.

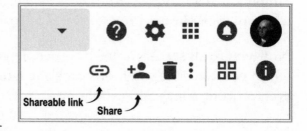

Sending from your phone is a cinch. Your daughter needs your chili recipe for a last-minute dinner party, but you're out doing errands. No problem since you have all your recipes on Google Drive. Open the app on your phone and you're ready to help her out.

1. Find the file you want to share.

2. Tap the More icon (three dots).

3. Select **Add people** or **Share**, depending on your phone. Type in the name or email address.

4. Add a note, such as "Here's my world-famous chili recipe. Enjoy!"

5. Choose what access to share (pencil icon).

6. Hit the Send icon (cute arrow, top right).

Share files with non-Google users. You can work on projects with your friends even if they don't use Google. If you type a non-Google email address and click on **Send**, you'll be offered two choices. One shares the normal way, but the person must log in to Google. But the second sends just a link to the file, so no login is required.

Easily manage your shared files. It's a little scary when you can't remember who you've shared your files with. But in Drive, files and folders are marked if shared. You'll see folders with a small share icon (a head) inside it and an icon with two heads next to the file name.

Teamwork made easy with 1 simple feature

Imagine you're working on a file with three other people, whether it's a report for work or a shopping list for your big Super Bowl party. If you email the file back and forth, you create multiple versions. In the end, someone might wind up using the wrong one.

Of course, that can be disastrous with a shopping list.

It's time to get in the driver's seat. With Drive, you all work on the same document or spreadsheet, so files don't get mixed up. What's more, you can view a file's "version history," which lists who has worked on it and when.

For example, if your shopping list is a Google Docs file, just click to open it in Docs. Then under **File**, top left, select **Version history**. You can see what changes your friends made and restore old versions if needed. This simple feature can save you a lot of time and trouble.

Create files and folders in an instant

You've uploaded lots of documents, pictures, and videos, possibly from your desktop, laptop, phone, and even tablet. You're creating more files using Google Docs, Sheets, and Slides.

For most people, things start getting messy around this point. And toggling between the Grid view and List view icons (try it, top right) doesn't clear the fog. Luckily, Google Drive is a powerful tool for organizing files as well as opening new ones.

Create folders with ease. Manage files on Drive the same way you do on a PC or Mac, sorting files into folders and subfolders.

To create a folder, just click the large **New** icon, top left, and select **Folder** from the drop-down menu. Then type in a name, whether it's "Invoices" or "Kitty Videos," click **Create**, and your folder awaits. Now you can drag and copy files into it, even from folders on your computer.

Want another easy way to create folders and files in Google Drive? Simply right-click in the work area, and make your choice from the menu that appears.

Open new files from Drive with a single click. Open new files fast, without pulling up a different window or opening other software. Click **New** and, holding your finger down, select **Docs**, and see a blank document pop open a new tab. The simplicity and speed is refreshing compared to other programs.

Get more than what meets the eye. Drive's magic **New** icon also lets you create forms, drawings, custom maps, and even websites. Click the icon and select **More** to view all your choices.

Make your files easy to find

Ever feel like you're staring at window after window of files and folders that all look alike? And realize you are? How can anyone find things like that?

Make items stand out — in color. There's always room for more color in the world, and Drive lets you add it to folders. Select any folder and right-click to get the menu.

One option in the drop-down menu is **Change color**. You might choose green for your gardening tips folder or light blue for your beach pictures to remind you of that beautiful ocean.

Give items star power. Likewise, right-click either a folder or file to add a star to the right, which will make it stand out.

Organize the way you like it. Move files and folders around either by right-clicking and selecting **Move to** or by dragging them around. Remember, you can toggle between List view and Grid view with the view icon top right.

You can also turn off the **Quick Access** preview panel along the top by clicking on the gear icon and going into **Settings.**

How to always find things. If all else fails, head to the search bar at the top of Drive. The down arrow on the right pulls up advanced search options that can help you along.

No worries — you can use Drive offline

These days, few things upset a household as much as an internet outage, even if you don't have teenagers. If you're considering using online software for work, possible outages can be a disaster.

But Google software lets you work offline. Here's how to set it up in a Chrome browser.

1. In Drive, click the gear icon and select **Settings**.

2. Next to **Offline**, click the checkbox for **Sync Google Docs, Sheets, Slides & Drawings files to this computer so that you can edit offline**.

3. Click **Done**.

To access your work offline, you'll need to install the Google Docs offline Chrome extension.

Double your peace of mind: Back up Drive files to your computer

Much as Drive has your back when it comes to securing files, you may still want to keep copies on your computer. In fact, one expert jokes that data doesn't exist if you don't have two or more copies of it.

So, yes, let Drive back up your files from the cloud and onto your computer. It may seem backward at this point, but you always want to have a copy to fall back on.

The best part is Drive will do all the backup work for you. You just need to download the program, either for Windows or Mac. In Drive, click the gear icon and choose **Get Backup and Sync**, and click **Download**. Once it's downloaded, install it as you do other software.

Here's how to back up in Windows 10. Look for these three steps in the backup program menu.

1. **Sign in.** Use your Google account.

2. **My computer.** Check the items you want Drive to automatically back up from your computer. Choose the options offered, or click **Choose folder** to make your own choices. When done, click **Next**.

3. **Google Drive.** Now you choose which items to back up from Drive to your computer. Select either **Sync everything** or **Sync only these folders** (and choose the folders you want).

Click **Start** and you're done. Drive does all the work from here, so you can kick back and relax. From now on it will automatically upload any data you put in the shared folders.

You can find your backed-up files in Windows Explorer (or File Explorer), where a Google Drive icon will appear among the folders in the left-hand panel. Return anytime to **Backup and Sync** to change your settings.

Docs, Sheets, and Slides
Free office tools for everyday tasks

Set yourself free from Office with G Suite

For many years you were forced to use — and pay a lot of money for — Microsoft Office because you had no good alternatives. But then Google came to the rescue with its Docs word processing software and now G Suite, which is Docs, Sheets, Slides, and other Google products. They let you open and edit files from Word and Office and even save new ones as Office files.

Google Docs is similar to Word, Sheets to Excel, and Slides to PowerPoint. The cost — free. Installation — none. Once you have a Google account, you're ready to go with all three. Just open a browser and head to Docs, Sheets, or Slides.

To get there, either open a file from Drive, or open it through the web.

- **Docs** — *docs.google.com*

- **Sheets** — *docs.google.com/spreadsheets*

- **Slides** — *docs.google.com/presentation*

As with other Google software, you can use Docs, Sheets, and Slides on your phone or tablet as well. Just open the device's app store and download the apps, all free. They all work together with the mobile app for Drive, and you can move and work on files seamlessly between your computer, phone, and tablet.

Convert files from Word in the blink of an eye

If you've ever had to struggle with different versions of Word, then you'll take pleasure in this step. Transferring Word and Office files to Docs takes just a simple upload.

How to move Office files to G-suite. In Google Docs, go to **File** and then **Open**, and you'll see more than the normal options. You can choose to open files from your Drive folders or upload them from your computer.

When the file opens, it's already converted. The same is true with Excel and PowerPoint files when you open them in Sheets and Slides.

Remember, you can just as easily open and convert files from Drive. Just right-click on the file, select **Open with** and then choose **Docs** for documents.

Simple way to change back to Word. If you send files, whether it's for work or volunteering at your grandkids' school, chances are the other person uses Microsoft Office. That means the document needs to be an Office or Word file.

No problem. Simply click **File** and **Download as**, and choose the format you want. You can save your file as a Word document, a PDF, a web page, and even an EPUB, which is an e-book file.

> When you're in the Google Chrome browser, keep in mind that the left-most icon on the toolbar pulls up shortcuts to your apps, including Docs, Sheets, Slides, Drive, Gmail, and more.

┌─ **Free software gives Google the edge** ──────────────

Google launched its Docs software in 2008, the first serious challenge to Microsoft Office's worldwide monopoly. One thing that made it a hit is its ability to let numerous people work on files. Up to 10 people can edit a Docs file at the same time, while 50 can edit a Sheets spreadsheet.

Office still dominates the market, but Google's success forced Microsoft to create its own online suite with the ability to share — Office 365. And while Microsoft works hard to add features, 365 is lacking in one key ingredient. Google's software is free.

Make your work look amazing with templates

Want to impress people with a spiffy newsletter, invitation, or resume? You'll find professional-quality templates at the top of the home pages of Docs, Sheets, and Slides that share a simple design. Click **Template Gallery**, top right, to see more. They include

- recipes, newsletters, resumes, and brochures in Docs.

- to-do lists, budgets, schedules, and team rosters in Sheets.

- presentations, photo albums, wedding invitations, and recipe books in Slides.

Let say you're planning to share a family recipe with friends, and you want to give it a true cookbook appearance. In Docs, choose a template that has an image and replace the image with a picture of the delicious family dish.

After opening the template, right-click the image and select **Replace image**. From there you can upload one from your computer or your Drive (or other options). Right-clicking also gives you the option to crop the image and edit its colors and brightness (click **Image options**).

As for text, just type in your own, replacing what's there, or copy text from another document and paste it in place. Next, change the text the way you like it. Select sections of text and enlarge the font, tweak the color, and change what you want in the columns and formatting the template comes with.

When you're done, you'll have a professional-looking recipe that you'll be proud to pass around.

Enhance your docs with easy-to-add images

A picture is worth a thousand words, but is it worth the clicks needed to download it, save it, find it on your computer, and then insert it into your document? You won't have that hassle with Docs.

No-sweat way to insert images. On a computer, open your document, click **Insert** and select **Image**, the top choice. You'll be able to get images from your computer, Google Drive, a camera, or a web address. Simple but powerful.

Insert a picture directly from the web. You can thank Google's tech team for allowing you to pull pictures right off the internet. They focused some of their efforts on making image insert in Google Docs a breeze to work with.

Just click **Insert**, select **Image**, and then **Search the web**. A new panel opens on the right with a search bar at the top and space for results underneath.

Do a search, and it's two clicks from a web page to your document — one click on an image result and one on **Insert** (at the bottom of the panel). Presto — the picture pops directly from a web page into your work.

Time to use your editing skills. Select an image you've inserted, and you're ready to resize it by dragging the corners. Underneath a selected image, you can choose **Wrap text**, which makes the words go around the image, or **Break text**, which divides text above and below the image.

Right-click for more options, to put the most useful tools at your fingertips. Literally.

Take the fear out of tables

Tables are a great way to explain something graphically without using a lot of text. But they can be a pain in the neck to create and use. In Docs, the simplicity of using tables makes you wonder why they are so complicated in other software.

To add a table to your document, click **Insert** and select **Table**. Instead of dealing with the complex drop-down menu you get in Word, you get just a simple grid. Move your mouse around the grid to choose the number of rows and columns you want. Click and your table is underway.

Once you create a table, you can resize its rows and columns right on the page by dragging its lines. Manage border lines by moving your cursor over the table cells and clicking the down arrow that will appear.

> With Google Docs, you'll never have to click **Save** again. That's right, once you've typed or made a change, your work is automatically saved. Since files live in the cloud, even if you have a power outage, you won't have to worry that your work is lost.

Find other essential functions and tools (**Add column, Delete row,** etc.) by right-clicking on the table. Easy as pie.

Bring documents to life with drawings, charts, and graphs

There's nothing like graphics when you're presenting sales figures or youth baseball statistics. Use Docs to insert colorful pie charts and line-and-bar graphs. And scare away remaining critics by adding textbook-quality math equations to back up your case. Just click **Insert** and you can add:

- drawings from Docs' built-in drawing tool. Simple but useful.

- charts and graphs, including bar, column, line, and pie charts.

- links to web pages.

- bookmarks — shortcuts to spots in a document.

- table of contents through auto-generated tables.

3 ways to make teamwork even more terrific

Google Drive makes it easy to share files when you work in Docs, Sheets, and Slides. It's even easier — and livelier — if you use these three features.

Chat with your team while working. When you work with people on a file at the same time, their images, along with a **Show chat** icon, appear at the top of the screen, next to the **Share** button. Click the icon to chat, so you can discuss edits — or the weather — while you work.

Make or suggest changes in real time. Directly under the **Share** button is a pencil icon that allows you to edit or suggest changes.

To the left of the **Share** button is a comment icon that allows you to view the file's comment history.

Easily keep track of revisions. To the left of the **Share** button and chat icon is a link to your file's version history. Depending on what you did last, it will read **See new changes** or **All changes saved**. Click the link to see who edited a document and when, and go back to older versions if needed.

Sheets — your data solution

So your New Year's resolution is to start budgeting your money and reining in spending. Put your computer to work. If you record expenses in a spreadsheet and not a document, you can sort them in different ways — by date, most expensive to least, by category (groceries, eating out, utilities, etc.), and other factors.

How to create a spreadsheet. It's easier than you think. Go to the Sheets home page (*docs.google.com/spreadsheets*) or Google Drive. In Sheets, click a template or the **Blank** icon with a large plus sign in the middle. You're ready to go.

Import work from a different program. Convert spreadsheets from Excel or other programs as easily as you do documents in Docs. In Drive, click **New** and then **File upload**. Choose existing spreadsheets (with extensions including .xls, .xlsx and .xlt) from your computer. Once a file is in Drive, right-click the file and select **Open with** and then **Google Sheets**.

Customize your data. Sheets allows you to do all the things you can in Excel, and the menus are similar to what you have in Docs and Slides.

Under **Insert**, in addition to charts, images, and drawings, you can add rows, columns, and even math. Many of these options are also available by right-clicking on cells. The added **Data** menu helps you work with data, such as sorting on a certain column, while the **Tools** menu offers advanced options.

Like other Google software, Sheets has extensions in its **Add-ons** menu. Here you'll find everything from more templates to tools for teachers.

Simple solution: Turn your device into a slideshow remote

If you've seen even a handful of slideshow presentations, then you've probably witnessed a confused presenter staring ahead, wondering what the next, or current, slide is.

Here's a great way to make sure that doesn't happen to you. If you present your slideshow on a TV that has a Google Chromecast device, you can use your tablet or phone as a remote. (Chromecast is a plug-in Bluetooth device that lets you stream content from a computer or phone to a TV.)

You'll get the best Slides remote experience on a tablet, where one pane shows the current, next, and last slides, and another shows speaker notes. Just open a slideshow in the Slides app on your device, and tap the Chromecast icon along the top (a tiny screen with waves on the bottom left).

In addition, you can find both free and paid apps that stream presentations to a PC or Mac. To see what's out there, visit your mobile device's app store.

Create a winning presentation with Slides

You may need to present a million-dollar project at work or display photos of a youth sports team at an end-of-season party. Either way, slideshows are an excellent tool. And with the ease and simplicity of Slides, you'll give your most impressive presentation yet.

Navigate easily around Slides. Docs, Sheets, and Slides share a simple design with similar menus along the top (**File**, **Edit**, **View**, etc.). This makes finding your way around easy. Slides has some icons under the menus, although you don't need a course in pictographs to understand them.

Moving PowerPoint files into Slides is the same as moving files into Docs and Sheets. Just upload files to Drive and open them.

Use ready-made slide layouts. In addition to the templates on Slide's home screen (*docs.google.com/presentation*), you can add new slides with custom layouts to a slideshow. Once a presentation is open, find the **New slide** icon (a large friendly plus sign), upper left, and click on the down arrow. Then choose slides with different column and title layouts.

Add charts, images, and videos. Since this is slideshow software, it's not surprising that the **Insert** menu has extra options. In addition to images, charts, and shapes, add videos from your Drive, a URL, or YouTube. From the **Insert** menu, you can also add diagrams, word art, and a variety of lines. (See graphic.)

View or show your presentation. Very importantly, you'll want to test your slideshow and show it when you finish. In Slides, go to the **View** menu and select **Present**. This menu also gives you different view options as well as an option to show or hide speaker notes.

Google Calendar
Fast and easy organizing on the go

Get the calendar that goes everywhere

It feels wonderful to get your life organized on calendar software — birthdays, appointments, events, vacations, all mapped out with reminders. It feels less wonderful two years later when the software is outdated or you switch phones — say, Apple to Samsung — and have to start all over. Again, Google software comes to the rescue.

Use your calendar on multiple devices. Google Calendar is an alternative you can rely on long-term, regardless of what phone or computer you use. Calendar provides a wonderful experience in a web browser (PC or Mac), and its mobile apps are just as functional on Apple and Android devices.

That's a key point for smartphone users — you can use Google Calendar on your iPhone but you won't find Apple's calendar app on either an Android phone or a PC. Apple wants to make you do everything only on Apple products, and that makes switching, if you ever decide to, even harder.

Check your calendar on someone else's device. Easily access your calendar on a friend's phone or tablet without installing the app. Simply open a browser and go to *calendar.google.com* and log in. Remember to log out when you're done.

Schedule events in a snap

Remember the old line "I'll have to check my calendar"? It was a handy one for unwanted invitations or appointments you weren't ready to commit to. These days, of course, most people carry calendars on their phones, so they can schedule events on the go.

Google Calendar's colorful, roomy design makes it a breeze to make quick appointments, whether you're in a doctor's waiting room or on the phone with your insurance agent.

How to create events. On either a computer or phone, click or tap any square on your calendar or the **Create event** icon (look for the plus sign) and you're ready to go. Here's an example of what your calendar might look like.

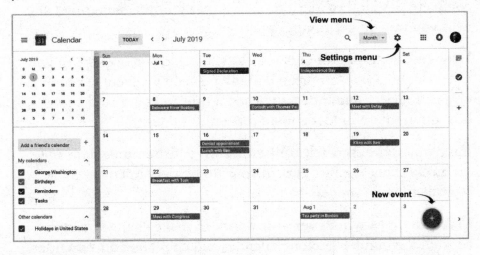

The interface is a little different by device, but it's easy to input the when, what, where, and even the how and why (in the description field). Other features on this menu allow you to:

- choose between one-time and repeat events.

- select how often events repeat.

- add video conferencing if you use Google's Hangouts.

- add guests to invite them by email.

- choose a color for your event.

Keep up to date with notifications. In the **Create event** menu, you can also set notifications to alert you on your phone, computer, and by email.

Jog your memory with reminders

It's one thing to mark a date on your calendar and another to actually remember it. That's where reminders come in. If you need to buy airline tickets later in the month, just add a reminder. It will carry over to the next day if you forget until you mark the task complete. It's kind of like a to-do list that follows you around and nags you till you get things done.

How to create personal reminders. Click on any square in your calendar and a pop-up menu will offer to add an event, a reminder, or a task. Select **Reminder**, then add a title and date, and choose how often the reminder should repeat, if it does.

Easy way to keep track of them. Turn your reminders on and off by checking the box next to your **Reminders** calendar, under **My calendars** in the left-hand panel.

Make changes whenever you want. To make changes, simply click on a reminder on your calendar and click the **Edit reminder** icon (a pencil).

If you have more than one reminder on the same day, click on the day and move your cursor over one of the reminder titles that comes up. That will make the **Edit reminder** icon appear. Click it to make your changes.

Convenience perk: Add events from everywhere

If you remember the days when you kept calendars by hand, then you'll appreciate how easy Google makes it to add events. Even if you're switching from another calendar program, you'll be surprised by what Calendar can do.

Enjoy Calendar's ability to search for events. Google has added technology to Calendar that can scan your email for events such as concerts, flights, and dinner reservations and automatically add them to your schedule.

For example, if someone shares an event with you from their Google Calendar by email, it will pop right into your calendar.

To make sure the feature is turned on, click the gear icon, top right, and select **Settings**. Then scroll down on the right until you see **Events from Gmail**. Check the box to turn it on.

Add events from around the web. Buying tickets to a concert or looking for art shows to visit? When you find them on the internet, you often have the option to add the event to a calendar.

Google Calendar is generally one of the choices — at times when calendars from Apple, Outlook, and Yahoo are not. Click the Google Calendar icon or link to add the event to your calendar.

Customize your calendar and make it your own

If you're switching to new calendar software, it can drive you crazy if it looks really different. And it may look even worse on your tiny cellphone screen.

Google has put impressive design features into its calendar that let you see more and make the best use of a screen's real estate, whether it's a monitor or phone. And your calendar will keep the same design across your different devices.

Choose your view. In a browser or on a smartphone app, Calendar lets you choose between views (day, week, month, year) with helpful design features that let you see more. For instance, the month view shows not just the limited four weeks of older software but six weeks, in six rows going down the page. In addition:

- in a browser, you can toggle open the left-hand menu panel that includes a mini-month view at the top. Toggle it off to see more of your calendar.

- you can choose to show weekends or hide them for more weekday space.

- you can decide whether to show declined events.

Make your events colorful. You can choose a color for an event when you create it in the **Create event** menu. Or right-click on an event you already created, and a pop-up menu will let you change the color.

This can be useful. You might choose red for important events like bills that must be paid, orange for work, and blue for family events. You'll know instantly which group each event is part of.

Simplify your life — put all your calendars together

If you like to put a lot of things on your calendar — birthdays, holidays, or days like National Coffee Day — it can become crowded pretty fast. That makes it hard to read. But Google lets you create multiple calendars you can turn on and off, so you see only the types of events you want.

Put calendars on top of calendars. In a browser, click the Main menu icon (three horizontal lines), top left, to open the menu in a left-hand panel. There you'll find special calendars for such things as birthdays and holidays.

You can turn these on and off by checking the box next to them. Some menu functions are also available on Calendar mobile apps, depending on your device.

Get a little help with birthdays. The Calendar app gathers dates of birth from your Google contacts where possible and lists them. This is great for friends, although it can be a little strange when the birthday of someone you don't know well pops up.

Never an excuse to forget holidays. As with your birthdays calendar, Google adds a calendar listing major U.S. holidays. Turn this calendar on when you need a reminder of the date Easter or Thanksgiving falls on. Or turn it off to make your own calendar easier to read.

Add calendars for sports and more. In the left-hand panel just above **My calendars**, you'll find an add calendar icon (plus sign). Its drop-down menu will let you create a new calendar, import a calendar, or add a calendar of interest, such as sports or holidays in different countries.

Are you a diehard fan of the Atlanta Falcons or the New England Patriots? Well, of course you need to know the dates of all their events. Simply add the calendar of your favorite team and never miss another game.

Calendar makes teamwork a walk in the park

Let's say you're helping organize a high school reunion. You hope to bring together hundreds of people who haven't seen each other in years and are scattered around the state. It would be great just to create a schedule in Word and send it out. But your reunion's six months away and schedules keep changing.

Solution — set up your events on the calendar that everyone can view on any device.

6 simple steps to sharing a calendar. Quickly make your calendar public to anyone on the web.

1. Click the gear icon and choose **Settings**.

2. On the left, click on the calendar you want to share.

3. On the right, scroll down to **Access permissions**.

4. Check the **Make available to public** box.

5. Click **Get shareable link**, bottom right, and copy the link that comes up.

6. Paste the link into an email to share it.

Now people will be able to view the calendar in a web browser. Once it's set up, you can do a lot more than schedule the reunion. You can invite guests, check RSVPs, reserve rooms and resources, check guest attendance, and more.

Share calendars only with certain people. Of course, you might not want to make a calendar available to the world. Scroll down a bit farther on the right to **Share with specific people**. Click **Add people** and type in their names or email addresses. Underneath you can choose what permissions to give them.

Set up and share team calendars. In the office, in a club, or just among a group of friends, getting everyone to use Google Calendar has amazing benefits.

If you need to work on a team project, here's an easy way to get everyone on the same page. Create and share a calendar that a group of people can access and even make changes to if needed. Remember, since Google Calendar works on any device, it doesn't matter what phone or device people use.

Discover the world with Google Maps

Use the Map app that goes everywhere

Remember the days when the first step of any journey was to stop by an AAA office to get free maps? Nowadays the first step is just typing — or speaking — a place name into your phone's Map app. And labeling places makes that even faster.

Include Google Maps on your devices. Like other Google software, Maps is browser-based on a computer, but on phones, you get much more out of the app. Check the app store on your phone if Maps didn't come with it. Google Maps is available for iPhones and iPads. You'll get a similar experience on the app that you get on your computer.

Put yourself on the map. There's no place like home. And work. Saving these places on Google Maps is a good way to start. On a computer, go to *google.com/maps*, or open the Maps app on your phone. Tap or click the Menu icon (three vertical lines, top left), select **Your places**, and type in addresses for your home and work.

Save your favorite places. Whether it's for a beach you love, your favorite restaurant, or an ice cream store you found across town, saving places as you go along makes them easier to find later.

Simply search on an address, business name, or if you happen to know it, the place's longitude and latitude (a lesser-used option, to be sure).

Choose a search result if more than one appear. Click or tap the **Save** icon. You can save it to an existing list (such as **Favorites**, **Want to go**, etc.) or make a new list, like "Great lunch spots." To view your saved places, return to **Your places**.

Learn to save from websites. You can often save places directly from maps on websites, when the site uses Google Maps. For example, if you're heading to Washington, D.C., you can save a map of the area to your computer or send it right to your phone.

3 tip-top ways to pinpoint your view

If you want to get away for a peaceful weekend, you might not be able to tell from a regular map whether the hotel you're considering is next to a stretch of forest or a small bus depot. With Google Maps you can.

Google has combined satellite images, aerial photos, and 360-degree images taken from Google's Street View cars, as well as by people hiking, boating, riding snowmobiles, and exploring underwater.

Here's how to fine-tune your viewing so you know exactly what you're looking at.

On a computer. Click the **Menu** icon, top left, to choose **Map** (for a simple view), **Satellite** (to identify any nearby bus depots) or **Terrain**. Lower down the menu you can add more details — **Traffic**, **Transit**, and **Bicycling**.

On a phone or tablet. Click the app's separate view icon, located at the top right, for the same options.

Put view options to work. You have three great tools in front of you to help you check out the area.

- Terrain. The terrain view comes in handy on road trips, for example to see if you're heading into hills or into desert. Choose your highway wisely.

- Satellite. Satellite view is great for finding many things — hidden stretches of beach, parking lots around parks and lakes, and even coffee shops with drive-throughs.

- Map. All the same, at times the simplicity of just the map view will keep you from getting lost, which is, after all, a map's main job.

Keep in mind that satellite view images may be a few years old, easily enough time to build a small bus depot. Check views of your home occasionally to see how old the satellite images are.

Take to the streets — and know what's there — with Street View

Look before you leap. Let Street View give you a firsthand, move-around view of a hotel, a neighborhood, or even a mountain highway before you commit to going anywhere near it. Street View puts you right there so you can stroll around and give the place the once-over.

Travel with Street View on your computer. Meet Pegman, Google's cute Street View icon. After you pull up a map for a place, you'll find Pegman at the bottom right corner of your screen. Drag Pegman out, and blue lines appear along streets where Street View is available.

Next, drag the icon to any spot on a blue line and drop it, and the street — right from that spot — pops up before you. Don't forget to zoom in close before choosing your spot. Aiming from a distance might land you in the middle of a freeway.

Now it's time to explore. Hold down your left mouse button and drag the image to look around 360 degrees. Or walk up the road by moving your cursor forward and clicking the arrow. The farther forward the arrow is when you click it, the farther you will go, and the faster you can race up a street.

Walk around different neighborhoods to get landscaping ideas, explore Times Square, or take a stroll right along the water on Hawaii's Waikiki Beach.

Use Street View in real time on your phone. Out sightseeing and looking for a nice neighborhood to eat in? You can search for a place and "drop a pin" on any road. Simply hold your finger down on the spot to make a pin appear.

> Take a Street View walk down memory lane. Check out the neighborhood you grew up in or the schools you went to. Go for a stroll in tourist spots you once visited or a park you brought your kids to. See what's changed and what's still there. Enjoy a little nostalgia in your life.

If Street View is available at the spot, a Street View icon will appear at the bottom of your screen, showing an image of the place with a tiny round-arrow icon. Tap that and your phone becomes a portal into another world. To navigate, drag the image to turn around, and double-tap points in front of you to walk.

Keep the feature in mind when you're out and about. Street View has a lot of uses. House hunting? Walk a few neighborhoods before climbing into your car. Considering a job across town? See what lunch options the area restaurants offer. Or simply look for a coffee shop with outside seating on a quiet street.

You can also bring Street View's 360-degree images indoors with Google's newer Street View app for phones and tablets. It's great for travel, letting you look around museums and landmarks, and even add your own destinations. See the story *Armchair travel anywhere in the world* later in this chapter for more on this great feature.

Make Maps your handy location guide

Explorers have never had such tools. If you're looking for a business, a travel destination, or a place to do some serious shopping, Google Maps tells you how to get there, and also whether you really want to go.

Get the scoop on a particular spot. Search on a place, and if necessary, select a result, and you'll get a map with a host of information. For a pizza parlor, you'll get a description, reviews, photos, hours ("open now" hopefully), and contact information. Search on a city name, and you'll get photos, quick facts (Boston is Massachusetts' capital), and hotels, with images and links.

Find what you need nearby. If you're in an area you don't know well, Maps will show you around. Looking for a restaurant? Open the app on your phone and tap the compass icon. That makes Maps zoom in on your location, showing the buildings around you.

Tap **Explore** at the bottom of the screen for quick searches of nearby restaurants, events, parks — and very importantly — coffee. Or if you want something more specific, for instance, Chinese food, type it into the search bar at the top of your screen.

Search out business and vacation sites. If you're going on a trip, you can explore your destination in advance. On a computer, do a Maps search on your vacation spot, and then click the **Nearby** icon in the left-hand panel. This allows you to search in the area as well as do quick searches on restaurants and hotels.

Or on any device, simply search on a place name and a type of business. For instance, look for "Seattle coffee shops," and you'll see Seattle is one city where coffee is taken very seriously.

Easy way to filter your searches. Want a coffee shop that's inexpensive but has good reviews? Depending on the search, you'll be offered filters for price, reviews, and hours. They appear in the left panel on a computer and on the bottom of the screen in the app.

Navigate the streets like a pro

It may not be the bridge of a starship, but you can put one screen on your car dashboard that would have seemed sci-fi-like not long ago — your cellphone. Google Maps has a reputation for turning your phone into the most-reliable navigation device you can buy, with graphics that show what you're passing as you drive as well as when you will arrive. Point to it every time your kids ask, "Are we there yet?"

Get reliable turn-by-turn directions. On a phone, open your Google Maps app and type a location into the search bar at the top. That can be an exact business name, a place name, an address, or a search on "beachfront restaurants." Choose the result on the map if there's more than one.

A map showing the destination will appear. Tap **Directions** at the bottom and the map will show you the recommended route

Google Maps steers you around accidents and traffic jams. Roads on maps change color to show traffic conditions. Blue is good, yellow is a slowdown, red is bad, and black is for roads you definitely want to avoid.

from your current location with a blue line. Additional routes may be offered with gray lines.

Revise your starting point. Once the route map appears, you can change the starting point at the top of your screen.

Change your transportation. Just above the route map are icons for types of transportation. Choose from driving, transit, walking, rides, and cycling. You'll get a time estimate for each. For example a journey from San Francisco to New York will take more than 60 hours by car, or about 40 days on foot.

Check your route. See the steps of the suggested route (turn right on Main St., etc.) at the bottom of your screen.

Start navigation. Ready to set out? Tap **Start** at the bottom of the screen and your phone will speak out the first step of your directions.

Get directions through your car audio. In cars with Bluetooth audio systems, you can get the voice directions through your car's speakers. You can still listen to music or the radio as you drive, although on some audio systems that can be tricky to set up. Hint — the first few times you use voice navigation through your car's audio, set it up and test it before you have to leave.

> Share your places and routes. This is especially helpful if you have two cars going on a road trip. Search for a place. At the bottom of your screen, tap the place name or address that appears for more options: Save, Share, Label, and Download. From your computer, you can also share directions to your phone.

Ask your phone questions. On Android phones, you ask questions and find places (gas stations, restaurants, etc.) by talking to your phone. Tap the small microphone and say "Find gas stations" for a search.

Stop navigation. When you get to where you no longer need help, simply tap the **Exit** button at the bottom of your screen. That sweet GPS voice you picked out can get irritating when you no longer need it.

Plan a trip with your computer. You can also get Google Maps directions on a computer. Do a Maps search and tap the **Directions** icon. Use your computer for planning road trips. On a computer it's easy to alter routes by moving your cursor over parts of the blue line route and dragging the line to a different roadway. Maps will tell you how long the different routes will take, as shown in this example.

Armchair travel anywhere in the world

You see an article about Buckingham Palace in London and think, "I'd like to go there one day." Why wait? Use Google Maps' satellite views to explore places from a bird's eye view, and use Street View to walk around the outside.

Imagine strolling around the palace grounds and checking out the monuments and parks, and even walking right by 10 Downing Street, home of the British prime minister.

With Google Maps in a browser (computer or phone) click or tap the pin on a place. In the information panel you'll find photos, sometimes including 360-degree images inside museums and other landmarks.

Get a closer look with the Street view app. Google's newer Street View app, which uses 360-degree images from Street View and others, is great for general exploring but also for travel. Visit landmarks, natural wonders, museums, and businesses and become an armchair tourist. No baggage fees required.

When you visit Buckingham Palace, Google's Pegman Street View icon changes into PegMa'am — the stick figure is decked out like the queen. Google added this Easter egg (a joke hidden inside an image or software) to honor Queen Elizabeth. So drag PegMa'am to let her show you around the palace wherever Street View is available.

Create your own Street View images. Go a step further and share your personal experiences. If you visit a national park, or maybe find a great fishing spot, you can make your own 360-degree images (there's an app for that) and put them on the map for others to enjoy. But give some thought to the fishing spot — you might not want to make that location public.

> Beware of Maps' surprises. Tap the microphone icon on an Android phone and ask, "Are we there yet?" several times and your phone will say, "If you ask me again, we won't stop for ice cream." Search on Loch Ness on your computer, and the Street View icon turns into the Loch Ness Monster. These are fun examples of Google Easter eggs, or jokes.

Travel back in time. Many places will let you go back in time using Street View, at least 10 years or so. Click the clock icon (if it's available) in the upper left-hand corner and choose your time.

Zip around the planet with Google Earth

Make armchair travel more lively with Google Earth. This software lets you quickly fly from location to location, soaring into the atmosphere and landing easily on each place you want to see.

Get the best view on a computer. Visit Google Earth (*google.com/ earth*) to launch the software in a browser, or download Google Earth Pro onto your computer. Start with just launching Google Earth. The opening is impressive, an interactive image of the planet rotating slowly in space. Zoom out to see Earth from a distance and in to explore.

You'll be able to visit the same places you can on Google Maps but with 3-D imagery that lets you view everything from the Eiffel Tower to your local supermarket from different angles. Then take tours of interesting places with Google Earth's Voyager feature.

Take it with you on your phone. Visit your phone or tablet's app store to get the Google Earth app. It's a small screen for a big planet, but the Google Earth app is still a useful tool.

Expand your sights to the universe. If you're really looking for something that's out of this world, try Google Moon (*google.com/moon*). Take tours of the lunar landing sites, narrated by Apollo astronauts, and explore the moon firsthand. If that doesn't quench your urge for exotic travel, try Google Mars (*google.com/mars*).

No Wi-Fi? Easy way to use Maps offline

Worried you might not get a decent signal when you need a map? Plan ahead and download maps to use offline.

Sign on to Google Maps, search on a place, and then tap the place name or address at the bottom of your screen. One option will be **Download**. Tap that button and you can resize the map and then tap the new download button that appears.

If your phone supports SD memory cards, you can save maps to them. Tap the Menu icon (three lines) top left and choose **Offline maps**. Then tap the gear icon, top right, and select **Storage preferences**.

Choose between **Device** (your phone) and **SD card**, if one is available. You can also manage other features of offline maps from the settings. Now you can use Maps normally, even if you don't have an internet signal.

The amazing cloud
Work, play, and share from anywhere

If you're confused by all the talk about "cloud computing," you're not alone. Although the concept has been around since the 1960s, it's only become widely known to the public for about 10 years.

But what, exactly, is it? It's really not that complicated. It's basically taking some of the things you used to do directly on your own computer, phone, or tablet — word processing, spreadsheets, file storage — and moving it onto other computers over the internet. That online network of computers is known as the cloud.

Think of it like a public utility such as electric power. You use electricity in your home every day. But you don't actually generate electricity in your home — you get it from outside. You don't have to own and maintain the expensive equipment used to generate power. You just have to connect to the service from your home and use it.

Same thing with cloud computing. Instead of buying large computer systems or expensive software, you rent a share of it from an online company, and move activities off your computer and into the "cloud." The big advantage of this network in the sky is that you can get to your information no matter where you are as long as you have a device with an internet connection.

You probably use some cloud services without even realizing it. Favorites like Netflix, Yahoo Mail, and YouTube all operate out of the cloud. So don't let it intimidate you. Read on to learn about the many ways the cloud can improve your life.

Cloud storage made easy
Everything you need to know

5 reasons to get your head in the cloud

Using the cloud is easier than you think. It's a great way to store pictures and files and a fun way to share them with your friends and relatives. And, most importantly, it keeps your files safe when you switch computers or cellphones.

That's because you store your photos and documents on the internet rather than on your own computer or phone. Need a little push? Here are some great reasons to make the cloud an essential part of your life.

It's free. Cloud storage sites usually give you a basic plan for free. Google Drive lets you store 15 gigabytes (about 5,000 photos). OneDrive and iCloud give you 5 gigabytes, Dropbox is 2 gigabytes. Amazon Drive gives Prime members unlimited space for photos and 10 gigabytes for everything else. All of them also offer paid storage that starts as low as about $2 per month.

You probably already have it. Large tech companies usually have their own cloud storage services, so chances are you already have one built into your favorite device. If you own a Mac or an iPhone, you have iCloud. If you own a Windows computer, you have OneDrive. If you are an Amazon Prime member, you have Amazon Drive. If you use Gmail, you have Google Drive.

The services are easy to use.
Most cloud storage services let you install an app to your computer, tablet, or phone to automatically save files and pictures to the cloud as easily as you save things now.

Computer scientists work long hours, and they also tend to have an odd sense of humor. The way they name things reflects that, hence the word byte, which is made up of two "nibbles."

It's a safe place. It's happened to most people at least once. Your computer or your phone dies and you lose everything on it. That's inconvenient at best and a tragedy at worst, losing some of your most precious pictures and videos forever. Using cloud storage keeps those memories safe. When your device dies, your files are still there waiting for you to connect to the internet from another device.

Sharing is fun. Because your photos and other files are on the internet, but in your private space, you get to choose who can see them, just by clicking the **Share** button in your cloud app.

Hey you get off of my cloud: Keep your data away from hackers

Should you store your documents in the cloud? Yes and no. As you consider cloud storage providers, you'll also want to consider the security of your files. Ask yourself these questions to help you decide how much or how little protection you're comfortable with.

How much security do you need? Your answer to this will depend partly on the kinds of files you're storing and partly on your level of comfort with security.

Obviously, you want your private documents and photos to be kept private. But if you're simply storing photos, videos, and documents that don't have confidential information, security may not be your first priority.

On the other hand, if you have financial information, tax records, confidential letters, photos, and videos, then you may need a higher level of security to ensure against hackers grabbing your information.

What security options does your provider offer? Each service provider should offer a few basic options to protect yourself from hackers.

- Two-Factor Authentication (2FA). 2FA goes beyond a simple username/password access. If your provider offers 2FA and you use it, you'll have to go through an extra step any time you access the site from a new device.

  This usually takes the form of entering a one-time access code or clicking a one-time link that is sent via text message, phone call, or email to an address you set up in your account. This protects you against people figuring out or finding your password and using it to access your account.

- Advanced Encryption Standard (AES). The U.S. government created AES as a secure standard that could generally only be decrypted by, well, the U.S. government. Sites using AES give your data an encryption key that has 1,077 combinations. This is generally adequate for most purposes.

- Zero-Knowledge Encryption (ZKE). The main advantage of ZKE is that your provider never has access to unencrypted versions of your files. All encryption takes place on your own computer or device, so theoretically only someone on your device could look at them.

  > Most cloud providers don't sell your email address to third-party advertisers. But, depending on your license agreement, they may have the right to do it. Read the fine print to find out where they stand before using their service.

How much extra trouble are you willing to go to? Obviously, some extra security can require more work on your side. For instance, Two-Factor Authentication makes you take an added step before you can access your files.

Creating a hard-to-remember password is another way to make it more difficult for hackers to get your files. But it makes it harder for you to access your files, too.

For help with remembering passwords, see *Password protection: How to pick them, remember them, and keep them safe* in the chapter *Protect your good name: How to fight fraud and stop identity theft.*

Your quick and easy guide to storage providers

With almost every major consumer tech company entering the cloud space, keeping track can be confusing. Here's a quick roundup of some of the major players and the benefits they offer.

OneDrive. If you use a Windows computer or Microsoft's online version of Office — Office 365 — you already have access to One-Drive. Windows computers have a OneDrive folder already built in, allowing you to save directly from your computer to OneDrive. OneDrive offers 5 gigabytes of storage free (25 gigs for Office 365 subscribers), with 50 gigabytes available for $1.99 per month.

iCloud. If you own a Macbook or an iPhone, you already have iCloud. Even if you don't have a Mac or iPhone, iCloud will give you 5 gigabytes of storage for free. Upgrade to 50 gigs for 99 cents per month, 200 gigs for $2.99, or 2 terabytes (2,000 gigabytes) for $9.99.

iCloud works seamlessly from your Macbook and iPhone, automatically backing up your information, photos, and files. Setting up from your Windows computer or Android tablet or phone is a little more complicated, but it can be done.

Amazon Drive. Its "free" plan is only for those with a paid Prime membership. If you're a member, you also receive unlimited photo storage and 5 gigabytes of storage for everything else. 100 gigabytes is $11.99 for a year, and 1 terabyte is $59.99 per year. An app on your phone lets you easily back up, and a simple download allows you to back up from your computer.

Dropbox. This provider's main focus is on business customers, but it offers a basic 2 gigabyte storage plan for free. You can upgrade to 16 gigabytes for free by connecting your account to social media or by getting friends to sign up as well.

Dropbox's least expensive paid plan is $8.25 per month for 1 terabyte of storage, $16.58 for 2. Dropbox lets you set up a special folder on your computer for automatic backups, with access to old versions of files for up to 120 days.

Google Drive. It works seamlessly with other Google apps, including Gmail. Google Drive supports multiple versions of files and automatic backup from your devices. A 15 gigabyte plan is free. Unlimited storage costs $10 per month. To learn more about this software, see the chapter *Google Drive: Sync, store, and share your files in the cloud.*

Other top services. Many lesser-known services can provide bargain storage options, although they're not always as easy to use as the well-known brands.

- Mega's basic free plan gives you 50 gigabytes of storage.

- Box works well with Google Docs and Office 365 with 10 gigabytes of free storage.

- iDrive is good if you want to back up from multiple home computers on your network easily. Its free plans give you 5 gigabytes of storage.

- pCloud is great if you need to upload large files (some services limit the size of your uploads) and offers 20 gigabytes for free.

- MediaFile gives you 10 gigabytes for free but lets you upgrade to 40 gigabytes by recruiting your friends to sign up, too.

How much is a gigabyte anyway?

You hear a lot about "gigabytes" and how many each cloud provider offers, but what does that mean? Well, a "byte" is the smallest practical unit of computer memory, what it takes to display one character, like the number 1.

Multiply a byte by 1,000 and you get a kilobyte. Multiply that by 1,000 to get a megabyte, and so on. Here's the progression: byte > kilobyte > megabyte > gigabyte > terabyte.

So a gigabyte is 1,000 megabytes, 1 million kilobytes, and 1 billion bytes. That sounds like a lot, but gigabytes add up pretty quickly depending on what you store. One gigabyte actually holds:

- 677,963 pages of text.

- 715 low-resolution photos.

- 130 high-resolution photos.

- 16 hours of music (about 230 songs).

- 15 minutes of standard video shot on a phone.

- 90 seconds of high-resolution video.

That means if home movies are your hobby, a free 5 gigabyte storage plan only lets you hold around 7 minutes and 30 seconds of cousin Floyd's wedding.

Cloud storage options: Find your silver lining

Nowadays, it seems like every big tech company has some set of cloud storage available. The sheer number and variety of options can be overwhelming when you try to choose the best solution for you.

The good news is you can't make a wrong choice, as almost all cloud storage providers have the same basic features. And if you decide down the line you didn't choose the best one for you, moving to a different provider is relatively painless. So what should you consider when picking a cloud storage service?

What devices and services do you use already? Because the big tech companies have their own cloud services, they naturally favor their own devices.

Own a Macbook and iPhone? Apple's iCloud may be best for you. Rely on Gmail and an Android phone? Google Drive may be the ticket. Use Microsoft Office on a Windows computer? You already have OneDrive ready and waiting.

What's your budget? Free is good, and many cloud providers offer a free version of their service. But free also comes with limitations on space and services. Some sites offer larger plans for around $5 per month, and unlimited space begins around $10 per month.

How much space do you need? Your storage needs vary depending on what you're doing with your phone and computer. Are you a poet who writes mainly haiku? Your ideas are vast, but your storage needs are small, and pretty much any free service will be enough.

Are you the one who's always behind the camera, snapping pictures at family events? If you take lots of pictures and videos that you want to keep forever, then your needs will be pretty big. Look for the most "gigs" for your buck.

How easy is it to use? If you're a power-user, ease of use may not be the most important factor. But if you're not comfortable with complex setups or don't have complicated needs, simpler and easier products are the choice for you. Your best bet is to turn to the big providers like Google, Microsoft, Amazon, and Apple.

Automatic uploads save time and trouble

You have two ways to save your computer documents to your preferred cloud provider. One is to log in on the provider's website and manually upload your files to back them up. The other is to install software on your computer to let you save your documents directly to the cloud. Why would that be better? Glad you asked.

It's easier. It's so easy, in fact, that you won't even know you're doing it. Once installed, it works exactly the same as if you were saving to your own computer. You can even drag files from other parts of your computer into your cloud folder and have them instantly backed up.

You can access your old versions. If you've created enough documents on your computer, at some point you've realized "Ah! I changed something I didn't mean to." If you've been saving your file directly to your computer, there may be no way to turn back the clock to an earlier version.

Not so if you're saving to the cloud. Most cloud storage sites automatically back up every version of your file, every time you save. OneDrive, for instance, keeps those versions for 30 days. And those old versions don't count against your storage quota.

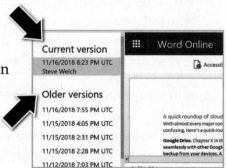

Makes it simple to work with a team. If you're working with others, your partners can see the latest version as soon as you save it. You don't need to send an email to tell them about changes. And you don't have to worry about several people making changes at the same time or on different versions of the same document.

No-cost, no-worry backup for phone and tablet

"New phone. Who's this?" If you've ever gotten this text message, then you have a friend who failed to back up their phone. Don't be that person. So much of everyone's life is now on their phones that when you lose or break it, you can feel lost for weeks.

Luckily, today it's easy to automatically back up everything on your phone or tablet — contacts, documents, apps, photos — so when you get a new one, you won't lose anything. And you can do it for free.

However, you may want to back up photos separately to save space in your preferred cloud system.

Apple devices. The easiest way to back up your iPhone or iPad is using the built-in iCloud. To set it up, just go into your phone or tablet settings and choose **iCloud** and then **Backup**. You can pick and choose which items (contacts, photos, etc.) that you want to back up.

Your devices will back up any time you're connected to Wi-Fi and plugged in. If you're out of iCloud space you could also back up to your computer. Simply connect with a charging cable and launch iTunes.

You can also get third-party apps (like Acronis) in the app store or from your mobile provider that back up your data and restore it to your device.

Android devices. Google's mobile operating system is used on most non-Apple phones and tablets. Android used to lag behind in a good backup system, but now is just as easy as the iPhone when it comes to securing your information.

In your system settings, simply go into **Backup** and choose **Backup to Google Drive**. That's pretty much it. When you get a new phone or tablet, you log in to the same Google account to download the data you've stored. If you've filled up your Google Drive, a number of apps are available to back you up.

Share files from the cloud simply and safely

Cloud platforms make it easy to share your photos and other documents with family and friends. Each is a little different but use similar techniques. Here are the steps you would take with OneDrive.

1. After you've logged into OneDrive with your username and password, first click **Files** to navigate to the specific document or entire folder you want to share.

2. Select the document or folder you wish to share. In OneDrive, a checkbox appears when you move your mouse cursor over the item. Click the checkbox to select the item.

3. Click the **Share** button in the top menu.

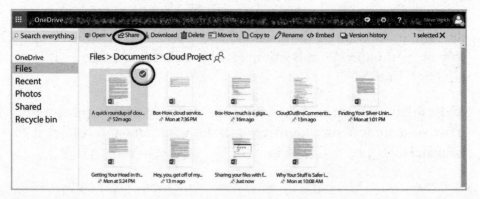

4. A sharing window will pop up. Check **Allow editing** to give your friend permission to make changes, or leave it unchecked to allow them only to see and download it. OneDrive lets you set an expiration date, after which the link will no longer work.

   You can also set a password that your friend must provide to get access. Without a password, anyone with the link can access your document. Click the link OneDrive creates and then share it with your friend or in your social media account. You could also click the **Email** button to create an email with the link in it.

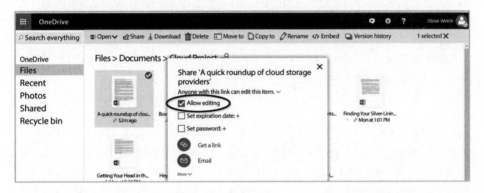

5. If you save your documents directly to a OneDrive folder on your computer, you can create a share link in Windows by right-clicking on what you want to share and choosing **Share a OneDrive link**.

Conserve space: Turn paper docs into cloud docs

Most people collect all sorts of things they don't know what to do with — old coins, extra pounds, photos, and papers. Lots and lots of papers. Before you buy another filing cabinet or put another box in storage, consider some options.

First, throw out what you don't need. Second, keep and file the ones you do need, whether for sentimental or legal reasons. For what's left, you have some good alternatives.

Find owner's manuals online. You know that drawer full of manuals for the TV, the refrigerator, the washing machine? You may want to empty it. Pretty much any manual you need is available online, just by searching the model number and the words "owner's manual."

Scan documents with your mobile phone. Covered up by old paperwork you just can't throw away? Try this modern method of storing important documents, and get used to having all that free space.

Simply use the camera on your smartphone to digitize your records. If you just have a few pages to deal with, take a picture with your phone. It's an easy way to preserve your priceless papers and photos.

For bigger jobs, you'll want to use one of the many apps available for that purpose. A good one — like Abbyy FineScanner or Adobe Scan — will let you capture multiple pages in the same document. It will even do text recognition so you can search your documents for words or phrases.

Scan with your all-in-one printer. Your home printer most likely has a built-in scanner and software to run it. If you can make photocopies on your printer, you can probably scan, too.

If your printer has a document feeder, it may be the easiest way to scan your documents. Just put all the pages into the feeder, hit the scan button, and wait for the document to appear on your computer. Then you can save it to your computer or to the cloud — wherever you want.

Use a scanning service. Not comfortable scanning things yourself? If you have enough of those old coins hanging around, you can kill two birds with one stone and send your documents to a professional scanning service. It can get expensive, but it's certainly cheaper than the monthly rent on a storage locker for all those old papers.

Save your hard-earned money — resist the pressure to upgrade

One of the things you're probably asking yourself is, "So what's the catch? Why do cloud providers give me these services for free?"

The catch is, they want to upsell you on more storage. They also want to sell to your friends and family.

When you start running out of space on your free plan — and most people do, eventually — you'll receive emails urging you to upgrade.

Whenever you visit the provider's website, you'll also see ads insisting it's time to buy more storage. When you share files and pictures with your friends and family, they'll get the same tough sell.

Don't get pressured into buying more storage if you don't want it. Simply delete or move items out of the cloud if you're close to your limit. Then you can ignore the provider's arm-twisting tactics and relax knowing you're not giving them any of your hard-earned money.

4 super strategies to get the most free storage

In the real world, clouds can come together and form one giant cloud covering. In the digital world, it's not so simple. Wouldn't it be great if you could combine your free 15-gigabyte storage from

Google with your free gigs from OneDrive, Dropbox, Amazon, and iCloud? Make one big free cloud?

Unfortunately, cloud providers don't want to make it that easy. After all, they make money when you run out of free space and have to buy more from them.

Fear not, penny-pinchers. There are ways to spread your information across several different free clouds. You just have to be creative and willing to do a little extra work. But "free" is worth it, right?

Use different backups for your phone and computer. Each smartphone has a "native" backup, either iCloud or Google Drive. Use that to back up your phone and a different cloud provider for your computer.

Choose separate providers for your media. Back up your photos to a specialized photo cloud like Shutterfly or Amazon Photos. Your videos can go to a video service like YouTube or Facebook. And your music can be backed up to your favorite music service. Everything else can go to a general cloud backup like iCloud or Google Drive.

Don't back up all folders to the same place. When you install cloud backup software to your computer, you can specify which folders on your computer should be backed up.

If you install more than one backup service, you can specify different folders to be backed up to each. You might have different project folders, or folders for different parts of your life, such as work, personal, and school.

Open several email accounts to get more service. You probably have a few different email addresses. Even if you don't, it's easy and free to create them. Most cloud providers let you sign up for a separate account with each email address. Combine this tactic with the others, and you'll boost your cloud cover in no time.

Looking for fame? 3 sites to achieve video stardom

It's never been easier to record and share video with family, friends, even the whole world if you're seeking video stardom. The most famous people you've never heard of are online video stars.

You can even broadcast live from your smartphone on Facebook, YouTube, and other sites. If you like to record video, you probably know that files can be huge and quickly fill up your computer or even your cloud storage space. Luckily, you have many cheap — and even free — options to share your videos in the cloud.

Facebook — more than just cat memes and angry politics. It's also a place for video which, granted, is sometimes about cats or politics. But if you already post on Facebook, adding video to your posts is simple.

- When you post an update, simply click the **Photo/Video** button to choose a video from your computer or phone to share. It takes Facebook a few minutes to process your video, but your post is available to your friends, family, and followers almost immediately.

- Facebook limits the length of your video to 45 minutes. But you have no limit on the number of videos you can store or the amount of storage you can use. That's a great way to get around storage limits on other cloud services.

- You can also click the **Live Video** button to broadcast directly to your Facebook audience. Share your vacation with the folks back home while sitting on the beach, or praise your favorite politician. It's your choice.

YouTube makes it easy and boasts a huge audience. YouTube is probably the best-known site for sharing and viewing videos, and for good reason. It's the third most-popular streaming site on the internet and accounts for more than 11 percent of all internet streaming traffic, according to *Variety*.

- Trusted users can upload videos that are up to 12 hours long. These are people whose videos have complied with YouTube's terms, especially regarding copyright. Until you're an established user, videos are limited to 15 minutes.

- You have no limits on the number of videos you can upload or the storage space you use. Your videos can be public, password-protected, or unlisted. Unlisted means no password is required for anyone who has the direct link to the video.

- Adding a video to your personal channel is easy. Click the camera icon to the left of your profile picture, and choose **Upload video** or **Go live**. Then follow the on-screen instructions. Use the **Go live** option to broadcast live video to your channel. Your live video is then available on demand. YouTube also has editing tools to let you add music, title screens, and even automatically generated closed captions to your video.

Vimeo — a well-known site for indie video producers and fans. Vimeo has always stressed high-resolution video and strong privacy controls for members who want to share their videos with specific people or groups.

Paid membership levels allow video-making teams to collaborate and provide feedback on posted videos. Free membership plans are limited to uploading 500 megabytes per week and total storage of 5 gigabytes. Live streaming is only available to Premium members, who pay $900 per year.

Store and play music in the cloud — for free

As a music lover, you may have invested long hours "ripping" your old CDs to the digital formats that today rule the music market. So now, instead of shelves full of discs, you may have hard drives full of MP3s. For many people, music libraries are their biggest need for cloud storage.

A single gigabyte holds about 230 songs — around 21 CDs. If you've spent your life collecting music, you'll soon run out of storage space on your device. Fortunately, you have a lot of ways to store — and play — your music from the cloud. Here are some of the top services.

Google Play Music. Part of Google's music streaming service, Google Play Music lets you upload up to 50,000 songs (more than 4,500 albums) from your personal collection and stream them to any device, from anywhere. And it's completely free.

Songs you buy from Google Play don't count toward the 50,000-song limit. Upgrade to a paid subscription to stream any of the 40 million songs in the Google library.

iCloud Music Library. Apple doesn't offer a free option beyond the free general storage that is part of iCloud. But if you subscribe to Apple Music ($9.99 per month), iCloud Music Library is included. Otherwise, for $24.99 a year, you can store your iTunes library (up to 100,000 songs) in iCloud. But it does require you to use iTunes to organize your library.

> If it weren't for the American obsession with good music, the smartphone might not exist. The first iPhone evolved from Apple's original music player, the iPod.

Amazon Prime Music. One of the goodies Amazon bundles in with its Prime service is Prime Music. Storage is a little limited compared to others, just 250 songs.

It also gives you access to more than 29 million songs in the Amazon Prime library. For $7.99 per month, you can store 250,000 songs and have access to more than 50 million songs with Amazon Music Unlimited.

Streaming services. A number of music streaming services also offer access to their music libraries. Pandora, Tidal, Slacker Radio, and Spotify are all well-known services that offer free plans as well as paid subscriptions with more songs and more features. But they don't include storage of your personal library.

For more on streaming music, see the chapter *Turn up the tunes: Stream music you love anywhere, any time.*

> Want another good reason to store your music in the cloud? If a song is in the music service's library, they will replace your file with their high-quality digital file. That saves them space and gives you a better listening experience. Win-win.

E-books and audiobooks
Your library in the cloud

10 ways e-books outshine print

Print books are great. The smell, the feel, even the sounds —
paper rustling, that solid "thump" when you close the hard cover
for the night. But if you haven't yet fallen for their modern, digital
counterpart, here are a few things that may change your mind.

Glasses are not required. If you rely on reading glasses for
browsing through your favorite book, chances are you won't need
them for e-books. You control the type size and style, so you can
make the letters as big as you need them to be.

Let your partner sleep. If you're a late-night reader with a partner who can't stand a bedside light, e-books are for you. Most of
them have their own internal light. So turn off the lamp and read
yourself to sleep.

Which books to bring? Why not all of them! You're heading
off for vacation and faced with one of the toughest decisions a
reader can face — how many books will fit in your luggage? With
e-books, you can bring as many as you want without going over
the airline weight limits.

Keep your selections private. You're reading in the local coffee shop and catch someone glancing at the racy cover of your romance novel. How embarrassing. With e-books, no one can tell if you're reading *The Flame and the Flower* or *War and Peace*.

Listen to a story. Some e-books can synchronize with their audiobook counterparts, so you can go back and forth between reading to yourself and being read to.

Never get caught without a book. Ever found yourself with an unexpected wait and nothing to do? Picking up a grandkid from soccer practice? Emergency dental visit? With your phone in your pocket, you're never without a good book to read.

¿Cómo se dice en inglés? It's frustrating when a book has a phrase in a language you don't speak, whether modern Spanish or ancient Latin. With an e-book, translation is only a click away.

Get help with words you don't know. Even if you do speak the book's language, sometimes authors throw around unfamiliar words. With a built-in dictionary, you can get the definition with just a tap.

Marking up is a "highlight." For many, writing notes or highlighting in a book can feel like blasphemy. And forget about dog-earing your place. In an e-book, you can do all that without damage — or guilt.

Simple to share on social media. Nowadays, how can you tell you've done something if you haven't shared it on social media? Sites like Goodreads exist so you can share your reading status right from within your e-book and have impromptu book club meetings with fellow readers. You can also share interesting quotes directly from your book to the social media site of your choice.

A handy guide to the e-book alphabet

When you want to download your favorite novel, you need to know whether it will run on the platform and software you use. Formats like .epub, .azw, .mobi, and .pdf can make your eyes cross with a confusion of letters. Here's what you need to know.

EPUB (or ePub). Almost every e-reader device and every e-reader software except for Kindle can read EPUB. It uses the same technology for formatting text and images that the web does.

Kindle. This format (file extension .azw) works only on Kindle devices and on Kindle software for Apple and Android phones and tablets. You need special software or an online service to convert Kindle files to work on other devices or software.

MOBI. All major e-readers can read the MOBI format, except Barnes and Noble's Nook.

IBA. Apple's iBooks Author app delivers content in the IBA format. Commercial books in the iTunes store are in EPUB, so you'll find relatively few books in IBA, which can only be read in iBooks.

PDF. Portable Document Format shows you the page exactly as it was designed by the publisher. The downside is it may be difficult to read comfortably on smaller screens.

E-reader 101: Choose the right type for you

Perhaps one of the most intimidating parts of getting into e-books is buying a device to read on. You have several basic types to choose from.

General-purpose tablets and phones. Most e-book sellers offer apps you can use to read their books on Android and iOS tablets and smartphones. If you already use one of these devices, this is the quickest and easiest way for you to start reading e-books. Simply download the Kindle app and you're ready to find some books.

E-reader tablets. The two largest e-book retailers are Amazon, which sells Kindle Fire, and Barnes and Noble, which sells the Nook. Both are Android-based tablets with their apps built in.

These are more than just e-readers, featuring many of the apps that are available for Android tablets, but not all. They also have a bias for their own company's content, so it may be difficult to read e-books from other providers on the tablet.

The big advantage is that the tablets tend to be less expensive than other tablets of comparable quality and features.

E-ink readers. Sometimes called "digital paper," these are simple e-readers that most closely imitate the experience of reading black ink on white paper.

Barnes and Noble's version is called the Nook GlowLight. Amazon's Kindle E-reader and Kindle Paperwhite series both use versions of the technology. Another company, Kobo, offers similar devices called Aura or Forma.

Unlike some other types of tablets, they are easy to read even in direct sunlight. They are lightweight and easy to hold in one hand. E-ink readers are designed almost exclusively for reading books and have limited other functions.

> One nice feature of e-readers is that you can use different devices and they will all sync. If you start a book on your Kindle Fire, for example, you can pick up where you left off on your smartphone's Kindle app. Each device knows which page you stopped on so you don't have to search for it.

5 e-book sellers you need to know

Are you a big Amazon fan? Have a place in your heart for Barnes and Noble? Those things may play into your decision on what e-book provider to choose. Here's a quick rundown of the major sellers to help you decide.

Amazon *(amazon.com/ebooks)*. The largest online retailer in the world, Amazon started life as an online bookseller. Books are still central to Amazon. They helped pioneer the e-reader, but you don't need a Kindle to buy e-books from Amazon.

- Kindle books can be read on most mobile devices and desktop computers, using the Kindle app from Amazon. However, they cannot easily be read in other apps.

- Amazon has a huge selection and is often less expensive than other e-book retailers.

- You can synchronize Amazon e-books with audiobooks from its sister company, Audible.

- The Kindle app lets Prime members loan e-books to friends the way you might lend a physical book.

Kobo Books *(kobo.com)*. Kobo sells its own e-readers and tablets and features a large online store. Kobo books are in a proprietary format, so they can't be read in other apps or other e-readers.

However, the Kobo app is available for all major platforms, so Kobo books can be read on most tablets and smartphones. The Kobo store features audiobooks as well as e-books.

Apple Books *(iTunes.com)*. Apple doesn't sell a dedicated e-reader. You read Apple Books on your Apple or Android phone or tablet using the iBooks app. The store features a broad selection, including audiobooks.

Apple Books has no website. You must purchase books either by having Apple's iTunes software installed on your computer or from inside the Books app.

Barnes and Noble *(Barnesandnoble.com)*. The largest brick-and-mortar book retailer in the world, Barnes and Noble also has a strong online presence for e-books. Barnes and Noble sells its own line of Nook e-readers and tablets, including ones for kids.

> Although there's some disagreement, the first e-book was probably the *Index Thomisticus*, an electronic index of the works of Thomas Aquinas, created by Roberto Busa. Busa started the work in 1949 but didn't finish it for almost 30 years. At first on a single computer, it's now on its own website.

Like other e-book sellers, Barnes and Noble's Nook app lets you read Nook books on any mobile device. But Nook books no longer support reading on your desktop computer.

Google Play *(play.google.com/books)*. Google is relatively new to the book business, but they've gone big. You read their books through the Google Play Books app on your phone or tablet, or through a web browser on your computer.

Because of Google's efforts to digitize most books that have been published, many of them are available for free through Google's bookstore.

Surprise — you can send personal documents to your e-reader

Chances are, most of what you'll read on your e-reader will be e-books you buy from the reader's store. But you don't have to limit yourself.

Depending on your e-reader software, you can add free books you download from the internet, e-books from your library, and even documents you create yourself. That can be useful if you want to read a large report on the train or keep a technical manual handy wherever you are.

Most e-readers let you open compatible files. You can do this either by emailing files to an email account you can open on the device, or by adding them to a cloud storage app you have on your phone.

When you open the file, your tablet or phone will ask what you want to do with it. Choose to open the file in your e-reader app. Here's how to do it on leading e-readers.

Kindle. Your Kindle e-reader and app can read MS Word documents, a variety of image files, PDFs, and .mobi-formatted ebooks.

- For automatic delivery, you can use your device's special email address to send yourself files. Every Kindle and Kindle app has a unique email address.

- You can find your "Send to Kindle" address by opening the Settings in your Kindle app. Or find it in your Amazon account under Manage Your Content and Devices > Preferences > Personal Document Settings. You can even change the email address to something easier to remember.

- If you have more than one Kindle (or more than one device with the Kindle app), each one has its own address. Attach your file to an email addressed to your Kindle. If you want to convert it to native Kindle format, rather than the original format you send, make the subject of the email "Convert." Within a few minutes, the file will show up on your Kindle.

Nook. Connect your computer to your Nook using the USB cable that came with your device. On the computer, drag the files you want to read on your e-reader from the computer to the Nook's **My documents** folder.

Kobo. You can send PDF documents to your Kobo two ways. Connect it to a computer with a USB cable and drag files to the Kobo, or put the files on an SD card and insert that card into the Kobo.

Keep more money in your pocket: Add free e-books to your library

Book lovers on a budget have always been creative about ways to read their favorites without spending a lot of money. The good news is, all of those old ways — libraries, bargain bins, borrowing from a friend — are available to e-book readers, too.

Take advantage of your public library. If you have a library card, chances are you also have access to free e-books. You'll need to log in to your library's online card catalog and search for books available in e-book format.

Many libraries deliver e-books through third-party sites, like OverDrive or RBdigital, so you may need to register with that site as well to gain access to the content. Typically, books are active on your device or computer for a set amount of time, after which they become unreadable.

Here's what a typical online library catalog listing of e-books looks like, showing a **Download** button you can use to get your e-book.

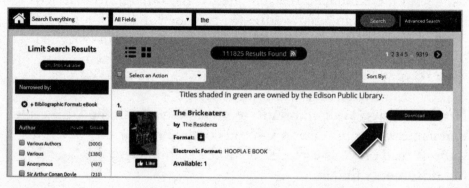

Get free books at Project Gutenberg. Founded in 1971, Project Gutenberg was named for the inventor of the movable-type printing press, which made books affordable for the first time. It aims to bring free electronic books to the world.

Before the invention of portable e-books, Project Gutenberg provided the "plain vanilla" text of classic, public domain books on a mainframe computer and then on the world wide web.

Today, their 57,000 titles are available in multiple formats, including Kindle and EPUB. Check them out at *gutenberg.org*.

Google Play Bookstore is in the game. Google has made it a mission to digitize every book ever published. Many of them are available for free as e-books in the Google Play store. Many classic, public domain books are available as well as a number of newer titles. You'll find them at *play.google.com/books*.

Borrow — or donate — at Open Library. As its name implies, Open Library styles itself as a community library, with e-books donated by people from around the world. This is not limited to out-of-print or public domain books but also includes more recent books.

Contributors add their legally owned physical copy of a book to a library, which is then converted to e-book format for others to borrow. The number of "copies" is limited to the number that have been donated, so many popular titles have waitlists to borrow.

Membership is free, and you are allowed to borrow up to five titles at a time. Go to *openlibrary.org*.

Take your grandkids to the International Children's Digital Library. Find hundreds of free e-books for young readers. Search by reader age, type of book, even the color of the book cover. Many titles are available in several languages. You'll find them at *childrenslibrary.org*.

Enjoy reading a Nook book. The Nook e-book library from Barnes and Noble at *barnesandnoble.com* features many free titles. These include both public domain classics and lesser-known modern books. Many are from independent publishers and authors.

First step to digital reading — pick your device

Trying to figure out which e-book provider you want to use? The first thing you should do is decide what device you prefer. (For help, see *E-reader 101: Choose the right type for you*.) Your choice will determine whether you're locked in to a particular provider or have some flexibility.

E-readers are most restrictive. If you own a Nook, you can pretty much only read e-books sold by Barnes and Noble. If you have a Kindle, you'll rely on books from Amazon. And Kobo supplies books from its own store. None of them work particularly well with books sold by other providers.

Other devices give you more choices. Apple and Android devices, on the other hand, have apps for each of these booksellers as well as most others. In fact, you can have books from multiple bookstores on those devices.

The downside is that each of your libraries will be separate, so you'll have to remember where you bought a particular e-book to find it on your device.

Amazing news — you can share your digital books

"Never lend books, for no one ever returns them; the only books I have in my library are books that other folks have lent me." — Anatole Franc

Does that sound like you? If you're like most people with shelves full of books, lending them out is one way to share your passion and bond with friends. That doesn't have to change in the era of e-books. You have a number of ways to lend e-books to your friends, some of which even guarantee you'll get them back.

Kindle allows you to lend some books. This service puts a fair amount of restrictions on lending books, but it can be done. Not all books are lendable, and even those that are can only be lent once. A loan period lasts 14 days, during which time you cannot access the book yourself.

To lend a book, go to **Manage My Content and Devices** at *amazon.com/mycd*. Click the **Actions** button. If a title allows you to loan it, the words **Loan this title** will appear in the menu. Simply click that to be brought to a page where you'll enter the recipient's email address.

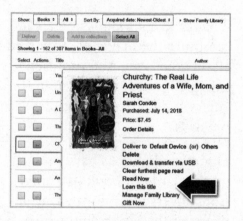

Nook loans are even easier. Barnes and Noble makes lending books a bit simpler. Log in to your B&N account and go to **My Library**. Any book that allows lending will have a green **Lend Me** tab on the edge of its cover.

Click the preferences gear icon near the center of the cover, and select **LendMe**. This brings up a form for sending the book to your friend. During the 14-day lending period, you will not be able to access the book in your own library.

Send your books to Open Library. It's not exactly a loan, but you can donate your physical print books to Open Library, which then

converts them to e-books and lends them to others on your behalf. It's a "one copy, one loan," model.

Every physical copy of a book in the Open Library is individually digitized, and that single digital copy is loaned out one at a time to comply with copyright laws.

Recapture your childhood with your own personal story time

Did you learn to love books because your parents read to you often as a child? That's how most people come to enjoy the written word. But when you learn to read for yourself, that cozy story-telling usually comes to an end.

Thanks to audiobooks, you can recapture the magic of story time all on your own. You can even snuggle up with a blanket and a cup of hot chocolate just like the old days.

In the days before digital audio, audiobooks were expensive and inconvenient. A large book might need a dozen CDs or audio cassettes and cost five times what a print book would. Audiobooks are now cheaper, more convenient, and higher quality than ever before.

Digital audiobooks have opened up the world of book listening. Book lovers listen in the car, on walks, at the beach, and while doing household chores. And where only one or two digital audiobook providers existed a few years ago, readers now have more options than ever. Here are three of the biggest.

Audible (*audible.com*). In 1995, several years before Apple released the first iPod, Audible introduced the first consumer digital audio player. The digital audiobook was born.

Today you can listen to Audible books on virtually any device — Apple and Android phones and tablets, desktop computers, and Amazon Echo digital assistant speakers. Audible remains the largest seller of audiobooks, and also includes newspapers, magazines, and other audio content.

Audible is now owned by Amazon, and many of its audiobooks sync with your reading position on Kindle e-books. That means you can go back and forth between listening and reading.

This service has the largest selection of audiobooks, including many original productions. Titles are sold either individually or via monthly subscription starting at $14.95 per month.

Google Audiobooks *(play.google.com/audiobooks)*. A relative newcomer to the audiobook market, Google positions itself a little differently than Audible.

Unlike Audible, Google offers no monthly or yearly subscription for audiobooks, which also means no member discount for books. Individual titles tend to be priced a little lower than Audible's non-member price, so if you don't listen to many books, Google may be a cheaper option than Audible.

Selection is a little smaller — especially lacking Audible's own content — but Google is certainly worth a look.

Kobo Audiobooks *(kobo.com/audiobooks)*. In addition to their e-book business, Kobo also offers an audiobook service similar to Audible. The selection at Kobo is not as large as Audible's, but if your main focus is on bestsellers, Kobo should meet most of your needs. Their subscription price — good for one book per month — is $9.99 per month.

An audiobook's 'voice' is your choice

Depending on the title, audiobooks may come in a number of "flavors." Which you choose is really just up to your personal preference. Most audiobook sellers offer samples you can listen to before you buy.

Unabridged. Every word that was in the print edition of the book is included.

Abridged. Books are edited to remove nonessential content. This generally makes an audiobook less expensive and quicker to listen to, but you miss part of the story.

Narrated. Books are read simply, usually by a single voice. The narrator may adopt a variety of voices to make characters more authentic, but production is simple and closest to the experience of someone reading the book to you. The producers may use some music at the beginning or ending of text sessions, but usually not.

Dramatized. Usually includes multiple voices acting the content in the book. It may also include sound effects and music. More like an old-style radio play than just listening to a book.

Text-to-Speech. On some e-readers, software will read your e-book aloud to you. Check the features and settings on your device to activate. Some e-book sites also offer recordings of computer-spoken books. These vary widely in quality. The best of them sound close to the way a human might read the book. The worst are very obviously computer-generated.

Download audiobooks for free — legally!

Audiobooks are great. But free audiobooks are even better. Luckily, you have a number of ways to get them, and not by asking Uncle Fred for his Audible password.

Participate in crowd-sourcing with LibriVox. Volunteers from around the world record public domain books and a few more-recent titles. The selection is not as large as other sites, and the recording qualities can vary a lot. But it's free, and it has a lot of the classics. Check it out at *librivox.org*.

Enjoy the resources of Open Culture. This site catalogs free audiobooks from a number of sources and brings them together. Mostly classics, but with some new titles from independent authors.

Because they link to resources on other sites, you can sometimes find some real gems, such as works by Maya Angelou and Neil Gaiman. Look for them at *openculture.com*.

Take advantage of the original free bookstore. In recent years Project Gutenberg at *gutenberg.org* has added audiobooks, mostly classics. As with other sites, quality can be good or not so good. Some text-to-speech computer-generated audio can be difficult to listen to.

Spotify offers more than just music. The well-known music-streaming service at *spotify.com* also features audiobooks, mostly classics but some modern titles as well. Available titles vary from month to month. Basic service — with ads — is free.

Don't forget your public library. Your library card gives you access to free audiobooks. You'll need to log in to your library's online card catalog and search for books available in audio format. Of course, you can also check them out from your local brick-and-mortar location.

The media you receive can be a mixed bag, anything from physical cassette tapes or CDs to digital files available from a variety of sites. You may have to transfer the files to the device of your choice.

Picture-perfect way to store your photos

Store your pictures in the right type of cloud

Storing your photos and videos on a photo-specific site has several advantages. These kinds of large files can quickly eat up the free storage limits on cloud sites, so it's a great way to increase your free storage.

Photo sites also feature tools for editing and enhancing your pictures and help you create new and interesting ways to share photos with your friends and family. Here's a look at some of the best sites.

Flickr — one of the oldest and best-known photo storage sites. Flickr's popularity has in part been due to its generous storage limits. Unfortunately, those free limits changed in 2019, dropping from a full terabyte of storage down to just 1,000 photos and videos.

- If you're a serious photographer, you'll run out of free storage pretty quickly. A monthly plan of around $6 ($4 if you pay annually) gets you unlimited storage and desktop auto-upload.

- Flickr is a sort of social media network for photographers. You can organize pictures in a variety of ways and build collections of photos from various photographers across the site.

- An easy-to-use photo editor can help turn ordinary pictures extraordinary. There's even a large database of public domain photographs if you're looking for pictures to illustrate a project.

Check out the Flickr community at *flickr.com*.

500px — a site for serious photographers. You're limited to uploading only seven pictures per week for free at *500px.com*. A $13 monthly plan gives you unlimited uploads.

But if you have really stellar pictures that you think other people might be willing to pay for, you can join the 500px marketplace to offer them. The site also features a well-respected photography blog to teach you tips and techniques. Unlike sites aimed at amateurs, there are no editing tools included.

Photobucket — built for the amateur photographer. Photobucket at *photobucket.com* limits its free users to just 2 gigabytes (around 400 photos). Paid plans range from around $4.50 per month for 25 gigabytes to around $11.50 monthly for 1 terabyte.

Photobucket features a powerful photo-editing tool. It's also highly integrated into a photo gift store and print store so you can easily use your photos on everything from coffee mugs to giant banners.

Google Photos — your best storage deal. Google Photos at *photos.google.com* offers unlimited storage for free. The catch is that free plans limit your photo resolution to 16 megapixels. You can store larger photos with a paid plan, which starts at $1.99 per month for 100 gigabytes.

> Want free photos? Check popular photo-printing sites like Shutterfly or Snapfish for promotions. Shutterfly, for example, will give you unlimited free prints if you download its app. Perfect way to get those pictures off your phone and into the hands of your loved ones.

A robust photo-editing tool helps you enhance your photos, and the site allows you to share photos easily.

Imgur — a good place to store high-definition photos. With a generous 20 gigabytes of free storage, Imgur at *imgur.com* is a good choice if you want a free spot to store your high-def photos.

An extremely easy-to-use photo editor includes a one-button **Enhance** feature to fix many problems instantly. There's also a meme generator and a tool to convert video to moving gif images if you want to have fun with your images.

All accounts from Imgur are now free, so there's never any pressure to upgrade. The downside is you can't pay to get rid of ads or for other features that used to be offered for higher-definition photos.

Share your favorite photos in a snap

Remember all those travel slideshows you were forced to sit through at your friends' homes? Back then, it was the only way they could share their massive stack of pictures.

Now it's so much easier. Most photo-sharing sites feature a quick-and-easy **Share** button. Clicking it usually brings up a dialogue box asking what social media site you'd like to share on.

You can also select a direct link to your photo that you can copy and then paste in your social media site. So you can share hundreds of photos with anyone you want to without having to email them. And it's free, too.

Probably the best range of sharing options comes from Imgur (*imgur.com*), a popular photo-sharing site. (See graphic.) Clicking the **Share** button on your photo gives you more than a dozen options for places on which to share your picture.

It also gives you the option to share at multiple sizes and even to embed your picture on your website.

Scan photos without spending a dime

Think it's expensive to scan all your photos? It doesn't have to be. There's a good chance you already own a photo scanner, although you may not be aware of it. And that would make scanning absolutely free.

Most home printers include an option for scanning photos and other documents, and they come with the software you need. If your printer allows you to photocopy, that means you can scan, too.

If you don't have a scanner — or don't want to do it yourself — most chain drugstores have walkup scanners in their photo departments. Or you can send your photos off to be scanned by a professional. But that's where it gets expensive.

In a pinch, you can use your digital camera or smartphone as a budget scanner, but it's hard to do well. Getting a straight photo, with good lighting, and completely in focus, is a challenge.

From print to pixels: No. 1 way to protect your family photos

Most people above a certain age have boxes and albums of old print photos lying around the house, fading, cracking, and eventually doomed for the trash.

Fortunately, it does not take a lot of skill or expensive equipment to save those old photos from the rubbish piles. All you have to do is scan them and save them to the cloud. The main requirements? Time and patience.

Use negatives if possible. If you have the negatives for your photos, this is usually best for getting quality scans. But you will need a special scanner for negatives. Otherwise you'll have to send them out to professionals.

Clean everything up. To scan your photos, you'll want to make sure both the scanner glass and the photos themselves are as clean as possible. Use a soft brush on the photos. Any spot, wrinkle, or dirt that's on your photo will be in your scanned version.

Pay attention to the options. Make sure your photo is straight on the glass. When you press the **Scan** button on your printer, your attached computer should automatically launch its scanning software, which will ask you to choose some options.

- Always scan in color, even if your photo is black and white. You'll capture more of the grays.

- Scan your photos at a minimum of 300 dpi (dots per inch); 600 dpi is better but will make for big files.

- You'll also have to choose what format to save your photo in. "TIF" files are higher quality, but also take up more storage space and are less easy to share. "JPEG" or "jpg" files use less storage space and are usually of high enough quality for home users.

Why your pictures are safer in the cloud

Every family has stories about Grandma's photo albums being lost in the fire, or the time the basement flooded and that prize-winning story dad wrote in 10th grade was destroyed. But those kinds of tragedies don't need to happen anymore. Here are some reasons your photos are safer when they're stored in the cloud.

No house fire can touch your precious photos. Uploading photos to the cloud means there's a perfect copy of them preserved forever. If your house burns down, they're still there. If you have a flood, they're still there. The movers lose a box? No problem. Your photos are waiting for you in the cloud.

The cloud doesn't fade or rip. No matter how careful you are, time is hard on your pictures and documents. They fade. They get scratched. Tacked to the refrigerator, little fingers smear them with mustard. But the versions you store on the cloud are perfect. You can print them again at any time.

Your cousin doesn't have to return them. You're proud of your grandchildren, or your nieces and nephews, or your kids. You want to show their pictures to everyone, and why not? Sometimes a picture is so precious, your cousin says, "Oh, that's lovely! Can I get a copy?"

If your photos are in the cloud, the answer is always yes. You can give them the printed photo and easily reprint it or send them a link so they can print their own copy.

They're easier to organize and to find. "Mom, remember that picture up at the lake when Jimmy fell in? Do you still have that?" Sometimes, the answer is "Yes, of course ... somewhere." That may lead to an hour digging through boxes trying to find the elusive picture.

Stored in the cloud, your pictures are easy to find. You can organize them in any way that makes sense to you — date, place, person, or any combination of those. And sometimes you can even search in plain language. Just type in "Jimmy, Lake Winnipesaukee," to find the right picture in a few keystrokes.

Even when you're gone, they're not. You may not like to think about it, but someday, you won't be here anymore. Your families will be left to go through your things, preserving what they feel is important — or have space for — and discarding the rest.

Those quick decisions have lasting effect. Thirty years from now, one of your kids may notice a resemblance between his youngest and Uncle Jimmy and want to see a picture of Jimmy at that same age.

Instead of searching through Grandma's attic, he can quickly search through Grandma's cloud and find the picture because nobody ever threw it away.

Cloud services help you edit like a pro

Even the best photographers can use a little help. Luckily, most photo storage sites also feature free and easy-to-use tools to enhance your photos and turn blah snapshots into true art.

The tools tend to be pretty similar. Here's an example of photo editing in Imgur and what some of the buttons do.

Enhance. Probably the most important tool in the box, the **Enhance** button performs an automatic correction for your picture, sharpening the focus, adjusting the exposure to the correct darkness, even sometimes turning the photo a little to make lines straight. Sometimes, all you need to do to fix your photo is click **Enhance.**

Orientation. Have you ever uploaded a photo and found it came in the wrong way or even upside down? The **Orientation** button rotates photos 90 degrees at a time. Simply click it until your picture appears right side up.

Crop. One of the most common errors amateur photographers make is standing too far away from their subject. The **Crop** button lets you focus in on the important parts of the picture and trim the rest away.

Effects. Sometimes called **Filters**, the **Effects** button lets you apply a variety of artistic elements to your photo. Depending on the particular photo editor, it could be anything from turning the picture sepia-toned or pastel to making it look like a cartoon or oil painting.

Blemish. Look for the **Smudge** or **Blemish** tool to help you smooth over cracks, creases, spots, and yes, even skin blemishes on portraits.

Preserve your memories — restore your family photos

As print photos get old, they fade. They pick up scratches and watermarks. They tear. Worst of all, they get lost forever.

Now that you've scanned your old photos and saved them from further decay, how about restoring them? Wouldn't you love to have a perfectly clear photo of your grandmother in her wedding dress? It's pretty easy to restore a lot of common problems yourself, even using free cloud-based photo editors.

Save the original. Before starting photo restoration, make sure you preserve the original scanned photo as well as the original photo print. You may make a mistake when restoring the photo. If you do, you'll want to go back to the original to start over.

Key editing tools you'll need. You have many features to choose from when using photo-editing software. But here are a few key tools you'll need to restore your family photos.

- Uncle Billy may not have been the best photographer in the family. If Aunt Gertie and Cousin Myrtle are surrounded by empty space, you may want to focus in on them. Use the **Crop** feature to retain just the part of the image you want to save.

> For more serious issues with old photos, such as multiple scratches, tears, and watermarks, you may want to bite the bullet and use a professional photo restoration service.

- Color faded? The **Enhance** button may correct faded color. However, if it doesn't do the whole job, you'll want to get in and manually adjust using the **Color** tool and the **Brightness** or **Contrast** tool to correct for years of fading.

- Physical damages to the original photo, such as scratches and stains, are the hardest to fix. Wherever there's a scratch, a bit of the original picture is missing. You have to find something to replace the missing bit, usually from the area closest to the scratch.

  Zoom in close on the damage and then select the **Blemish** or **Smudge** tool (called **Clone** in higher-end software). You then use your cursor to "paint over" the bad spots. This will work great on little scratches, particularly on backgrounds and clothes.

  Faces are more difficult — you can wind up erasing a person's facial features like a bad Botox injection. The trick is to zoom in close and use the smallest size "brush" available.

You'll be surprised how much damage you can mend to keep your precious memories from becoming just that — memories only.

Write, edit, and compute with powerful online software

Word wars — which program is best for you?

If you need to do some writing, Microsoft Word is probably the first program you turn to. And if you've used it on your computer, you'll be familiar with how it works online. The tools and menus are similar, with a few bonus features added in. Here's a rundown of the online version, along with three other word-processing programs you may want to try.

Word — a comfortable program you won't have to relearn. Take a look at the toolbars in the example on the next page. You may see a few things that are unfamiliar.

- At the top left is a menu that lets you switch between Office 365 programs, including Word, Excel, PowerPoint, and Outlook. (It looks like a grid.)

- Toward the top right is a button to launch Skype, a video-calling feature owned by Microsoft. Clicking the button from within a Word document will let you chat via text, voice, or full video while sharing the document with your friends. You can talk over changes as you make them, and all of you can see those changes as they happen.

- Below the Skype button is a more traditional **Share** button. Click this to get a link you can email to your friends. Or you can email them from directly within Word Online.

- The **Tell me what you want to do** box is self-explanatory. Simply type in what you're trying to do. It's pretty good at figuring out natural language, so typing "make bigger" works just as well as "change font size" to help you make the text larger.

Pages — Apple's simple and elegant word processor. If you have an iCloud account from Apple, you can use the Pages cloud-based word processor. Graphic design tools built into Pages make it easy for you to make your documents attractive, even if you don't have a lot of experience with page design.

You can even save your files directly to an Apple Books format so people can open your file as an e-book. Sharing tools are similar to other cloud tools. The major downside to Pages is that, like many Apple products, it doesn't play well with others. Files can't be saved as Word documents, and Word is a much more widely used format.

Evernote — fun and easy to learn. It may be less familiar to you than Word, but once you get used to working with Evernote, you may really enjoy it. Try it at *evernote.com.*

Along with traditional word processing, Evernote allows you to drop in all kinds of documents — pictures, PDFs, voice memos, video clips, handwritten notes — to build a single document. A **Share** button lets you send a link to friends and colleagues, who can work directly on your document.

Evernote also lets you organize your documents by using tags, which can be by format, topic, project, or team, to name a few. Each file can have multiple tags so it is easier to find depending on your need.

Zoho Writer — simple but rich in features. Not as well known as other online word processors, Zoho Writer is nevertheless a feature-rich, free alternative to other cloud tools. It works well with Microsoft Word and also lets you save files as ePub e-book format or as a PDF. You'll find it at *zoho.com/writer.*

Make the cloud your office in the sky

In the "good old days," working on computers meant you had to buy specialized software for everything you wanted to do. That software was expensive, it went out of date quickly, and it took up a lot of space on your computer.

Today, things are different. Most of the basic work functions you use computers for — email, word processing, spreadsheets, basic photo editing, presentations — are now easy to do with inexpensive (or free) software that lives in the cloud. If you're looking for one software program to tie everything together, here are some to try.

Office 365 includes all your old favorites. Microsoft's entry into cloud software, Office 365 features versions of Word for creating text documents, PowerPoint for creating presentations, Excel for creating spreadsheets, and other popular Microsoft apps for databases, email, note-taking, and team collaboration.

It works closely with OneDrive cloud storage. For instance, you can save a Word document from your computer into your OneDrive folder and then immediately edit it in a web browser on your iPad.

Office 365 is free to students and teachers. A personal subscription to Office 365 starts at around $70 per year, with family plans starting at $100 per year, including 1 terabyte of OneDrive storage per user. Learn more at *office365.com*.

G Suite is a sweet program from Google. Similar to Office 365, G Suite includes cloud storage, word processing, spreadsheets, and online meeting tools. You'll find all the details in the section *Google software: The free suite that does it all* or at *gsuite.google.com*.

Evernote is for more than just note-taking. Evernote organizes your text, photos, scanned documents, voice memos, and even handwritten documents, which it can turn into searchable text.

With Evernote, you can find your documents regardless of what device you created them on. With the Evernote app, you can scan hard-copy documents to add to your collection. Everything is available to you from any internet-connected device on the cloud.

The program also lets you quickly and easily share your notebooks or individual notes with other people. That makes it simple to organize a group project. Check it out at *evernote.com*.

The free version limits you to 60 megabytes of uploads per month and syncing on a maximum of two devices. Paid versions raise these levels to 10 gigabytes and unlimited devices, along with faster text recognition and enhanced editing abilities.

3 simple reasons it's better to write in the cloud

When you're ready to write your memoirs or that adventure novel you've been thinking about, turn to the cloud. Creating your document in an online program has a number of super benefits.

- You don't have to worry about computer software glitches destroying your documents — or worse, losing them. Everything happens in your web browser.

- Your files are safely stored in the cloud. No natural disasters can touch them.

- Working with others — like your editor — is a breeze. It's simple for more than one person to work on the same document at exactly the same time. And everyone can see the changes as they happen.

Spreadsheets make your data pop — and you can share them, too!

You don't need to feel left out if numbers are your thing. The cloud has tools for you, too. You've already read about Google Sheets, which is probably the most popular free online spreadsheet program. Here are a few others for you to play with.

Excel Online — a mainstay of Office 365. Microsoft may not have invented the spreadsheet program, but people are probably most familiar with Excel spreadsheets. The online version works closely with OneDrive cloud storage.

Excel Online is easy to share with others through a single button click. Microsoft also integrates Skype directly into Excel so you can have an impromptu video, audio, or chat meeting about a spreadsheet. All parties can see and edit it in real time.

Numbers — spreadsheets for the Apple crowd. This program, as the name implies, is a powerful spreadsheet application. As you might expect from such a graphics-focused company, Numbers really excels (no pun intended) at creating colorful, attractive charts and graphs from your data.

Unfortunately, sharing is not one of its strong points. Although it's easy to work in Pages with other iCloud users, it's not so easy to send editable data to your friends who use other spreadsheet programs.

Zoho Sheet — a free alternative. Zoho Sheet looks nearly identical to Excel, and also opens existing Excel documents and saves in that format as well. It is easy to share spreadsheets with other people through email or links. Look for it at *zoho.com/sheet*.

Create online forms like a pro

You're throwing a party and want to know who's coming and what they're bringing. You coach junior soccer and need parents to sign up to bring snacks. You're planning the group holiday party and want your friends to vote on the restaurant.

You need a form. And you want one that will make other people say "Wow!" because most of them still send around paper signup sheets. Online forms are your answer.

The cloud has many free tools available to create forms, which you can then share through email, social media, or with an easy link. After you design your masterpiece, simply send it to your friends and family to fill out and return. In general, most form-building sites have similar features.

- You can customize them with drag-and-drop templates.

- You can choose to create either information-gathering forms or opinion surveys.

- They have data-collection options that include spreadsheets, PDFs, even automatically generated graphs.

- You can send it either through a web link or by embedding it on your own website.

But there are some differences. Here's a quick rundown of some of the most popular tools.

FormStack. If you want to build professional-looking forms, you can't go wrong with FormStack at *formstack.com*. There are more than 40 customizable standard templates, each of which are available in multiple styles.

You can even test out two different versions of the same form and compare which gets better results. While FormStack doesn't offer a free plan, you can try it before you buy it with a 14-day free trial.

TypeForm. A fun and easy way to create forms using drag and drop, TypeForm is free at its basic level. You're limited to 100 responses per month and only 10 questions per form. But if you're just doing a few simple forms, this should meet your needs. Check it out at *typeform.com*.

Google Forms. If you already use G Suite, Google Forms works very closely with it. And it's completely free with unlimited forms and unlimited users. You'll find it at *forms.google.com*.

Formsite. Unlike most form services, Formsite provides free, full-color photos to help make your forms attractive. It's easy to use, and you can even accept PayPal payments. The free version limits you to five forms with only 10 responses per form.

Here's an example of how to create a "Volunteer Signup" form at *formsite.com*.

Help from the cloud
Simplify your life with a digital assistant

Choose the right home assistant for you

You may have noticed a strange box in your children's home that plays music and answers questions. That remarkable device is known as a smart speaker. Basically it's a wireless speaker with voice-control built into it. When you talk to it, it will respond to your commands.

The computerized "brains" in these speakers are known as digital assistants. They can do things like give you the weather or sports scores, read you a book, find your favorite radio station, or even turn on your TV.

There are a lot of smart speaker options available and more coming all the time. The most popular are Amazon's Alexa, Google's Google Assistant, and Apple's Siri. It can be confusing trying to decide which one is right for you. Here are two things you should think about before you buy.

Where do you already shop? Is most of your music and video purchased through iTunes? Do you own an Apple TV? Then you should look closely at HomePod, Apple's entry into the smart speaker market.

More of an Amazonian, a Prime member, with a lot of Alexa-enabled home gadgets? Then the Amazon Echo may be the smart speaker for you. If you shop with Google and use a Chromecast video device, then maybe you live in a Google Home.

How do you plan to use it? Different home assistants have different strengths, so knowing how you'll use yours should help you make your decision.

Simple web searches and offering general information are things any device can handle. If you do a lot of translation requests, devices from Google are best. Want to control your Apple TV video and audio library? Then you need an Apple HomePod.

Here's another helpful tip. When buying a digital assistant, find out what device your children or grandchildren have. If you buy the same one, they can explain how it works and help troubleshoot if anything goes wrong.

Do you have your lights, thermostat, washing machine, and other appliances on an automatic control? Alexa-enabled devices dominate home automation, so that makes the Echo series a natural choice.

Top 5 reasons you'll love your new device

A lot of people's first reaction when they hear about smart speakers or home digital assistants is "What the heck do I need that for?" Well, you may not need it, but it can be useful, not to mention lots of fun. Here are some of the benefits.

It's your own personal encyclopedia. Your know-it-all cousin can be pretty annoying, piping in with trivia and offering unwanted opinions all the time. Your home assistant, on the other hand, really does know everything. But it only speaks when you ask it to and never offers an opinion.

Watching a classic movie and want to know how many Oscars *Gone with the Wind* won? Just ask Siri. What's the difference between a badger and a bobcat? Alexa knows. How many fluid ounces in a liter? Ask Google Assistant.

You can control your home entertainment. You enjoy listening to music while you go about your daily chores. But it's so hard to find a radio station that plays the old songs you love.

Digital assistant to the rescue. Just ask her to play anything you want and she'll find it. You can listen to audiobooks, streaming music, podcasts, or news reports, all with a simple request. And if you want to hear the same internet radio station in every room in the house, no problem. Just add as many devices as you want and they'll sync together — no wires necessary.

Video is a little trickier because each assistant favors its own company's products and may not work with competitors. No matter which one you have, you can watch Netflix and Hulu. But only Alexa will pull up Fire TV and Amazon Prime Video. You'll need Google Home for Chromecast and Google Play, and Apple HomePod to access iTunes and Apple TV.

Home automation is a snap. Amazon's Alexa system is fast becoming a requirement for most home automation tools, so finding compatible devices for your Echo is easiest. But many major home automation systems work with all three smart-speaker systems — Amazon Echo, Google Home, and Apple HomePod.

This means you can use your device to control everything from your thermostat to your lights and even your appliances. Want to set a time for the laundry to start? How about scheduling when the porch lights go on and off? Just tell your digital assistant, and it will get done.

It keeps you on schedule. Smart speakers can connect to your digital calendar to help remind you of appointments and things you need to get done. You can even automate reminders.

So when you tell Alexa "good morning," she can read your appointments for the day and what time you need to leave. She'll list your to-dos, give you an update on the top news and current weather, and even turn on the coffee maker. How helpful is that?

Armchair shopping is a breeze. Both Google and Amazon have huge online storefronts, so it's no surprise their digital assistants make shopping easy. That's especially true for items you order on a regular basis. When you run low on Fido's kibble, you can simply say, "Alexa, reorder dog food," and it's done in under 30 seconds.

3 handy ways to narrow down your choices

So you've decide to take the plunge and see what all the fuss is about. After you've decided which provider works best for you, it's time to pick your digital assistant device. Here are some things you'll want to consider.

Sound quality makes a difference. As you might expect, the more expensive the device is, the better the sound quality.

- The weakest sound comes from the smallest devices, Amazon's Echo Dot and the Google Home Mini.

- Music enthusiasts will want to consider larger devices that focus on sound quality, such as the Apple HomePod and the Google Home Max.

- Somewhere in the middle of sound quality are the larger Amazon Echo and Google Home. Amazon devices also allow you to connect to external speakers if you want a boost in sound quality.

You'll find a wide range of prices. You can dip your toe in the water with a low-cost Echo Dot, then graduate to a pricier Apple HomePod once you feel more comfortable.

- Google and Amazon each offer smart-speaker devices for under $30. As new versions are released, sometimes devices can even dip under $20.

- Mid-range devices, whose primary advantage over cheaper ones is the sound quality, run between $65–$150.

- Devices built for sound — such as Apple HomePod, Sonos One, or Google Home Max — cost between $170–$400.

- Devices that feature video-calling functions are in a different category, ranging from around $130 for the tiny Amazon Echo Spot to around $400 for the Portal Plus from Facebook, which also features Amazon's Alexa as its "brain."

Don't forget to factor in how many devices you want. If you plan to put one in the living room and another in the bedroom, you'll need to include that in your cost.

Appearance is a personal decision. Unlike computers and tablets, these devices are on display in your home all the time. Most devices are some variety of small, round, and black. Google devices have a somewhat different style, with white and gray dominating. Google and Amazon offer decorative sleeves to cover up the black with whatever color you prefer.

Video devices look mostly like tablet computers. The exception is Amazon Echo Spot, which looks a little like an 8-ball cut in half with a video screen on one side.

The future is here: Make calls without using your phone

Remember the days when calling your Mom meant using a dial-up phone? Nowadays, even a smartphone may be passé with the arrival of smart speakers and digital assistants.

- Making audio and even video calls to your friends and loved ones has never been easier. If you have an Alexa-enabled device, you can call anyone else in your contacts whether or not they have one too. Just say, "Alexa, call Uncle Steve."

- Both Google and Alexa devices let you use them as home intercoms if you have more than one device. No more shouting from the second floor to the basement.

- They can also be used as hands-free devices that connect wirelessly to your smartphone, so you can make phone calls or listen to audio from your phone through your smart speaker.

Here are some tips, tricks, and techniques for different kinds of assistants.

Apple HomePod. To make calls on the HomePod, you'll need either an iPhone, an iPad or a Mac computer to make the actual connection. But you can use the HomePod as a high-quality hands-free speakerphone.

Just say, "Hey Siri, call Mom" to start the connection. If Mom isn't stored in your contacts, you can speak the phone number you want to call out loud. When you're done, say "Hey Siri, hang up."

Google Home. Google has some advantages for voice calls. Unlike HomePod, you don't need a phone to make calls. That's because Google Home connects to Google Voice, a free service that gives you an internet phone number, which can be used from an app, a computer, or from Google Home.

And while Google doesn't offer a true intercom system between devices, its "Broadcast" feature is pretty cool, allowing you to choose prerecorded messages or record your own to be broadcast to all your devices at the same time.

This includes the ability to send a message from an app on your phone to all the Google smart speakers in your house. A great way to let everyone know you're on your way home.

Amazon Echo. Amazon's Echo devices, as well as other Alexa-enabled devices, let you make voice calls to any contact stored on your connected mobile phone and some tablets.

Amazon also has video calling on its Echo Spot and Echo Show, which lets you make video calls to anyone with a similar device, Skype, or the Alexa app.

Echo devices can be used as a home intercom system to make voice calls from one room to another. Remember the horror movie where they say, "They're calling from inside the house!"? Well, that can be you.

You can also use the device to "drop in" on another device in your home. You can hear what's going on in the other room even if no one's there to answer. Useful as a baby monitor and to find out if the dog is upstairs chewing your shoes.

Is your digital assistant eavesdropping on you?

Technically, no. Much like your kids, your digital assistant is always listening, but it isn't always paying attention.

Smart speakers are programmed to listen for the "wake" word, such as "Alexa," "OK Google," or "Siri." Until you say it, it ignores you. Everything after you speak the wake word is sent over the internet to be analyzed and converted into text. Your little device doesn't have enough computing power to do that itself. It recognizes its wake word but nothing else.

Some people are concerned that, since the device is always on, there's room for abuse — or mistakes. One person claims his Echo device called a person mentioned in his conversation without him knowing it. It's possible Alexa mistook a similar word for its wake word. But that's highly unusual.

A smart speaker lights up when in use and sounds chimes to alert you to a new call, so you should always know when it's activated. If you're concerned, you can turn off the microphone so it no longer hears what you say. But you'll have to turn it back on when you want to use it again.

Index

A

Accessibility, computer
  dictation 64-65
  earbuds 79-80
  magnifier 29
  narrator 29
  predictive text 67-68
  speakerphone 79
  voice typing 63-65, 82
  zoom in 66-67, 80-81
Alexa, Amazon 363-370
Amazon
  Alexa 363-370
  Drive 313, 317
  e-books 335
  Echo 364-370
  Fire TV 147-148
  Kindle 334
  Outlet 47
  Prime Music 330
  Prime Video 157
  Warehouse 46-47
Android
  Find My Device feature 239
  operating system, explained 3
Antennas, digital
  broadcast towers and 132
  direction of 134
  indoor vs. outdoor 133
  troubleshooting 134-135
Anti-virus software. *See Also* Viruses,
  protecting against
  benefits of 198-199
  for smartphones 238
  programs 201-203
Apple. *See Also* iPhones
  app store 7, 20-21
  Books 335-336

  Health app 37
  HomePod 363-369
  iCloud 313, 316, 321
  ID account 10
  iTunes 177
  iWorks, software package 4
  Music Library 329
  Notes 57
  operating system, iOS 3
  Pages 356
  refunds for apps 19-20
  Siri 365, 368-369
  TV 124, 148
Applications (apps)
  Calendar, Google 294-300
  definition of 2
  deleting 17-18, 24-25
  downloading 8-12
  Drive, Google 278-279
  for coupons 39-46, 56
  for email 271
  for health 26-38, 52, 56
  for medical emergencies 30
  for medication management 30
  for mental stimulation 50-52
  for network TV 161
  for news 60, 263-264
  for organization 57-59
  for personal safety 30
  for seniors 55-57
  for smart TV 139-141
  for sports 158
  for traveling 56, 57, 59-60
  for weather 56, 59
  free 12-14, 20-24, 50-51
  hidden costs of 12
  Kindle 334-335
  Maps, Google 301
  payment methods 10

371